150 RECIPES FOR YOUR
BREAD MACHINE

150 RECIPES FOR YOUR BREAD MACHINE

The complete practical guide to using your bread machine, fully revised and updated, with a collection of step-by-step recipes shown in over 650 photographs

Jennie Shapter

southwater

This edition is published by Southwater, an imprint of Anness Publishing Ltd,
108 Great Russell Street, London WC1B 3NA; info@anness.com

www.southwaterbooks.com; www.annesspublishing.com

If you like the images in this book and would like to investigate using them for publishing,
promotions or advertising, please visit our website www.practicalpictures.com for more information.

A CIP catalogue record for this book is available from the British Library.

PUBLISHER: Joanna Lorenz
EDITORS: Rebecca Clunes and Kate Eddison
DESIGNER: Nigel Partridge
PHOTOGRAPHERS AND STYLISTS: Nicki Dowey and Toby Scott
HOME ECONOMIST: Jennie Shapter
TYPESETTER: Diane Pullen
PRODUCTION CONTROLLER: Rosie Anness

NOTES
Bracketed terms are intended for American readers.
For all recipes, quantities are given in both metric and imperial measures and, where appropriate, in standard cups and
spoons. Follow one set of measures, but not a mixture, because they are not interchangeable.
Standard spoon and cup measures are level. 1 tsp = 5ml, 1 tbsp = 15ml, 1 cup = 250ml/8fl oz.
Australian standard tablespoons are 20ml. Australian readers should use 3 tsp
in place of 1 tbsp for measuring small quantities.
American pints are 16fl oz/2 cups. American readers should use 20fl oz/2.5 cups in place of
1 pint when measuring liquids.
Electric oven temperatures in this book are for conventional ovens. When using a fan oven,
the temperature will probably need to be reduced by about 10–20°C/20–40°F. Since ovens vary,
you should check with your manufacturer's instruction book for guidance.
The nutritional analysis given for each recipe is calculated per loaf or portion, unless otherwise stated.
If the recipe gives a range of serving sizes, such as Serves 4–6, then the nutritional analysis
will be for the smaller portion size, i.e. 6 servings. The analysis does not include optional ingredients,
such as salt added to taste.
Medium (US large) eggs are used unless otherwise stated.

PUBLISHER'S NOTE
Although the advice and information in this book are believed to be accurate and true at the time
of going to press, neither the authors nor the publisher can accept any legal responsibility or liability
for any errors or omissions that may have been made nor for any inaccuracies nor for any loss,
harm or injury that comes about from following instructions or advice in this book.

CONTENTS

INTRODUCTION

In recent years there has been a huge upsurge in the popularity of home-baked bread. Men and women are coming home from work to the comforting aroma of freshly baked bread once only associated with an idyllic childhood. But making and eating home-baked bread is not only the stuff of dreams. No. The bread that stands cooling in many of our kitchens is real. It has a beautiful golden crust, an even crumb and a delicious flavour. It

BELOW: To many people, a Farmhouse Loaf is the traditional bread they associate with their childhood.

looks and tastes as if aching effort went into its making, but nothing could be further from the truth. Much of today's tastiest bread is made at home with the aid of an easy-to-operate machine, which takes the hard work out of bread making while retaining all the pleasure.

The first automatic domestic bread-maker appeared on the market in Japan in the late 1980s, and since then bread machines have gained popularity all over the world. These excellent appliances have helped to rekindle the pleasure of making home-made bread, by streamlining the process and making it incredibly

simple. All the "home baker" needs to do is to measure a few ingredients accurately, put them into the bread machine pan and push a button or two.

At first it is easy to feel overwhelmed by all the settings on a bread machine. These are there to help you bake a wide range of breads, both sweet and savoury, using different grains and flavourings. In time you'll get to grips with them all, but there's no need to rush. Start by making a simple white loaf and watch while your machine transforms a few ingredients first into a silky, smooth dough and finally into a golden loaf of bread.

No matter what make of machine you have, it is important to focus on the bread, not the machine. Even the best type of machine is only a kitchen aid. The machine will mix, knead and bake beautifully, but only after you have added the necessary ingredients and programmed it. The machine cannot think for itself; it can only carry out your instructions, so it is essential that you add the correct ingredients in the right proportions, in the order specified in the instructions for your particular breadmaking machine, and that you choose the requisite settings. Do not become frustrated if your first attempts do not look one hundred per cent perfect; they will probably still taste wonderful. Get to know your bread machine and be willing to experiment to find the correct ratio of dry ingredients to liquids. There are a number of variables, including the type of ingredients used, the climate and the weather, which can affect the moisture level, regardless of the type of machine you are using.

When you make bread by hand you can feel whether it is too wet or dry, simply by kneading it. However, when you use a bread machine, you need to adopt a different strategy to determine if your bread has the right moistness and, if not, how you may adjust it to produce a perfect loaf.

After the machine has been mixing for a few minutes, take a quick look at the dough – it should be pliable and soft. When the machine stops kneading, the

dough should start to relax back into the shape of the bread machine pan. Once you have made a few loaves of bread you will soon recognize what is an acceptable dough, and you will rapidly progress to making breads with different grains, such as rye, buckwheat or barley, or breads flavoured with vegetables such as potatoes or parsnips. The range of both savoury and sweet breads you ultimately will be able to produce will only be limited by your imagination. Creative thinking can produce some magical results.

The breads in this book are either made entirely by machine or the dough is made in the machine, then shaped by hand and baked in a conventional oven. Teabreads are mixed by hand and baked in the bread machine.

It is very pleasurable to shape your own loaves of bread, and setting the machine to the "dough only" cycle takes all the hard work out of the initial mixing and kneading. The machine provides an ideal climate for the initial rising period, leaving you to bring all your artistry to bear on transforming the dough into

LOAF SIZES
Where loaves are made automatically you will find three lists of ingredients, each relating to a different size of machine. Small is recommended for machines that are designed for loaves using 350–375g/12–13oz/3–3¼ cups of flour, medium for machines that make loaves using 450–500g/ 1lb–1lb 2oz/ 4–4½ cups of flour and large for machines that can make loaves using up to 600g/1lb 5oz/5¼ cups of flour. Refer to your manufacturer's handbook. If only one set of ingredients is given for a loaf that is to be baked automatically, relate these to the size of your machine to make sure it is suitable for the job. Where a bread machine is used solely for preparing the dough, which is then shaped by hand and baked conventionally, only one set of ingredients is given.

ABOVE: Babka is a traditional Polish Easter cake.

BELOW: Mix the dough for Pistolets in the machine and shape by hand.

rolls, shaped breads or yeast cakes. Once you master the technique, you can make breads from all around the world, including Middle Eastern flatbreads, American Doughnuts, French Bread, and Jewish Challah – to name but a few. Sourdoughs and breads made from starters are becoming increasingly popular, and there is a chapter illustrating how the bread machine can be used to help you make them. It is also possible to make gluten-free breads. There are recipes for both ready mixes and gluten-free flours. If you need more details for your machine contact the manufacturer's helpline.

A BAKERY IN YOUR KITCHEN

Bread making is a tremendously satisfying activity. With the help of your machine, delectable breads you will not find at the bakery or supermarket can be made with very little effort. From basic breads containing little more than flour, yeast and water to more elaborate loaves based on stoneground flours milled from a variety of grains – the possibilities are endless. What's more, you know precisely what goes into the bread, and can tailor loaves to your family's own tastes, adding sweet or savoury ingredients.

For everyday use, basic white loaves, possibly enriched with milk or egg, or flavoursome Granary and Light Wholemeal Breads are perfect for breakfast, whether freshly baked or toasted, and these can also be used for sandwiches and quick snacks. These types of bread are the easiest to make in your machine and are the ones you are likely to make over and over again. In time, however, you will probably progress to baking loaves with added ingredients such as potato, to provide, for example, an enhanced lightness to the dough. Leftover rice makes a tasty bread; and another delicious treat is the New England Anadama Bread, made with white, wholemeal (whole-wheat) and corn meal flours flavoured with molasses.

ABOVE: Hazelnut Twist Cake

With the addition of other grains, you can make more complex, hearty loaves. Breads containing oats, rye, wheatgerm and wild rice, perhaps with added whole seeds and grains, can all be baked in the bread machine. These provide extra fibre and are a good source of complex carbohydrates, and are thus a wonderfully healthy option as well as being simply scrumptious. Try Multigrain Bread, a flavour-packed healthy loaf made from Granary (whole-wheat), rye and wholemeal flours with whole oats. Alternatively, experiment with a mixed-seed bread such as Four Seed Bread. The added seeds not only contribute crunchiness and flavour, but are also very nutritious.

The bread machine will happily incorporate such ingredients as caramelized onions, sun-dried tomatoes, chargrilled (bell) peppers, crispy bacon, slivers of ham and other cured meats, fresh chopped herbs and grated or crumbled cheese, to produce mouthwatering vegetable and other savoury breads. Spices and nuts, and dried, semi-dried and fresh fruits can also be added to make classic malted fruit loaves. Try succulent Cranberry and Orange Bread or Mango and Banana Bread. Other sweet breads include crunchy Buckwheat and Walnut Bread and – every chocolate lover's dream – Three Chocolate Bread.

You can also cook succulent teabreads, Soda Bread, Gingerbread, Madeira Cake and Passion Cake, to name but a few,

BELOW: Strawberry Teabread

which provides an alternative to using your traditional oven for one cake. Fresh fruits such as strawberries and raspberries plus more exotic offerings can also be used as flavourings for these tea-time treats, as can traditional dried fruits, such as apricots, dates, prunes and raisins.

These breads, mixed, proved and baked automatically, illustrate just a part of the bread machine's capabilities. You

BELOW: A flavoured bread, such as Grainy Mustard and Beer Loaf, is delicious served with cheese and pickle as a simple lunch.

can also use the "dough only" setting to make an endless variety of doughs for hand-shaping. Classic French breads, such as Fougasse, Couronne and baguettes, or rustic breads, such as Pain de Campagne and Pain de Seigle are all possible, as are Italian breads, such as Ciabatta, Pan all'Olio and Breadsticks (grissini). You will be able to experiment in making flatbreads such as Indian Naan, Middle Eastern Lavash and Pitta Breads, or Italian Focaccia, Stromboli, Sfincione or pizzas.

Sweet yeast doughs also work well in a bread machine. Try making Strawberry Chocolate Savarin, Peach Brandy Babas

or Austrian Coffee Cake, as well as strudels and classic festive breads such as Polish Babka (Easter bread) or a Finnish Festive Wreath. You can even impress your friends by baking the traditional Italian Christmas bread, Mocha panettone.

There are endless shaped rolls, buns and pastries to try out, from American Breakfast Pancakes to English Chelsea Buns, and the Chinese-style Chicken Buns, topped with sesame seeds. These breads can be easily shaped by hand after the machine has mixed and proved the dough, and then baked to golden perfection in a conventional oven.

GETTING DOWN TO BASICS

A bread machine is designed to take the hard work out of making bread. Like most kitchen appliances, it is a labour-saving device. It will mix the ingredients and knead the dough for you, and allows the bread to rise and bake at the correct time and temperature.

For most breads, all you will need to do is to measure the ingredients for your chosen bread, put them into the pan in the correct order, close the lid, select a suitable baking programme and opt for light, medium or dark crust. You may also choose to delay the starting time, so that you have freshly baked bread for breakfast or when you return from work. Press the Start button and in a few hours you will have a beautifully baked loaf, the machine having performed the kneading, rising and baking cycles for you.

Bread machines offer a selection of programmes to suit different types of flour and varying levels of sugar and fat. You can explore making a whole variety of raw

BELOW: The three different sizes of bread machine pans that are available. From left to right: large, small and medium.

ABOVE: The shape of the kneading blade varies. Some blades are articulated and drop down after kneading for easier removal and less damage to the loaf.

doughs for shaping sweet and savoury breads, sourdough breads, mixed-grains, Continental-style breads and many more.

All bread machines work on the same basic principle. Each contains a removable non-stick bread pan, with a handle, into which a kneading blade is fitted. Most kneading blades are removable, but a few are permanently fixed.When inserted in the machine, the pan fits on to a central shaft, which rotates the blade. A lid closes over the bread pan so that the ingredients are contained within a controlled environment. The lid includes an air vent and may have a window, which can be useful for checking the progress of your bread. The machine is programmed by using the control panel.

The size and shape of the bread is determined by the shape of the bread pan. There are two shapes currently available; one rectangular and the other square. The rectangular pan produces the more traditional shape, the actual size varying from one manufacturer to another. The square shape is mostly to be found in smaller machines and produces a tall loaf, which is similar to a traditional rectangular loaf that has been stood on its end. The vertical square loaf can be turned on its side for slicing, if preferred, in order to give smaller slices of bread.

The size of the loaf ranges from around 500g/1lb 2oz to 1kg/2¼lb depending on the machine. Most machines have the option of cooking different sizes of loaves; the large machines making up to three sizes on the basic programmes.

BUYING A BREAD MACHINE
There is plenty of choice when it comes to selecting a bread machine to buy. Give some thought to which features would prove most useful to you, then shop around for the best buy available in your price range. First of all, consider the size

of loaf you would like to bake, which will largely be governed by the number in your family. Remember that a large bread machine will often make smaller loaves but not vice versa.

You will need to consider whether the shape of the bread is important to you, and choose a machine with a square or rectangular bread pan accordingly.

Are you likely to want to make breads with added ingredients? If so, an automatic dispenser may be useful. You don't have to wait around to add the extra ingredients, the machine will do it automatically. Does the machine have a special gluten-free cycle? Would this matter to you? Does it have the option for you to self programme the machine? Are you likely to want to? Extra features, such as jam-making and pasta dough programmes, are very specialized and only you know whether you would find them worth having.

BUILT-IN SAFETY DEVICES

Most machines include a power failure override mode which can prove to be extremely useful. If the machine is inadvertently unplugged or there is a brief power cut the programme will continue as soon as the power is restored. The maximum time allowed for loss of power varies from 8 to 30 minutes, or more. Check the bread when the power comes back on; depending on what stage the programme had reached at the time of the power cut, the rising or baking time of the loaf may have been affected.

An over-load protection is fitted to some models. This will cut in if the kneading blade is restricted by hard dough and will stop the motor to protect it. It will automatically re-start after about 30 minutes, but it is important to rectify the problem dough first. Either start again or cut the dough into small pieces and return it to the bread pan with a little more liquid to soften the dough.

One important consideration is whether the manufacturer offers a well-written manual and an after-sales support system or help line. If these are available, any problems or queries you might have can be answered quickly, which is particularly useful if this is your first machine.

A bread machine takes up a fair amount of room, so think about where you will store it, and buy one that fits the available space. If the bread machine is to be left on the work surface and aesthetics are important to you, you'll need to buy a machine that will be in keeping with your existing appliances. Most bread machines are available in white or black, or in stainless steel.

Jot down the features important to you, listing them in order of your preference. Use a simple process of elimination to narrow your choice down to two or three machines, which will make the decision easier.

BELOW: A typical bread machine. Although each machine will have a control panel with a different layout, most of the basic features are similar. More specialist cycles vary from machine to machine.

How to Use Your Bread Machine

The instructions that follow will help you to achieve a perfect loaf the first time you use your bread machine. The guidelines are general, that is they are applicable to any bread machine, and should be read in conjunction with the handbook provided for your specific machine. Make sure you use fresh, top quality ingredients; you can't expect good results with out-of-date flour or yeast.

1 Stand the bread machine on a firm, level, heat-resistant surface. Place away from any heat source, such as a stove or direct sunlight, and also in a draught-free area, as these factors can affect the temperature inside the machine. Do not plug the bread machine into the power socket at this stage. Open the lid. Remove the bread pan by holding both sides of the handle and pulling upwards or twisting slightly, depending on the design of your particular model.

2 Make sure the kneading blade and shaft are free of any breadcrumbs. Fit the kneading blade on the shaft in the base of the bread pan. The blade will only fit in one position, as the hole in the blade and the outside of the shaft are D-shaped. Some machines are fixed blade only.

3 Pour the water, milk and/or other liquids into the bread pan, unless the instructions for your particular machine require you to add the dry ingredients first. If so, reverse the order in which you add the liquid and dry ingredients, putting the yeast in the bread pan first.

4 Sprinkle over the flour, ensuring that it covers the liquid completely. Add any other dry ingredients specified in the recipe, such as dried milk powder. Add the salt, sugar or honey and butter or oil, placing them in separate corners so they do not come into contact with each other.

SPECIAL FEATURES

Extra programmes can be found on more expensive machines. These include cooking jam and making pasta dough. While these facilities would not be the main reason for buying a bread machine they can be useful extras. For instance, jam-making couldn't be easier: you simply add equal quantities of fresh fruit and sugar to the bread machine pan, set the jam programme and, when the cycle ends, you will have jam ready to pour into clean sterilized jars.

EASY MEASURING

If you have a set of electronic scales with an add and weigh facility, then accurate measuring of ingredients is very easy. Stand the bread pan on the scale, pour in the liquid, then set the display to zero. Add the dry ingredients directly to the pan, each time zeroing the display. Finally, add the fat, salt, sweetener and yeast and place the bread pan in your machine.

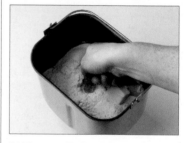

5 Make a small indent in the centre of the flour (but not down as far as the liquid) with the tip of your finger and add the yeast. If your indent reached the liquid below the dry ingredients, then the yeast would become wet and would be activated too quickly. Wipe away any spillages from the outside of the bread pan.

6 Place the pan inside the machine, fitting it firmly in place. Depending on the model of your machine, the pan may have a designated front and back, or clips on the outer edge which need to engage in the machine to hold the bread pan in position. Fold the handle down and close the lid. Plug into the socket and switch on the power.

7 Select the programme you require, followed by crust colour and size. Press Start.

8 Towards the end of the kneading process the machine will beep to alert you to add any additional ingredients. Open the lid, add the ingredients, and close the lid. If you have an automatic dispenser, add ingredients to this before starting the machine; it will add them at the correct time. Ingredients that may melt or stick should be added manually as described above. Check with your instructions.

9 At the end of the cycle, the machine will beep once more to let you know that either the dough is ready or the bread is cooked. Press Stop. Open the lid of the machine. If you are removing baked bread, remember to use oven gloves to lift out the bread pan, as it will be extremely hot. Avoid leaning over and looking into the bread machine when you open the lid, as the air escaping from the machine will be very hot and could cause you discomfort.

BELOW: A basic white bread is an excellent choice for the novice bread maker. If you follow these instructions and weigh the ingredients carefully, you are sure to achieve a delicious loaf of bread. Once you have gained confidence, try experimenting with the basic recipe, by adding other ingredients or changing the colour of the crust.

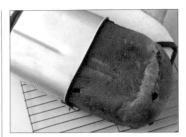

10 Still using oven gloves, turn the pan upside down and shake it several times to release the bread. If necessary, tap the base of the pan on a heatproof board.

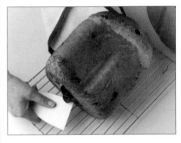

11 If the kneading blade for your bread machine is not of the fixed type, and comes out inside the bread, use a heat-resistant utensil to remove it, such as a wooden spatula. It will come out easily.

12 Place the bread on a wire rack to cool. Unplug the bread machine and leave to cool before using it again. A machine which is too hot will not make a successful loaf, and many will not operate if they are too hot for this reason. Refer to the manufacturer's manual for guidance. Wash the pan and kneading blade and wipe down the machine. All parts of the machine must be cool and dry before you store it.

BASIC CONTROLS

It will take you a little while and some practice to become familiar with and confident about using your new bread machine. Most manufacturers now produce excellent manuals, which are supplied with their machines. The manual is a good place to start, and should also be able to help you if you come up against a problem. Programmes obviously differ slightly from machine to machine, but an overview will give you a general idea of what is involved.

It is important to understand the function of each control on your bread machine before starting to make a loaf of bread. Each feature may vary slightly between different machines, but they all work in a basically similar manner.

START AND STOP BUTTONS

The Start button initiates the whole process. Press it after you have placed all the ingredients required for the bread-making procedure in the bread pan and after you have selected all the required settings, such as loaf type, size, crust colour and delay timer.

The Stop button may actually be the same control or a separate one. Press it to stop the programme, either during the programme, if you need to override it, or at the end to turn off the machine. This cancels the "keep warm" cycle at the end of baking.

TIME DISPLAY AND STATUS INDICATOR

A window displays the time remaining until the end of the programme selected. In some machines the selected programme is also shown. Some models use this same window or a separate set of lights to indicate what is happening inside the machine. It gives information on whether the machine is on time delay, kneading, resting, rising, baking or warming.

PROGRAMME INDICATORS OR MENU

Each bread machine has a number of programmes for different types of bread. Some models have more than others. This function allows you to choose the appropriate programme for your recipe and indicates which one you have selected. These programmes are discussed in more detail later.

DELAY TIMER

This button allows you to pre-set the bread machine to switch on automatically at a specified time. So, for example, you can have freshly baked bread for breakfast or when you return from work. The timer should not be used for dough that contains perishable ingredients such as fresh dairy products or meats, which deteriorate in a warm environment.

CRUST COLOUR CONTROL

The majority of bread machines have a default medium crust setting. If, however, you prefer a paler crust or the appearance of a high-bake loaf, most machines will give you the option of a lighter or darker crust. Breads high in sugar, or that contain eggs or cheese, may colour too much on a medium setting, so a lighter option may be preferable for these.

WARMING INDICATOR

When the bread has finished baking, it is best to remove it from the machine immediately. If for any reason this is not possible, the warming facility will switch on as soon as the bread is baked, to help prevent condensation of the steam, which otherwise would result in a soggy loaf. Most machines continue in this mode for an hour, some giving an audible reminder every few minutes to remove the bread.

LEFT: *French Bread can be baked in the machine on a French bread setting, or the dough can be removed to make the traditional shape by hand.*

INTERIOR LIGHT

This button can be pressed to switch on a light within the machine. It lets you see clearly what is happening inside the machine through the viewing window and avoids opening the lid. The light will automatically switch off after 60 seconds.

LOAF SIZE

You have the option of making two or three sizes of loaf on most machines. Options vary according to the selected programme. The actual sizes vary between machines but approximate to small, medium and large loaves that range from around 500g/1lb 2oz to 1kg/2lb 4oz in weight. Some machines have medium, large and extra large settings, but the extra large is still smaller than the 1kg or 2lb loaf made by large machines. Check with the manufacturer's instructions for recommended quantities for each loaf size and then choose the closest setting.

BAKING PROGRAMMES

All machines have a selection of programmes to help ensure you produce the perfect loaf of bread. The lengths of kneading, rising and baking times are varied to suit the different flours and to determine the texture of the finished loaf.

WHITE OR BASIC

This mode is the most commonly used programme, ideal for white loaves and mixed grain loaves where white bread flour is the main ingredient.

RAPID

This cycle reduces the time to make a standard loaf of bread by about 1 hour and is handy when speed is the main criterion. The finished loaf may not rise as much as one made on the basic programme and may therefore be a little more dense.

WHOLE WHEAT

This is a longer cycle than the basic one, to allow time for the slower rising action of doughs containing a high percentage

ABOVE: Sun-dried tomatoes can be added to the dough at the raisin beep to make deliciously flavoured bread.

of strong wholemeal (whole-wheat) flour. Some machines also have a multigrain mode for breads made with cereals and grains such as Granary and rye, although it is possible to make satisfactory breads using either this or the basic mode, depending on the percentages of the flours.

FRENCH

This programme is best suited for low-fat and low-sugar breads, and it produces loaves with an open texture and crispier crust. More time within the cycle is devoted to rising, and in some bread machines the loaf is baked at a slightly higher temperature.

SWEET BREAD

A few bread machines offer this feature in addition to crust colour control. It is useful if you intend to bake breads with a high fat or sugar content which tend to colour too much.

CAKE

This setting can be used to mix and bake cakes. Most machines require a dry mix and a liquid mix to be added to the bread pan. The machine will then mix and bake. If your machine does not have this facility, teabreads and non-yeast cakes

can be easily mixed in a bowl and then baked in the bread pan on the bake or bake only cycle.

BAKE

This setting allows you to use the bread machine as an oven, either to bake cakes and ready-prepared dough from the supermarket or to extend the standard baking time if you prefer your bread to be particularly well done.

GLUTEN-FREE

A programme designed for gluten-free flour bread recipes and mixes.

RYE

A feature offered on one machine for making rye and spelt flour breads. Includes a kneading blade especially suited to kneading these doughs.

RAISIN BEEP

Some machines have an automatic dispenser, which can be filled with the extra ingredients before commencing the programme.

DOUGH PROGRAMMES

Most machines include a dough programme: some models have dough programmes with extra features.

DOUGH

This programme allows you to make dough without machine-baking it, which is essential for all hand-shaped breads. The machine mixes, kneads and proves the dough, ready for shaping, final proving and baking in a conventional oven. If you wish to make different shaped loaves or rolls, buns and pastries, you will find this facility invaluable.

OTHER DOUGH PROGRAMMES

Some machines include cycles for making different types of dough, such as a rapid dough mode for pizzas and Focaccia or a longer mode for wholemeal dough and bagel dough. Some "dough only" cycles also include the raisin beep facility.

Baking, Cooling and Storing

A bread machine should always bake a perfect loaf of bread, but it is important to remember that it is just a machine and cannot think for itself. It is essential that you measure the ingredients carefully and add them to the bread pan in the order specified by the manufacturer of your machine. Ingredients should be at room temperature, so take them out of the refrigerator in good time, unless your machine has a pre-heat cycle.

Check the dough during the kneading cycles; if your machine does not have a window, open the lid and look into the bread pan. The dough should be slightly tacky to the touch. If it is very soft add a little more flour; if the dough feels very firm and dry add a little more liquid. It is also worth checking the dough towards the end of the rising period. On particularly warm days your bread may rise too high. If this happens it may rise over the bread pan and begin to travel down the outside during the first few minutes of baking. If your bread looks ready for baking before the baking cycle is due to begin, you have two options. You can either override and cancel the programme, then re-programme using a bake or bake only cycle, or you can try pricking the top of the loaf with a cocktail stick to deflate it slightly and let the programme continue.

Different machines will give different browning levels using the same recipe. Check when you try a new recipe and make a note to select a lighter or darker setting next time if necessary.

BELOW: Use a cocktail stick to prick dough that has risen too high.

Removing the Bread from the Pan
Once the bread is baked it is best removed from the bread pan immediately. Turn the bread pan upside down, holding it with oven gloves or a thick protective cloth – it will be very hot – and shake it several times to release the bread. If removing the bread is difficult, rap the corner of the bread pan on a wooden board several times or try turning the base of the shaft underneath the base of the bread pan. Don't try to free the bread by using a knife or similar metal object, or you will scratch the non-stick coating.

If the kneading blade remains inside the loaf, you should use a heat-resistant plastic or wooden implement to prise it out. The metal blade and the bread will be too hot to use your fingers.

ABOVE: Multigrain Bread is made with honey which, like other sweeteners, acts as a preservative. The loaf should stay moist for longer.

BELOW: Use a serrated bread knife when slicing bread so that you do not damage the texture of the crumb.

TO SERVE BREAD WARM

Wrap the bread in foil and place in an oven preheated to 180°C/350°F/Gas 4 for 10–15 minutes, to heat through. This is also a method that can be used to freshen bread.

COOLING

Place the bread on a wire rack to allow the steam to escape and leave it for at least 30 minutes before slicing. Always slice bread using a serrated knife to avoid damaging the crumb structure.

STORING

Cool the bread, then wrap it in foil or place it in a plastic bag and seal it, to preserve the freshness. If your bread has a crisp crust, this will soften on storage, so until it is sliced it is best left uncovered. After cutting, put the loaf in a large paper bag, but try to use it fairly quickly, as bread starts to dry out as soon as it is cut. Breads containing eggs tend to dry out even more quickly, while those made with honey or added fats stay moist for longer.

BELOW: Parker House Rolls can be frozen after baking, as soon as they are cool. They taste delicious warm, so refresh them in the oven just before serving.

ABOVE: If you are freezing bread to be used for toasting, slice the loaf first.

Ideally, freshly baked bread should be consumed within 2–3 days. Avoid storing bread in the refrigerator as this causes it to go stale more quickly.

Freeze cooked breads if you need to keep them for longer. Place the loaf or rolls in a freezer bag, seal and freeze for up to 3 months. If you intend to use the bread for toast or sandwiches, it is easier

ABOVE: Store bread with a crispy crust in a large paper bag.

to slice it before freezing, so you can remove only the number of slices you need. Thaw the bread at room temperature, still in its freezer bag.

With some loaves, however, freezing may not be a sensible option. For example, very crusty bread, such as French Couronne, tends to come apart after it has been frozen and thawed.

STORING BREAD DOUGHS

If it is not convenient to bake bread dough immediately you can store it in an oiled bowl covered with clear film (plastic wrap), or seal it in a plastic bag. Dough can be stored in the refrigerator for up to 2 days if it contains butter, milk or eggs and up to 4 days if no perishable ingredients are included.

Keep an eye on the dough and knock it back (punch it down) occasionally. When you are ready to use the dough, bring it back to room temperature, then shape, prove and bake it in the normal way.

You can make dough in your machine, shape it, then keep it in the refrigerator overnight, ready for baking conventionally next morning for breakfast. Cover with oiled clear film as usual.

Bread dough can be frozen in a freezer-proof bag for up to 1 month. When you are ready to use it, thaw the dough overnight in the refrigerator or at room temperature for 2–3 hours. Once the dough has thawed, place it in a warm place to rise, but bear in mind that it will take longer to rise than freshly made dough.

ABOVE: Store dough in the refrigerator in an oiled bowl covered in clear film or in a plastic bag.

ABOVE: Prepare rolls the night before and store in the refrigerator, ready to bake the following morning.

HAND-SHAPED LOAVES

One of the most useful features a bread machine can have is the dough setting. Use this, and the machine will automatically mix the ingredients, and will then knead and rest the dough before providing the ideal conditions for it to rise for the first time. The whole cycle, from mixing through to rising, takes around 1¾ hours, but remember it will vary slightly between machines.

KNOCKING BACK

1 At the end of the cycle, the dough will have almost doubled in bulk and will be ready for shaping. Remove the bread pan from the machine.

2 Lightly flour a work surface. Gently remove the dough from the bread pan and place it on the floured surface. Knock back (punch down) or deflate the dough to relieve the tension in the gluten and expel some of the carbon dioxide.

3 Knead the dough lightly for 1–2 minutes; shape into a tight ball. At this stage, a recipe may suggest you cover the dough with oiled clear film (plastic wrap) or an upturned bowl and leave it to rest for a few minutes. This allows the gluten to relax so dough will be easier to handle.

SHAPING

Techniques to shape dough vary, depending on the finished form of the bread you wish to make. The following steps illustrate how to form basic bread, roll and yeast pastry shapes.

BAGUETTE

1 To shape a baguette or French stick, flatten the dough into a rectangle about 2.5cm/1in thick, either using the palms of your hands or a rolling pin.

2 From one long side fold one-third of the dough down and then fold over the remaining third of dough and press gently to secure. Repeat twice more, resting the dough in between folds to avoid tearing.

3 Gently stretch the dough and roll it backwards and forwards with your hands to make a breadstick of even thickness and the required length.

4 Place the baguette dough between a folded floured dishtowel, or in a banneton, and leave in a warm place to prove. The dishtowel or banneton will help the baguette to keep the correct shape as it rises.

BLOOMER

1 Roll the dough out to a rectangle 2.5cm/1in thick. Roll up from one long side and place it, seam side up, on a floured baking sheet. Cover and leave to rest for 15 minutes.

2 Turn the loaf over and place on another floured baking sheet. Using your fingertips, tuck the sides and ends of the dough under. Cover; leave to finish rising.

TIN LOAF

Roll the dough out to a rectangle the length of the bread tin (pan) and three times as wide. Fold the dough widthways, bringing the top third down and the bottom third up. Press the dough down well, turn it over and place it in the tin.

COTTAGE LOAF

1 To shape a cottage loaf, divide the dough into two pieces, approximately one-third and two-thirds in size. Shape each piece of dough into a plump round ball and place on lightly floured baking sheets. Cover with inverted bowls and leave to rise for 30 minutes, or until 50 per cent larger.

2 Flatten the top of the large loaf. Using a sharp knife, cut a cross about 4cm/ 1½in across in the centre. Brush the area lightly with water and place the small round on top.

3 Using one or two fingers or the floured handle of a wooden spoon, press the centre of the top round, penetrating into the middle of the dough beneath.

TWIST

1 To shape bread for a twist, divide the dough into two equal pieces. Using the palms of your hands, roll each piece of dough on a lightly floured surface into a long rope, about 4–5cm/1½–2in thick Make both ropes the same length.

2 Place the two ropes side by side. Starting from the centre, twist one rope over the other. Continue in the same way until you reach the end, then pinch the ends together and tuck the join underneath. Turn the dough around and repeat the process with the other end, twisting the dough in the same direction as the first.

BREADSTICK

To shape a breadstick, roll the dough to a rectangle about 1cm/½in thick, and cut out strips that are about 7.5cm/3in long and 2cm/¾in wide. Using the palm of your hand, gently roll each strip into a long thin rope.

It may help to lift each rope and pull it very gently to stretch it. If you are still finding it difficult to stretch the dough, leave it to rest for a few minutes and then try again.

COURONNE

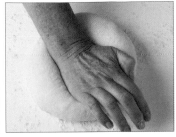

1 Shape the dough into a ball. Using the heal of your hand make a hole in the centre. Gradually enlarge the centre, turning the dough to make a circle, with a 13cm 15cm/5 6in cavity.

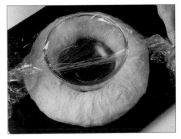

2 Place on a lightly oiled baking sheet. Put a small, lightly oiled bowl in the centre of the ring to prevent the dough from filling in the centre during rising.

SCROLL

Roll out the dough using the palms of your hands, until it forms a rope, about 25cm/10in long, with tapered ends. Form into a loose "S" shape, then curl the ends in to make a scroll. Leave a small space to allow for the final proving.

CROISSANT

1 To shape a croissant, roll out the dough on a lightly floured surface and then cut it into strips that are about 15cm/6in wide.

2 Cut each strip along its length into triangles with 15cm/6in bases and 18cm/7in sides.

3 Place with the pointed end towards you and the 15cm/6in base at the top; gently pull each corner of the base to stretch it slightly.

4 Roll up the dough with one hand from the base while pulling, finishing with the dough point underneath. Finally, curve the corners around in the direction of the pointed end to make the curved croissant shape.

BRAIDED ROLL

1 To shape a braided roll, place the dough on a lightly floured surface and roll out. Divide the dough into balls, the number depending on the amount of dough and how many rolls you would like to make.

2 Divide each ball of dough into three equal pieces. Using your hands, roll into long, thin ropes of equal length and place them side by side.

3 Pinch one of the ends together and plait the pieces of dough. Finally, pinch the remaining ends together and then tuck the join under.

FILLED BRAID

1 Place the dough for the braid on a lightly floured surface. Roll out and shape into a rectangle. Using a sharp knife, make diagonal cuts down each of the long sides of the dough, about 2cm/⅝in wide. Place the filling in the centre of the uncut strip.

2 Fold in the end strip of dough, then fold over alternate strips of dough to form a braid over the filling. Tuck in the final end to seal the braid.

PROVING

After the dough has been shaped, it will need to be left to rise again. This is sometimes referred to as proving the dough. Most doughs are left in a warm place until they just about double in bulk. How long this takes will vary – depending on the ambient temperature and richness of the dough – but somewhere between 30 and 60 minutes is usual.

Avoid leaving dough to rise for too long (over-proving) or it may collapse in the oven or when it is slashed before baking. Equally, you need to leave it to rise sufficiently, or the finished loaf will be heavy.

To test if the dough is ready to bake, press it lightly with your fingertip; it should feel springy, not firm. The indentation made by your finger should slowly fill and spring back.

ABOVE: A dough that has been shaped and placed in a bread tin to rise. The unproved dough should reach just over halfway up the tin.

ABOVE: Leave the dough in a warm, draught-free place to rise. This should take between 30 and 60 minutes. Once risen, the dough will have almost doubled in bulk.

SLASHING

Slashing bread dough before baking serves a useful purpose as well as adding a decorative finish, as found on the tops of traditional loaf shapes such as bloomers and French sticks. When the dough goes into the oven it has one final rise, known as "oven spring", so the cuts or slashes allow the bread to expand without tearing or cracking the sides.

The earlier you slash the dough the wider the splits will be. Depth is important, too: the deeper the slashes the more the bread will open during baking. Most recipes suggest slashing just before glazing and baking. If you think a bread has slightly over-proved keep the slashes fairly shallow and gentle to avoid the possibility of the dough collapsing.

Use a sharp knife or scalpel blade to make a clean cut. Move smoothly and swiftly to avoid tearing the dough. Scissors can also be used to make an easy decorative finish to rolls or breads.

SLASHING A SPLIT TIN OR FARMHOUSE LOAF

A long slash, about 1cm/½in deep, can be made along the top of the dough just before baking. You can use this slashing procedure for both machine and hand-shaped loaves. Using a very sharp knife, plunge into one end of the dough and pull the blade smoothly along the entire length, but make sure you do not drag the dough.

If flouring the top of the loaf, sprinkle with flour before slashing.

SLASHING A BAGUETTE

To slash a baguette, cut long slashes of equal length and depth four or five times along its length. A razor-sharp blade is the best tool for slashing breads. Used with care, a scalpel is perfectly safe and has the advantage that the blades can be changed to ensure you always have a sharp edge.

USING SCISSORS TO SLASH ROLLS

Rolls can be given quick and interesting finishes using a pair of sharp-pointed scissors. You could experiment with all sorts of ideas. Try the following to start you off.

• Just before baking cut across the top of the dough first in one direction then the other to make a cross.
• Make six horizontal or vertical cuts equally spaced around the sides of the rolls. Leave for 5 minutes before baking.
• Cut through the rolls in four or five places from the edge almost to the centre, just before baking.

ABOVE: Top rolls: making a cross; middle rolls: horizontal cuts around the side; bottom rolls: cuts from the edge almost to the centre.

BAKING BREAD WITH A CRISP CRUST

For a crisper crust, it is necessary to introduce steam into the oven. The moisture initially softens the dough, so that it can rise, resulting in a crispier crust. Moisture also improves the crust colour by encouraging caramelization of the natural sugars in the dough. Standing the loaf on a baking stone or unglazed terracotta tiles also helps to produce a crisp crust, the effect being similar to when breads are cooked in a clay or brick oven. The porous tiles or stone hold heat and draw moisture from the bread base while it is baking.

1 About 30 minutes before you intend to bake, place the baking stone on the bottom shelf of the oven, then preheat the oven. Alternatively line the oven shelf with unglazed terracotta tiles, leaving air space all around to allow for the free circulation of the hot air.

2 When ready to bake, using a peel (baker's shovel), place the bread directly on the tiles or baking stone.

3 Using a water spray bottle, mist the oven walls two or three times during the first 5–10 minutes of baking. Open the oven door as little as possible, spray the oven walls and quickly close the door to avoid unnecessary heat loss. Remember not to spray the oven light, fan or heating elements.

GLAZES

Both machine-baked breads and hand-shaped loaves benefit from a glaze to give that final finishing touch. Glazes may be used before baking, or during the early stages of baking to give a more golden crust or to change the texture of the crust. This is particularly noticeable with hand-shaped breads but good results may also be obtained with machine-baked loaves. Glazes may also be applied after baking to give flavour and a glossy finish. Another important role for glazes is to act as an adhesive, to help any topping applied to the loaf stick to the surface of the dough.

For machine-baked breads, the glaze should either be brushed on to the loaf just before the baking cycle commences, or within 10 minutes of the start of the baking cycle. Apply the glaze quickly, so there is minimal heat loss while the bread machine lid is open. Avoid brushing the edges of the loaf with a sticky glaze as this might make the bread stick to the pan.

Glazes using egg, milk and salted water can also be brushed over freshly cooked loaves. Brush the glaze over as soon as the baking cycle finishes, then leave the bread inside the machine for 3–4 minutes, to allow the glaze to dry to a shine. Then remove the loaf from the machine and pan in the usual way. This method is useful if you want to sprinkle over a topping.

For hand-shaped loaves, you can brush with glaze before or after baking, and some recipes, such as Parker House Rolls will suggest that you do both.

GLAZES USED BEFORE OR DURING BAKING

For a crust with an attractive glossy shine, apply a glaze before or during baking.

MILK

Brush on loaves, such as potato breads, where a softer golden crust is desired. Milk is also used for bridge rolls, buns (such as teacakes) and flatbreads where a soft crust is desirable. It can also be used on baps and soft morning rolls before dusting with flour.

OLIVE OIL

This is mainly used with Continental-style breads, such as Focaccia, Stromboli and Fougasse. It adds flavour and a shiny finish; and the darker the oil the fuller the flavour, so use extra virgin olive oil for a really deep taste. Olive oil can be used before and/or after baking.

BELOW: French Fougasse is brushed with olive oil just before baking.

BUTTER

Rolls and buns are brushed with melted butter before baking to add colour, while also keeping the dough soft. American Parker House Rolls are brushed before and after baking, while Bubble Corn Bread is drizzled with melted butter before being baked. Butter adds a rich flavour to the breads glazed with it.

SALTED WATER

Mix 10ml/2 tsp salt with 30ml/2 tbsp water and brush over the dough immediately before baking. This gives a crisp baked crust with a slight sheen.

EGG WHITE

Use 1 egg white mixed with 15ml/1 tbsp water for a lighter golden, slightly shiny crust. This is often a better alternative to egg yolk for savoury breads.

EGG YOLK

Mix 1 egg yolk with 15ml/1 tbsp milk or water. This classic glaze, also known as egg wash, is used to give a very golden, shiny crust. For sweet buns, breads and yeast cakes add 15ml/1 tbsp caster (superfine) sugar, for extra colour and flavour.

GLAZES ADDED AFTER BAKING

Some glazes are used after baking, often on sweet breads, cakes and pastries. These glazes generally give a glossy and/or sticky finish, and also help to keep the bread or cake moist. They are suited to both machine and hand-shaped breads.

BUTTER

Breads such as Italian Panettone and stollen are brushed with melted butter after baking to soften the crust. Clarified butter is also sometimes used as a glaze to soften flatbreads such as Naan.

HONEY, MALT, MOLASSES AND GOLDEN SYRUP

Liquid sweeteners can be warmed and brushed over breads, rolls, teabreads and cakes to give a soft, sweet, sticky crust. Honey is a traditional glaze and provides a lovely flavour, for example. Both malt and molasses have quite a strong flavour, so use these sparingly, matching them to compatible breads such as fruit loaves and cakes. Or you could mix them with a milder-flavoured liquid sweetener, such as golden (light corn) syrup, to reduce their impact slightly.

SUGAR GLAZE

Dissolve 30–45ml/2–3 tbsp granulated sugar in the same amount of milk or water. Bring to the boil then simmer for 1–2 minutes, until syrupy. Brush over fruit loaves or buns for a glossy sheen. For extra flavour, use rose water.

SYRUPS

Yeast cakes, such as Savarin, are often drizzled with sugar syrup, flavoured with liqueurs, spirits or lemon juice. The syrup moistens the bread, while adding a decorative topping at the same time.

PRESERVES

Jam or marmalade can be melted with a little liquid. Choose water, liqueur, spirits (such as rum or brandy) or fruit juice, depending on the bread to be glazed. The liquid thins the preserve and adds flavour. It can be brushed over freshly baked warm teabreads, Danish Pastries and sweet breads to a give a glossy, sticky finish. Dried fruit and nuts can then be sprinkled on top.

Select a flavoured jam to complement your bread or teacake. If in doubt, use apricot jam.

ICING SUGAR GLAZE

Mix 30–45ml/2–3 tbsp icing (confectioners') sugar with 15ml/1 tbsp fruit juice, milk, single (light) cream (flavoured with natural vanilla essence/extract) or water and drizzle or brush over warm sweet breads, cakes and pastries. You can also add a pinch of spice to the icing sugar to bring out the flavour of the loaf.

LEFT: The glossy top to Hot Cross Buns is achieved by glazing after baking with a mixture of milk and sugar.

TOPPINGS

In addition to glazes, extra ingredients can be sprinkled over breads to give the finished loaf further interest. Toppings can alter the appearance, flavour and texture of the bread, so are an important part of any recipe. They also allow you to add your own individual stamp to a bread by using a topping of your own invention.

MACHINE-BAKED BREADS

A topping can be added at various stages: at the beginning of the baking cycle, about 10 minutes after baking begins, or immediately after baking while the bread is still hot. If you choose to add the topping at the beginning of baking, only open the lid for the shortest possible time, so heat loss is limited to the minimum. Before you add a topping, brush the bread with a glaze. This will ensure that the topping sticks to the loaf. Most machine breads are brushed with an egg, milk or water glaze.

If applying a topping to a bread after baking, remove the bread pan carefully from the machine and close the lid to retain the heat. Using oven gloves, quickly loosen the bread from the pan, then put it back in the pan again (this will make the

ABOVE: *Flaked almonds have been sprinkled over the top of this Raspberry and Almond Teabread, giving a broad hint of its delicious flavour and adding extra crunch.*

final removal easier) then brush the loaf with the glaze and sprinkle over the chosen topping. Return the bread in the pan to the bread machine for 3–4 minutes, which allows the glaze to bake on and secure the topping. With this method, the chosen topping will not cook and brown in the same way it would were it added at the beginning of baking.

When using grain as a topping, the general rule is to match it to the grain or flour used in the bread itself; for example, a bread containing millet flakes or millet seeds is often sprinkled with millet flour.

If a flavouring has been incorporated into the dough, you may be able to top the loaf with the same ingredient, to provide a hint of what is inside. Try sprinkling a little grated Parmesan on to a cheese loaf about 10 minutes after baking begins, or, for a loaf flavoured with herbs, add an appropriate dried herb as a topping immediately after baking.

LEFT: *Rolled oats and wheat grain are sprinkled on to Sweet Potato Bread just before it begins to bake to give the loaf a delightful rustic look.*

FLOUR

To create a farmhouse-style finish, brush the loaf with water or milk glaze within 10 minutes of the start of baking and dust lightly with flour. Use white flour, or wholemeal (whole-wheat) or Granary (whole-wheat) for a more rustic finish.

SMALL SEEDS

Seeds can be used to add flavour and texture in addition to a decorative finish. Try sesame, poppy, aniseed, caraway or cumin seeds. If adding sesame seeds immediately after baking, lightly toast until golden before adding.

SALT

Brush the top of a white loaf with water or egg glaze and sprinkle with a coarse sea salt, to give an attractive and crunchy topping. Sea salt is best applied at the beginning of baking or 10 minutes into the baking cycle.

CORN MEAL OR POLENTA

Use corn meal, polenta, semolina or other speciality flours as a finish for breads containing these flours, such as Courgette Country Grain Bread.

LARGE SEEDS

Gently press pumpkin or sunflower seeds on to the top of a freshly glazed loaf to give an attractive finish and a bonus crunch.

WHEAT AND RYE FLAKES

These add both texture and fibre to bread as well as visual appeal. Sprinkle them over the top of the loaf after glazing at the beginning of baking.

ROLLED OATS

These make a decorative finish for white breads and breads flavoured with oatmeal. Rolled oats are best added just before or at the very beginning of baking.

PEPPER AND PAPRIKA

Freshly ground black pepper and paprika both add spiciness to savoury breads. This tasty topping can be added before, during or after baking.

ICING SUGAR

Dust cooked sweet breads, teabreads or cakes with icing (confectioners') sugar after baking for a finished look. If you like, add 2.5ml/½tsp spice before sprinkling

HAND-SHAPED BREAD

All of the toppings used on machine-baked breads can also be added to breads that are hand-shaped and baked in an oven. There are several methods that can be used for adding a topping to hand-shaped rolls and breads.

SPRINKLING WITH FLOUR

If you are using flour, this should be sprinkled over the dough immediately after shaping and again before slashing and baking, to give a rustic finish. Match the flour to the type of bread being made. Unbleached white bread flour is ideal for giving soft rolls and breads a fine finish. Use corn meal, ground rice or rice flour for crumpets and muffins, and brown, wholemeal and Granary (whole-wheat) flours on wholegrain breads.

GROUND RICE OR RICE FLOUR

Muffins are enhanced with a ground rice or rice flour topping.

WHOLEMEAL FLOUR

Wholemeal (whole-wheat) flour toppings complement wholegrain dough whether made into loaves or rolls.

ABOVE: An Easter Tea Ring is glazed with an icing made from icing sugar and orange juice, then sprinkled with pecan nuts and candied orange.

ROLLING DOUGH IN SEEDS

Sprinkle seeds, salt or any other fine topping on a work surface, then roll the shaped but unproved dough in the chosen topping until it is evenly coated. This is ideal for coating wholegrain breads with pumpkin seeds or wheat flakes. After rolling, place the dough on the sheet for its final rising.

SESAME SEEDS

Dough sticks can be rolled in small seeds for a delicious crunchy topping.

ADDING A TOPPING AFTER A GLAZE

Some toppings are sprinkled over the bread after glazing and immediately before baking. In addition to the toppings suggested for machine-baked breads, these toppings can be used:

CANDIED FRUITS

Candied fruits make an attractive topping for festive breads and buns. Add the fruits after an egg glaze. Candied fruits can also be used after baking, with a jam or icing (confectioners') sugar glaze to stick the fruits to the bread.

NUTS

Just before baking, brush sweet or savoury breads and rolls with glaze and sprinkle with chopped or flaked (sliced) almonds, chopped cashews, chopped or whole walnuts or pecan nuts.

MILLET GRAIN, BLACK ONION SEEDS AND MUSTARD SEEDS

These small grains and seeds all add texture and taste to breads. Try them as a topping for loaves and flatbreads such as Lavash and Naan.

VEGETABLES

Brush savoury breads and rolls with an egg glaze or olive oil and then sprinkle with finely chopped raw onion, raw (bell) peppers, sun-dried tomatoes or olives for an extremely tasty crust.

CHEESE

Grated cheeses, such as Parmesan, Cheddar or Pecorino, are best for sprinkling on to dough just before baking, resulting in a chewy, flavoursome crust.

FRESH HERBS

Use fresh herbs, such as rosemary, thyme, sage or basil for Italian-style flatbreads. Chopped herbs also make a good topping for rolls.

USING SUGAR AS A TOPPING

Sugar is available in many forms, so choose one appropriate for your topping.

DEMERARA SUGAR

Before baking, brush buns and cakes with butter or milk, then sprinkle with demerara (raw) sugar for a crunchy finish.

SUGAR COATING

Yeast doughs that are deep-fried, such as Doughnuts and Saffron Braids can be sprinkled or tossed in a sugar coating. Toss doughnuts in caster (superfine) sugar which has been mixed with a little ground cinnamon or grated nutmeg, or flavoured using a vanilla pod (bean).

DUSTING WITH ICING SUGAR

Use a fine sieve to sprinkle cooked buns and yeast cakes, such as Devonshire Splits and Calas, with icing sugar. Large cakes and breads such as Panettone, Kugelhopf and Strudel also benefit from a light dusting of icing sugar, as do fruit-filled Savarins. If serving a bread or cake warm, dust with icing sugar when ready to serve to avoid the topping soaking into the bread.

USING SOURDOUGHS AND STARTERS

For bread to rise, some sort of raising agent – or leaven – must be used. In most cases, this will be yeast, or perhaps bicarbonate of soda (baking soda), but it is also possible to initiate the fermentation process naturally, by the action of wild yeasts, present in the air, on a medium such as flour or potatoes. When this is done, the mixture that results is called a starter.

There are two basic starters: a natural leaven and a yeasted starter. The former uses only airborne yeast spores, which create a lactic fermentation, as when milk turns sour. A yeasted starter includes a small amount of baker's yeast to kick-start the fermentation and develop a desired strain of yeast.

Sourdoughs are made using starters which develop over several days to produce a distinctive tanginess or "soured" flavour. Depending on how starters are made, how long they are left to ferment and how they are used, different flavours as well as textures can be achieved. Many of the Continental breads owe their flavours and textures to starters, which also influence their keeping qualities.

BREADMAKING METHODS

There are three basic methods of making breads: the direct method, the sourdough method, and the sponge method.

In the direct method, the flour, water and yeast are mixed, and once the dough has risen, the bread is baked in the shortest possible time. This is the conventional way of bread making.

The sourdough method is a much lengthier process. First, a starter must be made – this takes several days – and then this must be mixed with additional flour and other ingredients, often in several stages, called "refreshments", a process that takes at least 24 hours.

The sponge method is a compromise between the previous two. The dough is made using baker's yeast. A portion of the dough is mixed and allowed to ferment before the remaining ingredients are added. The process enhances the flavour and texture of the finished bread.

THE SOURDOUGH METHOD

Sourdough breads can be made from either a natural leaven or a yeasted starter. Most natural sourdough cultures can be turned into a starter within about 5 days. Flour and water are the basic ingredients, but other ingredients may be added to encourage the fermentation, such as honey, malt extract, soured milk, ground cumin or even a little baker's yeast.

The French term for this flour and water mixture is a "chef". The chef is left to ferment for 2–3 days, which brings about a lactic acid action, giving rise to the basic sour flavour. Once this dough is aerated and slightly sour, it is mixed or "refreshed" with more flour and water, to feed the fermentation process. After another 24 hours or so it is refreshed again, and becomes a natural leavener, or levain. This is left to ferment for about 8 hours more, when it is ready for use in the final bread dough.

Bread made by this method will taste slightly sour and will have a dense moist crumb, chewy crust and extremely good keeping qualities. Sourdough starters have varying textures, so do not worry if you come across different consistencies. Often American starters tend to be less stiff.

THE FRENCH SPONGE METHOD

The French sponge or poolish is made with yeast and some of the flour and water from the bread recipe, but no salt to retard the fermentation. The poolish is usually fermented for a minimum of 2 hours, and for up to 8 hours. Usually less yeast is used than with the direct method so the dough rises more slowly, giving it time to ripen and develop a springy texture. It combines the chewiness of a sourdough with the lightness of a basic bread.

The wetter the mix, the quicker it will rise, as the flour and water will provide less resistance for the yeast.

THE ITALIAN SPONGE METHOD

The Italian sponge or biga takes at least 12 hours, often longer, to ripen, allowing time for the dough to develop and rise to three times its original bulk before collapsing. The longer it is left the more developed the flavour will be. These breads have an open, holey, slightly moist and chewy texture. Their flavour and aroma tend to be yeasty and champagne-like. Ciabatta is a perfect example.

MAKING AN ITALIAN SPONGE

1 The flour, water and yeast for the biga are added to the bread machine and mixed as usual.

2 It is allowed to rise for several hours until it has tripled in size. After 12 hours it should be starting to collapse.

3 When the dough collapses, it is ready to be combined with the remaining ingredients for the bread.

THE OLD DOUGH METHOD

A variation of the direct method, this approach is exactly what its name suggests. A small piece of dough is removed from a batch of risen dough and set aside for adding to the dough for the next loaf of bread. This is a quick and easy alternative to making a starter and will add texture and improve the taste of the bread to which it is added.

The old dough method is perfect for the bread machine. Make a batch of dough using the regular dough cycle. When the bread is ready for shaping, pull off about 115g/4oz of the dough, place it in a bowl and cover with clear film (plastic wrap). If using within 4 hours leave at room temperature; if not, put the bowl in the refrigerator, but let the dough return to room temperature before using it. It can either be kneaded into a batch of dough for shaping by hand or added with the ingredients for a machine-baked bread.

If you are adding old dough to a loaf which is to be baked in a machine, reduce the flour and liquid slightly when you make up the new batch of dough. The following recipe is suitable for a medium or large machine. If you have a smaller machine reduce the quantities by a quarter. You can increase the quantities by a quarter for a large machine if you like.

USING THE OLD DOUGH METHOD

ABOVE: San Francisco-style Sourdough is made from airborne spores of yeast, and has no baker's yeast added to it. The variety of yeast strains in the atmosphere will mean that the bread tastes slightly different from place to place.

1 Tear about 115g/4oz dough off bread that is ready for shaping. Place in a bowl and cover with clear film. Set aside at room temperature or, if not using within 4 hours, in the refrigerator. Return to room temperature before using.

2 Pour 280ml/10fl oz/1¼ cups water into the bread machine pan. Add the old dough which has been reserved. However, if the instructions for your machine specify that the dry ingredients are to be placed in the bread pan first, reverse the order in which you add the dry ingredients and the water and reserved dough.

3 Sprinkle over 450g/1lb/4 cups unbleached white bread flour. Add 7.5ml/1½ tsp salt, 15ml/1 tbsp granulated sugar and 25g/1oz butter, placing these ingredients in separate corners of the bread pan.

4 Make a small indent in the centre of the flour and add 5ml/1 tsp easy bake (rapid-rise) dried yeast.

5 Set the bread machine to the basic/normal setting, medium crust. Size: large/750g for medium or 1kg/2lb for large. Press Start. At the end of the cycle, turn the bread out on to a wire rack to cool.

MAKING A YOGURT STARTER

Variations on the basic flour and water starter can be made to add complexity and uniqueness to the flavour and texture of bread. This yogurt starter will give a flavour similar to that of San Francisco-style Sourdough because the lactose in the milk products sours in a similar way.

1 Place 75ml/5 tbsp natural (plain) yogurt in a bowl. Pour 175ml/6fl oz/¾ cup skimmed milk into a pan and heat gently.

2 Stir the milk into the yogurt. Cover with clear film and leave in a warm place for 8–24 hours, or until thickened. Stir in any clear liquid which may have separated and risen to the surface.

REPLENISHING A STARTER

After making the starter for the first time, use or replenish within 3–4 days. When half has been used, replenish with 50g/2oz/½ cup white bread flour and 45ml/3 tbsp skimmed milk and 15ml/1 tbsp natural yogurt or 60ml/ 4 tbsp skimmed milk. If used daily, the starter can be kept at room temperature. If not, store in the refrigerator; bring back to room temperature before use.

3 Gradually mix in 115g/4oz/1 cup organic white bread flour, stirring to incorporate evenly.

BELOW: French Couronne is made using a chef starter which becomes a levain, a natural leavener.

4 Cover and leave in a warm place for 2–3 days, until the mixture is full of bubbles and smells pleasantly sour. (Uncover to check the aroma of the starter.) Use instead of the usual starter for San Francisco-style Sourdough or incorporate into a basic bread recipe.

2 Stir the starter and use the amount required in the recipe. If your purpose in bringing the starter to room temperature is just so that you can feed it, pour half of the starter into a measuring jug (cup), note the volume, then throw it away. This is so you will know how much to replenish.

USING A STARTER IN YOUR BREAD MACHINE

You can try adding a sourdough starter to one of your favourite recipes for a more complex flavour. Add it to a basic white, wholemeal (whole-wheat), mixed grain or rye bread. Here are a few pointers:

• Always bring the starter back to room temperature before using if it has been stored in the refrigerator.

• If your starter was made from a mixture of roughly half flour and half liquid, when you add it to the recipe, reduce the liquid in the recipe by the quantity of liquid in the starter, that is by half the total volume of the starter.

• The starter can be used in two ways. Try it in doughs that are made in the bread machine but shaped by hand and baked in the oven, or use it in a dough that is made and baked in the machine. If the latter, check the dough during the rising stage to make sure it is not rising too high; you can always override the programme and set the machine to the bake only programme.

• If the dough hasn't risen as much as you would like, you will need to bake it in the oven. Remove the dough from the bread machine and shape it by hand. Leave to rise until it has almost doubled in size, then bake in the normal way.

ABOVE: Ciabatta is made using the Italian sponge method.

REFRESHING A SOURDOUGH STARTER

Each time you use a sourdough starter, it needs to be replenished. Also, if you are not likely to be using it for some time, it is important to "feed" the starter regularly, with flour and liquid, to keep it active. The amount of flour and water you add to the starter to replenish it should equate to what was removed, either to be used in dough or discarded.

Once established, a sourdough starter can be kept in the refrigerator almost indefinitely. In fact, the flavour of the sourdough starter gets better with age. If your starter begins to turn pink or develops a mould, however, discard it and start again.

3 Replenish the starter by adding a quantity of flour and water (in equal parts by volume). Use organic white or wholemeal (whole-wheat) bread flour, or a combination of both. Wholemeal flour develops a more intense sour flavour. Add a quantity that equates to the amount of starter that has been removed. Mix until smooth.

1 Remove the starter from the refrigerator. It should be at room temperature before it's added to a recipe or fed to keep it active.

4 Cover and leave in a warm place for a few hours until it starts to bubble and ferment. Place in the refrigerator until needed.

GETTING THE BEST FROM YOUR MACHINE

Even the most comprehensive bread-machine manual cannot possibly cover all the hints and tips you will need. As you gain experience and confidence you will be able to solve more and more of any little problems that crop up. Here are a few pointers to help you along the road to successful baking.

TEMPERATURE AND HUMIDITY

The bread machine is not a sealed environment, and temperature and humidity can affect the finished results. On dry days, dry ingredients contain less water and on humid days they hold more.

The temperature of the ingredients is a very important factor in determining the success of machine-baked bread. Some machines specify that all ingredients should be at room temperature; others state that ingredients can be added from the refrigerators. Some machines have preheating cycles to bring the ingredients to an optimum temperature of around 20–25°C/68–77°F, before mixing starts. It is recommended that you use ingredients at room temperature. Water can be used straight from the cold tap. Lukewarm water may be beneficial for the rapid bake cycle on cold days.

Hot weather can mean that doughs will rise faster, so on very hot days start with chilled ingredients, using milk or eggs straight from the refrigerator.

Icy winter weather and cold draughts will inhibit the action of the yeast, so either move your machine to a warmer spot, or warm liquids before adding them to the bread pan. On very cold days, let the water stand at room temperature for about half an hour before adding the other ingredients to the pan, or add a little warm water to bring it up to a temperature of around 20°C/68°F, but no hotter.

QUALITY PRODUCE

Use only really fresh, good quality ingredients. The bread machine can not improve poor quality produce. Make sure the yeast is within its use-by date. Yeast beyond its expiry date will produce poor results.

MEASURING INGREDIENTS

Measure both the liquids and the dry ingredients carefully. Most problems occur when ingredients are inaccurately measured, when one ingredient is forgotten or when the same ingredient is added twice. Do not mix imperial and metric measurements, as they are not interchangeable; stick to one set for the whole recipe.

Do not exceed the quantities of flour and liquid recommended for your machine. Mixing the extra ingredients may overload the motor and if you have too much dough it is likely to rise over the top of the pan.

FOLLOW THE INSTRUCTIONS

Always add the ingredients in the order suggested by the manufacturer. Whatever the order, keep the yeast dry and separate from any liquids added to the bread pan.

ADDING INGREDIENTS

Cut butter into pieces, especially if it is fairly firm, and/or when larger amounts than usual are required in the recipe. If a recipe requires ingredients such as cooked vegetables or fruit or toasted nuts to be added, leave them to cool to room temperature before adding them.

USING THE DELAY TIMER

Perishable ingredients such as eggs, fresh milk, cheese, meat, fruit and vegetables may deteriorate, especially in warm conditions, and could present a health risk. They should be only be used in breads that are made immediately. Only use the delay timer for bread doughs that contain non-perishable ingredients.

CLEANING YOUR MACHINE
Unplug the machine before starting to clean it. Wipe down the outside regularly using a mild washing-up liquid (detergent) and a damp, soft cloth. Avoid all abrasive cleansers and materials, even those that are designated for use on non-stick items, and do not use alcohol-based cleansers.

BREAD PAN AND KNEADING BLADE
Clean the bread pan and blade after each use. These parts should not be washed in the dishwasher as this might affect the non-stick surface and damage the packing around the shaft. Avoid immersing the bread pan in water. If you have difficulty extracting the blade from the pan, fill the base of the pan with lukewarm water and leave it to soak for a few minutes. Remove the blade and wipe it with a damp cloth. Wash the bread pan with mild washing-up liquid. Rinse thoroughly. Always store the bread machine with the kneading blade removed from the shaft. The bread machine and components must be dry before putting away. Some pans have a fixed blade.

ABOVE: A Granary loaf should be baked on the whole wheat setting, which has a longer rising cycle.

SPECIAL CONSIDERATIONS

Breads made with whole grains and heavier flours such as wholemeal (wholewheat), oatmeal or rye, or with added ingredients such as dried fruits and nuts, are likely to rise more slowly than basic white loaves and will be less tall. The same applies to breads with a lot of fat or egg. Breads that include cheese, eggs or a high proportion of fats and/or sugar are more susceptible to burning. To avoid over-cooked crusts, select a light bake crust setting.

WATCHING THE DOUGH

Keep a flexible rubber spatula next to the machine and, if necessary, scrape down the sides of the pan after 5–10 minutes of the initial mixing cycle. The kneading blade sometimes fails to pick up a thick or sticky dough from the corners of the pan.

COOLING THE BREAD

It is best to remove the loaf from the pan as soon as the baking cycle finishes, or it may become slightly damp, even with a "stay warm" programme.

CHECKING THE DOUGH

Check the dough within the first 5 minutes of mixing, especially when you are trying a recipe for the first time. If the dough seems too wet and, instead of forming a ball, sticks to the sides of the pan, add a little flour, a spoonful at a time. However, the bread machine requires a dough that is slightly wetter than if you were mixing it by hand. If the dough is crumbly and won't form a ball, add liquid, one spoonful at a time. You will soon get used to the sound of the motor and notice if it is labouring due to a stiff mix. It is also worth checking the dough just before baking, to make sure it isn't about to rise over the top of the bread machine pan.

ABOVE: Dough is too wet and requires more flour.

ABOVE: Dough is too dry and requires more water.

ADAPTING RECIPES FOR USE IN A BREAD MACHINE

After you have cooked a number of the recipes from this book you may wish to branch out and adapt some of your own favourites. This sample recipe is used to explain some of the factors you will need to take into consideration.

INGREDIENTS

Read the list of ingredients carefully before you start, and adjust if necessary.

MALT EXTRACT AND GOLDEN SYRUP

High sugar levels and/or dried fruit may cause the bread to over-brown. Reduce the malt extract and golden (light corn) syrup quantities by one-third and increase other liquids to compensate. Machine breads require the inclusion of sugar. Allow 5–10ml/1–2 tsp per 225g/8oz/2 cups flour.

BUTTER

High fat levels mean that the bread will take longer to rise. Reduce to 50g/2oz/¼ cup per 450g/1lb/4 cups flour. You may need to add an extra 30ml/2 tbsp liquid.

FLOUR

This recipe uses white flour, but remember that a wholemeal (whole-wheat) loaf works better if you replace half the wholemeal flour with strong white flour.

YEAST

Replace fresh yeast with easy bake (rapid-rise) dried yeast. In a wholemeal bread, for example, start by using 5ml/1 tsp for up to 375g/13oz/3¼ cups flour or 7.5ml/1½ tsp for up to 600g/1lb 5oz/5¼ cups flour.

MILK

Use skimmed milk at room temperature where possible. If you wish to use the time delay cycle you should replace with fresh milk with milk powder.

DRIED FRUIT

Additions that enrich the dough, such as dried fruits, nuts, seeds and wholegrains, make the dough heavier, and the bread will not rise as well. Limit them to about a quarter of the total flour quantity.

MALTED FRUIT LOAF

50g/2oz/scant ¼ cup malt extract
30ml/2 tbsp golden (light corn) syrup
75g/3oz/6 tbsp butter
450g/1lb/4 cups unbleached white bread flour
5ml/1 tsp mixed (apple pie) spice
20g/¾oz fresh yeast
150ml/5fl oz/⅔ cup lukewarm milk
50g/2oz/¼ cup currants
50g/2oz/⅓ cup sultanas (golden raisins)
50g/2oz/¼ cup ready-to-eat dried apricots
25g/1oz/2 tbsp mixed chopped (candied) peel
30ml/2 tbsp milk
30ml/2 tbsp caster (superfine) sugar

MAKES 2 LOAVES

1 Grease two 450g/1lb loaf tins (pans).
2 Melt the malt extract, syrup and butter in a pan. Leave to cool.
3 Sift the flour and spice into a large bowl; make a central well. Cream the yeast with a little of the milk; blend in the rest. Add the yeast mixture with the malt extract to the flour and make a dough.
4 Knead on a floured surface until smooth and elastic, about 10 minutes. Place in an oiled bowl; cover with oiled clear film (plastic wrap). Leave in a warm place for 1½–2 hours, until doubled in bulk.
5 Turn the dough out on to a lightly floured surface and knock back (punch down).
6 Gently knead in the dried fruits.
7 Divide the dough in half; shape into two loaves. Place in the tins and cover with oiled clear film. Leave to rise for 1–1½ hours or until the dough reaches the top of the tins.
8 Meanwhile, preheat the oven to 200°C/400°F/Gas 6. Bake the loaves for 35–40 minutes, or until golden. When cooked, transfer to a wire rack.
9 Gently heat the milk and sugar for the glaze in a pan. Brush the warm loaves with the glaze.

METHOD

Use a similar bread machine recipe as a guide for adapting a conventional recipe.

STEP 1

Obviously, you can only make one machine-baked loaf at a time. Make 1 large loaf or reduce the quantity of ingredients if your machine is small.

STEP 2

There is no need to melt the ingredients before you add them, but remember to chop the butter into fairly small pieces.

STEP 3

When adding ingredients to the bread pan, pour in the liquid first then sprinkle over the flour, followed by the mixed spice. (Add the liquid first unless your machine requires dry ingredients to be placed in the bread pan first.)

Add easy bake dried yeast to a small indent in the flour, but make sure it does not touch the liquid underneath.

Place salt and butter in separate corners of the pan. If your recipe calls for egg, add this with the water or other liquid.

Use water straight from the tap and other liquids at room temperature.

STEPS 4–8

Ignore these steps, apart from step 6. The bread machine will automatically mix, rise and cook the dough. Use a light setting for the crust due to the sugar, fat and fruit content of the Malted Fruit Loaf. Ordinary breads, such as a white loaf, need a medium setting; loaves that contain wholemeal flour should be baked on the whole wheat setting.

If you are adding extra ingredients, such as dried fruit, set the bread machine on raisin setting and add the ingredients when it beeps. If you do not have this facility, add approximately 5 minutes before the end of the kneading cycle.

STEP 9

Make the glaze as usual and brush over the loaf at the end of the baking cycle.

USEFUL GUIDELINES

Here are a few guidelines that are worth following when adapting your own favourite recipes.

• Make sure the quantities will work in your machine. If you have a small bread machine it may be necessary to reduce them. Use the flour and water quantities in recipes in the book as a guide, or refer back to your manufacturer's handbook.

• It is important that you keep the flour and the liquid in the correct proportions, even if reducing the quantities means that you end up with some odd amounts. You can be more flexible with spices and flavourings such as fruit and nuts, as exact quantities are not so crucial.

• Monitor the recipe closely the first time you make it and jot down any ideas you have for improvements next time.

• Check the consistency of the dough when the machine starts mixing. You may need to add one or two extra spoonfuls of water, as breads baked in a machine

ABOVE: Some conventional recipes call for you to knead ingredients, such as fried onions, into a dough. When adapting for a bread machine, add to the dough at the raisin beep.

BELOW: Use a similar bread machine recipe to help you adapt a bread you usually make conventionally. For example, if you have a favourite swede bread recipe, try adapting a machine recipe for parsnip bread.

require a slightly softer dough, which is wet enough to relax back into the shape of the bread pan.

• If a dough mixes perfectly in your machine but then fails to bake properly, or if you want bread of a special shape, use the dough cycle on your machine, then shape by hand before baking in a conventional oven.

• Look through bread machine recipes and locate something that is similar. This will give you some idea as to quantities, and which programme you should use. Be prepared to make more adjustments after testing your recipe for the first time.

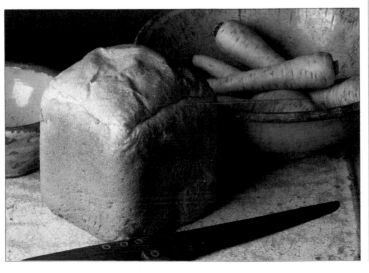

Packaged bread mixes can be used in your machine. Check your handbook, as some manufacturers may recommend specific brands.

• Check that your machine can handle the amount of dough the bread mix makes. If the packet quantity is only marginally more than you usually make, use the dough cycle and then bake the bread conventionally.

• Select an appropriate setting; for instance, use the white/basic or rapid/fastbake setting for white bread.

1 Place the recommended amount of water in the bread pan.

2 Spoon over the bread mix and place the pan in the machine.

3 Select the programme required and press Start. Check the consistency of the dough after 5 minutes, adding a little more water if the mixture seems too dry.

4 At the end of the baking cycle, remove the cooked bread from the bread pan and turn out on to a wire rack to cool.

TROUBLESHOOTING

Bread machines are incredibly easy to use and, once you have become familiar with yours, you will wonder how you ever did without it. However, they are machines and they cannot think for themselves. Things can go wrong and you need to understand why. Here are a few handy troubleshooting tips.

BREAD RISES TOO MUCH

• Usually caused by too much yeast; reduce by 25 per cent.
• An excess of sugar will promote yeast action; try reducing the quantity of sugar.
• Did you leave out the salt or use less than was recommended? If so, the yeast would have been uncontrolled and a tall loaf would have been the likely result.
• Too much liquid can sometimes cause a loaf to over-rise. Try reducing by 15–30ml/ 1–2 tbsp next time.
• Other possibilities are too much dough or too hot a day.

BREAD DOES NOT RISE ENOUGH

• Insufficient yeast or yeast that is past its expiry date.
• A rapid cycle was chosen, giving the bread less time to rise.

• The yeast and salt came into contact with each other before mixing. Make sure they are placed in separate areas when added to the bread pan.
• Too much salt inhibits the action of the yeast. You may have added salt twice, or added other salty ingredients, such as ready-salted nuts or feta cheese.
• Wholegrain and wholemeal breads tend not to rise as high as white flour breads. These flours contain bran and wheat germ, which makes the flour heavier.
• You may have used a plain white flour instead of a strong bread flour, which has a higher gluten content.
• The ingredients were not at the correct temperature. If they were too hot, they may have killed the yeast; if they were too cold, they may have retarded the action of the yeast.
• Insufficient liquid. In order for dough to rise adequately, it needs to be soft and pliable. If the dough was dry and stiff, add more liquid next time.
• The lid was open during the rising stage for long enough to let warm air escape.
• No sugar was added. Yeast works better where there is at least 5ml/1 tsp sugar to feed it. Note, however, that high sugar levels may retard yeast action.

BREAD DOES NOT RISE AT ALL

• No yeast was added or it was past its expiry date.
• The yeast was not handled correctly and was probably killed by adding ingredients that were too hot.

THE DOUGH IS CRUMBLY AND DOESN'T FORM A BALL

• The dough is too dry. Add extra liquid a small amount at a time until the ingredients combine to form a pliable dough.

THE DOUGH IS VERY STICKY AND DOESN'T FORM A BALL

• The dough is too wet. Try adding a little extra flour, a spoonful at a time, waiting for it to be absorbed before adding more. You must do this while the machine in still mixing and kneading the dough.

BREAD MIXED BUT NOT BAKED

• A dough cycle was selected. Remove the dough, shape it and bake it in a conventional oven or bake it in the machine on the "bake only" cycle.

BREAD COLLAPSED AFTER RISING OR DURING BAKING

• Too much liquid was added. Reduce the amount by 15–30ml/1–2 tbsp next time, or add a little extra flour.
• The bread rose too much. Reduce the amount of yeast slightly in the future, or use a quicker cycle.
• Insufficient salt. Salt helps to prevent the dough from over-proving.
• The machine may have been placed in a draught or may have been knocked or jolted during rising.
• High humidity and warm weather may have caused the dough to rise too fast.
• Too much yeast may have been added.
• The dough may have contained a high proportion of cheese.

THERE ARE DEPOSITS OF FLOUR ON THE SIDES OF THE LOAF

• The dry ingredients, especially the flour, stuck to the sides of the pan during kneading, and then adhered to the rising dough. Next time, use a flexible rubber spatula to scrape down the sides of the pan after 5–10 minutes of the initial mixing cycle, if necessary, but take care to avoid the kneading blade.

CRUST IS SHRIVELLED OR WRINKLED

• Moisture condensed on top of the loaf while it was cooling. Remove from the bread machine as soon as it is cooled.

CRUMBLY, COARSE TEXTURE

• The bread rose too much; try reducing the quantity of yeast slightly next time.
• The dough didn't have enough liquid.
• Too many whole grains were added. These soaked up the liquid. Next time, either soak the whole grains in water first or increase the general liquid content.

BURNT CRUST

• There was too much sugar in the dough. Use less or try a light crust setting for sweet breads.
• Choose the sweet bread setting if the machine has this option.

PALE LOAF

• Add milk, either dried or fresh, to the dough. This encourages browning.
• Set the crust colour to dark.
• Increase the sugar slightly.

CRUST TOO CHEWY AND TOUGH

• Increase the butter or oil and milk.

BREAD NOT BAKED IN THE CENTRE OR ON TOP

• Too much liquid was added; next time, reduce the liquid by 15ml/1 tbsp or add a little extra flour.
• The quantities were too large and your machine could not cope with the dough.
• The dough was too rich; it contained too much fat, sugar, eggs, nuts or grains.
• The bread machine lid was not closed properly, or the machine was used in too cold a location.
• The flour may have been too heavy. This can occur when you use rye, bran and wholemeal (whole-wheat) flours. Replace some of it with white bread flour next time.

CRUST TOO SOFT OR CRISP

• For a softer crust, increase the fat and use milk instead of water. For a crisper crust, do the opposite.
• Use the French bread setting for a crisper crust.
• Keep a crisper crust by lifting the bread out of the pan and turn it out on to a wire rack as soon as the baking cycle finishes.

AIR BUBBLE UNDER THE CRUST

• The dough was not mixed well or didn't deflate properly during the knock-down cycle between risings. This is likely to be a one-off problem, but if it persists, try adding an extra spoonful of water.

ADDED INGREDIENTS WERE CHOPPED UP INSTEAD OF REMAINING WHOLE

• They were added too soon and were chopped by the kneading blade. Add on the machine's audible signal, or 5 minutes before the end of the kneading cycle.
• Leave chopped nuts and dried fruits in larger pieces.

ADDED INGREDIENTS NOT MIXED IN

• They were probably added too late in the kneading cycle. Next time, add them a couple of minutes sooner.

THE BREAD IS DRY

• The bread was left uncovered to cool too long and dried out.
• Breads low in fat dry out rapidly. Increase the fat or oil in the recipe.
• The bread was stored in the refrigerator. Next time place in a plastic bag when cool and store in a bread bin.

BREAD HAS A HOLEY TEXTURE

• The dough was too wet; use less liquid.
• Salt was omitted.
• Warm weather and/or high humidity caused the dough to rise too quickly.

A STICKY LAYERED UNRISEN MESS

• You forgot to put the kneading blade in the pan before adding the ingredients.
• The kneading blade was not correctly inserted on the shaft.
• The bread pan was incorrectly fitted.

SMOKE EMITTED FROM THE MACHINE

• Ingredients were spilt on the heating element. Remove the bread pan before adding ingredients, and add any extra ingredients carefully.

OTHER FACTORS

Creating the ideal conditions for your bread machine is largely a matter of trial and error. Take into account the time of year, the humidity and your altitude. Bread machines vary between models and manufacturers, and flour and yeast may produce slightly different results from brand to brand or country to country. Breads made in Australia, for example, often need slightly more water than those made in Britain.

You will soon get to know your machine. Watch the dough as it is mixing and check again before it begins to bake. Make a note of any tendencies (do you generally need to add more flour? does the bread often over-rise?) and adapt recipes accordingly.

FLOUR

The largest single ingredient used in bread, the right flour is the key to good bread making. Wheat is the primary grain for grinding into flour. Apart from rye, wheat is the only flour with sufficient gluten to make a well-leavened bread.

WHEAT FLOURS

Wheat consists of an outer husk or bran that encloses the wheat kernel. The kernel contains the wheat germ and the endosperm, which is full of starch and protein. It is these proteins that form gluten when flour is mixed with water. When dough is kneaded, gluten stretches like elastic to trap the bubbles of carbon dioxide, the gas released by the action of the yeast, and the dough rises.

Wheat is defined as either soft or hard, depending on its protein content, and is milled in various ways to give the wide range of flours we know today.

Wheat is processed to create many sorts of flour. White flours, for example, contain about 75 per cent of the wheat kernel. The outer bran and the wheat germ are removed to leave the endosperm, which is milled into a white flour. Unbleached flour is the best type to use, as it has not been chemically treated to make it unnaturally white. This type is gradually replacing much of the bleached flour.

RIGHT: Clockwise from top: strong, French, self-raising and plain flour

PLAIN WHITE FLOUR

Plain white (all-purpose) flour contains less protein and gluten than bread flour, typically around 9.5–10 per cent. Sometimes a small amount of this type of flour is mixed with bread flour to achieve a closer-grained texture, but the main use for plain white flour is in quick teabreads, when chemical raising agents such as baking powder are added to give a light, airy crumb.

STRONG WHITE FLOUR

This flour is milled from hard wheat flour, which has a higher protein level than soft wheat flour. Levels vary between

ABOVE: Clockwise from top left: Granary, stoneground strong wholemeal, strong brown, stoneground wholemeal

millers but the typical figure is around 12 per cent. Some types of bread flour have lower levels – around 10.5–11 per cent – but these have ascorbic acid added to act as a dough enhancer.

SELF-RAISING FLOUR

Called self-rising in the USA, this is not used in traditional breads, but is ideal for quick teabreads and cakes cooked in the bread machine. Sodium bicarbonate and calcium phosphate are mixed into the flour and act as raising agents.

FINE FRENCH PLAIN FLOUR

Used principally for baking in France, this unbleached light flour is very fine and thus free-flowing. A small amount is often added to French bread recipes to reduce the gluten content slightly and achieve the texture associated with French specialities.

ORGANIC FLOURS

Organic white flour is produced using only natural fertilizers, and the wheat has not been sprayed with pesticides. Organic bread flours are recommended when developing natural yeasts for starters and sourdoughs.

WHOLEMEAL FLOURS

Because it is made from the complete wheat kernel, including the bran and wheat germ, wholemeal (whole-wheat) is coarse textured and full-flavoured with a nutty taste. For making machine breads, you should use strong wholemeal bread flour, with a protein content of around 12.5 per cent. Plain wholemeal flour can be used with baking powder or bicarbonate of soda (baking soda) for teabreads. Loaves made with 100 per cent wholemeal bread flour tend to be very dense. The bran inhibits the release of gluten, so the dough rises slower. For these reasons, many machine recipes recommend blending wholemeal bread flour with some white bread flour.

Stoneground flour results when complete wheat grain is ground between two stones. Wholemeal flours that are not stoneground have the bran and wheat germ removed during milling, then replaced after processing.

BROWN BREAD FLOUR

This flour contains about 80–90 per cent of the wheat kernel, with some of the bran removed. It is a good alternative to wholemeal flour, as it produces a loaf with a lighter finish, but with a denser texture and fuller flavour than white bread.

GRANARY FLOUR

A combination of wholemeal, white and rye flours mixed with malted wheat grains, it has a slightly sweet and nutty flavour. Malthouse is similar to Granary flour.

SEEDED WHITE BREAD FLOUR

This is an easy to use ready blended white bread flour with seeds. It contains golden and brown linseeds, sunflower seeds and millet.

SPELT FLOUR

Rich in nutrients, this is made from spelt grain, an ancient precursor of modern wheat. It is best used in combination with

ABOVE: Left to right: semolina, spelt and seeded white bread flour

white bread flour. Even though it contains gluten, some gluten-intolerant people can digest it, so it is included in some diets for people who are allergic to wheat.

SEMOLINA

A high gluten flour, semolina is made from the endosperm of durum or hard winter wheat before it is fully milled into a fine flour. It can be ground to a coarse granular texture or a finer flour. The finer flour is traditionally used for making pasta, but also makes a delicious bread when combined with other flours. If 100 per cent semolina is used, a heavy loaf will result.

OTHER WHEAT GRAINS

WHEAT BRAN

This is the outer husk of the wheat, which is separated from white flour during processing. It adds fibre, texture and flavour. You can add a spoonful or two to your favourite recipe or use it in place of part of the white bread flour.

WHEAT GERM

The germ is the embryo or heart of the wheat grain kernel. Use in its natural state, or lightly toasted, giving a nutty flavour. Wheat germ is a rich source of vitamin E and increases the nutritional value of bread. However, it inhibits the action of gluten, so do not use more than 30ml/ 2 tbsp for every 225g/8oz/2 cups flour.

CRACKED WHEAT

This is whole wheat kernel, broken into rather large pieces. It is quite hard, so you may like to soften it. Simmer in hot water for 15 minutes, then drain and cool. Add 15–30ml/1–2 tbsp to a dough 5 minutes before the end of the kneading cycle.

BELOW: Clockwise from top left: bran, bulgur wheat, wheat germ, cracked wheat

BULGUR WHEAT

This is made from the wheat grain. It is partially processed by boiling, which cracks the wheat kernel. Add to bread doughs, to give a crunchy texture. There is no need to cook it first. However you may wish to soak it in water first, to soften it further.

NON-WHEAT FLOURS
RYE FLOUR

Rye flour is used extensively in breads, partly because it grows well in climates that are cold, wet and not suitable for wheat cultivation. This is why so many of the Russian and Scandinavian breads include rye. Light and medium rye flours are produced from the endosperm while dark rye includes all the grain, resulting in a coarser flour which adds more texture to the bread. Rye contains gluten, but when used on its own produces a very heavy bread. Rye dough is very sticky and difficult to handle. For machine-made breads, rye flour must be combined with other flours. Even a small amount adds a distinctive tang.

MILLET FLOUR

Another high-protein, low-gluten grain, millet produces a light yellow flour with a distinctly sweet flavour and a slightly gritty texture. It tends to give breads a dry, crumbly texture, so you may need to add extra fat when using it. If using millet flour, boost the gluten content of the dough by using at least 75 per cent white bread flour.

BARLEY

Barley seeds are processed to remove the bran, leaving a product called pearl barley. This is ground to make barley flour, which is mild, slightly sweet and earthy. It gives breads a soft, almost cake-like texture, as it has a very low gluten content. White flour must be combined with barley flour in a ratio of at least 3:1 for machine bread.

BUCKWHEAT FLOUR

This greyish-brown flour has a distinctive, bitter, earthy flavour. Buckwheat is the seed of a plant related to the rhubarb family. It is rich in calcium and vitamins A and B, high

ABOVE: Left to right: polenta, corn meal, millet

in protein but low in gluten. Traditionally used to make pancakes, Russian blinis and French galettes, it is best used in combination with other flours, to produce full-bodied and tasty multigrain breads.

GLUTEN-FREE FLOURS
POTATO FLOUR

An ultra-fine, soft white powder obtained from soaking grated or pulped potatoes. This starch is used in conjunction with other gluten-free flours as a replacement for wheat-based flour in gluten-free breads.

BROWN RICE FLOUR

Another gluten-free flour, often used with potato starch and sometimes tapioca flour. It is made from brown rice, which is finely ground and pulverized.

GLUTEN- AND WHEAT-FREE BREAD FLOUR

This is a blend of gluten- and wheat-free flours and contains milled rice, potato and tapioca flour. They are mixed with xanthum gum, which helps to stabilize and strengthen the flours for breadmaking. It is very absorbant so extra liquid is needed when used in breadmaking to replace conventional gluten-rich flours.

GLUTEN-FREE MIXES

These prepared mixes are an option for people who cannot tolerate gluten. They are available from pharmacies and health food stores, or on prescription if you are a coeliac. They are a blend of gluten-free wheat starch with skimmed milk powder, sugar and raising agents, including yeast. There are several brands available.

ABOVE: Top to bottom: millet, buckwheat, barley

ABOVE: Top to bottom: oatmeal, rye

OTHER GRAINS

OATMEAL

When oats are cleaned and the outer husk has been removed, what remains is the oat kernel or groat. This is cut into pieces to make fine, medium or coarse oatmeal, or ground to make flour. All of these ingredients can be used in multigrain breads, adding flavour and texture. The coarser the oats, the more texture they will contribute. Oatmeal contains no gluten, so it needs to be combined with wheat flour for bread making. The coarser textured oatmeal makes an attractive topping.

POLENTA AND CORN MEAL

Dried corn kernels are ground to make coarse, medium and fine meal. The medium grain is known as polenta and the fine grain is known as corn meal. For bread making, this gluten-free flour has to be combined with white bread flour. It gives a sweet flavour and attractive yellow colour. For shaping bread by hand, use polenta, which is coarser and adds a pleasant finish.

MILLET GRAIN

This tiny, golden yellow, round grain is used in breads in Europe and Russia to give texture. Include 15–30ml/1–2 tbsp in a multi-grain

bread, or even in a simple basic white loaf, for added interest. Millet grains make an attractive topping for breads such as Lavash. Millet flakes are also used in some breads.

RICE

Rice grains can be used in a variety of ways. Cooked long grain rice can be added to doughs for bread with a moist crumb. Wild rice will add a texture and flavour. Add it near the end of the kneading cycle to keep the grain intact and give attractive flecks of colour. Ground rice and rice flour are milled from rice grains. Both brown and white rice flour are used, brown flour being more nutritious. Ground rice is more granular, similar to semolina. Either can replace some white bread flour in a recipe; they will add a sweet flavour and chewy texture. Ground rice and rice flour can also be used as toppings; they are often dusted over English muffins or crumpets.

As rice is gluten-free, use only a small percentage of it with the bread flour, otherwise your loaf will be rather dense.

ROLLED OATS

The inedible husk is removed from the oat kernel and the grain is then sliced, steamed and rolled to produce rolled oats. You can get jumbo-size oat flakes as

ABOVE:
Clockwise from top left:
ground rice, rice flour,
wild rice, long grain rice

well as old-fashioned rolled porridge oats. For bread making, use old-fashioned oats rather than "quick cook" oats. Add rolled oats to bread doughs to give a chewy texture and nutty taste, or use as a topping.

OAT BRAN

High in soluble fibre, this is the outer casing of the oat kernel. It acts in a similar way to wheat bran, reducing the elasticity of the gluten, so use a maximum of 15ml/1 tbsp per 115g/4oz/1 cup flour. You may need to add a little extra liquid to the dough.

ABOVE: Left to right:
Brown rice flour,
potato flour

RIGHT: Clockwise from top right:
jumbo oats, rolled oats, oat bran

LEAVENS AND SALT

Yeast is a living organism which, when activated by contact with liquid, converts the added sugar or sucrose, and then the natural sugars in the flour, into gases. These gases cause the bread to rise. As yeast is live, you must treat it with respect. It works best within the temperature range 21–36°C/70–97°F. Too hot and it will die; too cold and it will not activate. Yeast must be used before its use-by date, as old yeast loses its potency and eventually dies.

In most bread machine recipes dried yeast is used. In this book, all the recipes have been tested using easy bake (rapid-rise) dried yeast, which does not need to be dissolved in liquid. It is also called fast-action bread yeast or quick yeast for bread. If you can find dried yeast especially made for use in bread machines, this will produce good results. You may need to adjust the quantities in individual recipes as variations occur between different makes of yeast.

ABOVE: Place dried yeast in a shallow indent in the flour.

ABOVE: Fresh yeast is dissolved before placing in the bread pan.

ABOVE: Yeast is available in two forms, fresh and dried. From top to bottom: fresh yeast, dried yeast.

ABOVE: Add liquid to dissolve and activate fresh yeast.

Fresh yeast is considered by some bakers to have a superior flavour. It can be used with caution when baking in a bread machine, but is best used in the "dough only" cycle. It is hard to give exact quantities for breads, which will be made using a range of machines operating in different temperatures. The difficulty lies in preventing the bread from rising over the top of the bread pan during baking; doughs made from easy-blend dried yeast are easier to control where uniform results are required.

NATURAL LEAVENS

Long before yeast was sold commercially, sourdough starters were used to make breads. These were natural leavens made by fermenting yeast spores that occurred naturally in flour, dairy products, plant matter and spices. Breads are still produced by the same method today. Breads made using natural leavens have different flavours and textures from the breads made with commercial yeast.

BELOW: Buckwheat and Walnut Bread is made using easy-blend dried yeast, which gives good, uniform results.

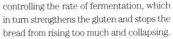

RIGHT: Left to right: cream of tartar, baking powder, bicarbonate of soda

CHEMICAL LEAVENS

Raising agents other than yeasts can be used for bread. When using a bread machine, other raising agents are best used for teabreads and cakes that are mixed in a bowl, then baked in the bread pan.

Bicarbonate of soda (baking soda) is an alkaline raising agent that is often used for quick breads. When moistened with liquid it gives off carbon dioxide, which makes the cake or quick bread rise. The heat from the oven cooks and sets the risen batter before it has a chance to collapse.

Cream of tartar is an acid, which is often combined with bicarbonate of soda to boost the latter's leavening qualities. It also helps to neutralize the slightly soapy taste from the bicarbonate of soda.

BELOW: Bicarbonate of soda is the raising agent used to make this Soda Bread.

Baking powder is a ready-made mixture of acid and alkaline chemicals, usually bicarbonate of soda and cream of tartar, but sometimes bicarbonate of soda and sodium pyrophosphate. All these raising agents are fast acting. The bubbles are released the moment the powder comes into contact with a liquid, so such breads must be mixed and baked quickly.

SALT

Bread without salt tastes "flat". While it is possible to make a saltless bread (there is a famous saltless Tuscan bread which is eaten with salty cheese or preserved meats), salt is normally an indispensable ingredient. Salt has two roles. one is to improve the flavour and the other is to act as a yeast retardant, controlling the rate of fermentation, which in turn strengthens the gluten and stops the bread from rising too much and collapsing.

When adding salt to the bread pan, it is vital to keep it away from the yeast, as concentrated salt will severely impede the activity of the yeast.

Fine table salt and sea salt can both be used in bread that is to be baked in a machine. Coarse sea salt is best used as a topping. It can be sprinkled on top of unbaked breads and rolls to give a crunchy texture and agreeable flavour.

Salt substitutes are best avoided as few of these contain sodium.

DOUGH CONDITIONERS

These are added to breads to help stabilize the gluten strands and hold the gases formed by the yeast. Chemical conditioners are often added to commercially-produced bread, and you will find bread improvers in the ingredients on fast-action yeast packets.

Two natural dough conditioners which help to ensure a higher rise, lighter texture, and stronger dough are lemon juice and malt extract. Gluten strength can vary between bags of flour, so you can add some lemon juice to the dough to help to strengthen it, particularly when making wholegrain breads. You can add 5ml/1 tsp lemon juice with every 225g/8oz/2 cups bread flour without affecting the flavour of the bread.

Malt extract helps to break down the starch in wheat into sugars for the yeast to feed on and so encourages active fermentation. If you use up to 5ml/1 tsp malt extract with every 225g/8oz/2 cups bread flour you will not effect a noticeable flavour change. If you like the flavour of malt extract, you can increase the amount used.

On some wholewheat programmes the dough collapses slightly before the machine starts to bake. Lemon juice can solve this problem, or you can add 1 x 100mg vitamin C tablet, crushed.

LIQUIDS

Some form of liquid is essential when making bread. It rehydrates and activates the yeast, and brings together the flour and any other dry ingredients to make the dough. Whatever the liquid, the temperature is important for successful machine breads. If your machine has a preheating cycle, cold liquids, straight from the refrigerator, can be used. If not, use liquids at room temperature, unless it is a very hot day. Water from the tap, providing it is merely cool, is fine. On a very cold day, measure the water and leave it to stand in the kitchen for a while so that it acclimatizes before you use it.

WATER

Water is the most frequently used liquid in bread making. Bread made with water has a crisper crust than when milk is included. Tap water is chemically treated, and if it has been heavily chlorinated and fluorinated this may well slow down the rising. Hard water can also affect the rise,

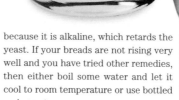

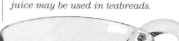

BELOW: Cranberry juice and orange juice may be used in teabreads.

because it is alkaline, which retards the yeast. If your breads are not rising very well and you have tried other remedies, then either boil some water and let it cool to room temperature or use bottled spring water.

ABOVE: Clockwise from top left: milk, buttermilk, milk powder

MILK

Milk helps to enrich the dough and produces a creamy-coloured, tender crumb and golden crust. Use full-cream (whole), semi-skimmed (low-fat) or skimmed milk, according to your preference. You can also replace fresh milk with skimmed milk powder. This can be useful if you intend using the timer to delay the starting time for making bread, as, unlike fresh milk, the milk powder will not deteriorate. Sprinkle it on top of the flour in the bread pan to keep it separated from the water until mixing starts.

BUTTERMILK

Used instead of regular milk, this makes bread more moist and gives it an almost cake-like texture. Buttermilk is made from skimmed milk which is pasteurized, then cooled. After this a cultured bacteria is added which ferments it under controlled conditions to produce its slightly tangy, acidic, but pleasant flavour. This flavour is noticeable in the finished loaf.

Yogurt and Other Dairy Products

Another alternative to milk, yogurt also has good tenderizing properties. Use natural (plain) yogurt or try flavoured ones, such as lemon or hazelnut in similarly flavoured breads.

Sour cream, cottage cheese and soft cheeses such as ricotta, fromage frais and mascarpone can all be used as part of the liquid content of the bread. They are valued more for their tenderizing properties than for their flavour.

Coconut Milk

Use 50:50 with water to add flavour to sweet breads and buns.

Fruit Juices

Fruit juices such as orange, mango, pineapple or cranberry can be added to the dough for fruit-flavoured breads to enhance their fruitiness.

Vegetable Juices and Cooking Liquids

The liquid left over from cooking vegetables will add flavour and extra nutritional value to breads and is particularly useful when making savoury breads. Potato water has several benefits. The extra starch acts as an additional food for the yeast, and produces a greater rise and also a softer, longer-lasting loaf.

Vegetables themselves contain liquid juices and when added to a bread machine will alter the liquid balance.

Soaking Juices

When dried vegetables such as mushrooms, especially wild ones, and sun-dried tomatoes are rehydrated in water, a

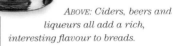

ABOVE: Ciders, beers and liqueurs all add a rich, interesting flavour to breads.

flavoursome liquid is produced. This is much too good to waste. Rehydrate the vegetables, drain off the liquid and add it as part of the liquid in a savoury bread. In sweet breads, the liquid drained from dried fruits that have been plumped up in fruit juices, spirits and liqueurs is equally useful.

Beers, Ales, Ciders and Liqueurs

All of these can be added to bread recipes. Beers and ales, in particular, have a great affinity with dark, heavy flours. The added sugars stimulate the yeast by providing more food. Dark beers and ales impart a stronger flavour.

Eggs

If a bread recipe includes eggs, these should be considered part of the liquid content. Eggs add colour, improve the structure and give the bread a rich flavour, although they are inclined to dry out more quickly than plain bread. It is worth adding extra fat to compensate for this. All the recipes in this book use medium eggs unless stated otherwise.

ABOVE: Use soaking and cooking liquids in savoury breads.

FATS AND SWEETENERS

FATS

Whether solid (butter, margarine) or liquid (oil), small amounts of fats are often added to breads. They enrich doughs and add flavour, and, with eggs, they give a soft, tender texture to the crumb. Fats help to extend the freshness of the loaf, and in rich doughs, help to cancel out the drying effect that eggs can cause.

In small amounts, fat contributes to the elasticity of the gluten, but use too much and the opposite effect will result. The fat coats the gluten strands and this forms a barrier between the yeast and flour. This slows down the action of the yeast, and hence increases the rising time. For this reason it is best to limit the amount of fat in a machine-baked bread, or risk a heavy, compact loaf.

When making rich, brioche-style bread, it is best to use the bread machine only for making the dough. It may be necessary to use the cycle twice. Afterwards, shape the dough by hand and leave it to rise for as long as required, before baking the bread conventionally.

SOLID FATS

Butter, margarine or lard (shortening) can all be used in small quantities (of up to 15g/½oz/1 tbsp) without adding any noticeable flavour to the dough. Where a recipe calls for a larger quantity of fat, use butter, preferably unsalted (sweet). If you only have salted butter, and you are using quite a lot of it, you may need to reduce the amount of salt added to the dough. Cut the butter into small pieces so that it will mix in better. Avoid letting the fat come into contact with the yeast as it may inhibit the dissolving of the yeast.

BELOW: Left to right: olive oil, sunflower oil, hazelnut oil and walnut oil can all be used to impart a slightly different flavour to bread.

Where butter is layered in yeast pastry for croissants and Danish pastries, it is important to soften it so it has the same consistency as the dough. Although it is possible to use low-fat spreads in breadmaking, there is not much point in doing so, as they may contain up to 40 per cent water and do not have the same properties as butter.

LIQUID FATS

Sunflower oil is a good alternative to butter if you are concerned about the cholesterol level, while olive oil can be used where flavour is important. Use a fruity, full-flavoured extra virgin olive oil from the first pressing of the olives.

Nut oils, such as walnut and hazelnut, are quite expensive and have very distinctive flavours, but are wonderful when teamed with similarly flavoured breads.

Fats and oils are interchangeable in many recipes. If you wish to change a solid fat for a liquid fat or oil the amount of liquid in the dough needs to be adjusted to accommodate the change. This is only necessary for amounts over 15ml/1 tbsp.

LEFT: Left to right: margarine, butter, lard

*ABOVE: Left to right:
dark brown sugar,
light muscovado (brown) sugar, light
brown soft sugar, granulated sugar,
caster sugar*

SWEETENERS

Sugars and liquid sweeteners accelerate the fermentation process by providing the yeast with extra food. Modern types of yeast no longer need sugar; they are able to use the flour efficiently to provide food. Even so, it is usual to add a small amount of sweetener. This makes the dough more active than if it were left to feed slowly on the natural starches and sugars in the flour. Enriched breads and heavy whole-grain breads need the increased yeast action to help the heavier dough to rise.

Sugar helps delay the staling process in bread because it attracts moisture. It also creates a tender texture.Too much sugar can cause dough to over-rise and collapse. Sweet breads have a moderate sugar level and gain extra sweetness from dried fruits, sweet glazes and icings.

*BELOW: Left to right: treacle, golden
syrup, molasses, malt extract,
maple syrup, honey*

Sweeteners contribute to the colour of the bread. A small amount enhances the crust colour. Some bread machines over-brown sweet doughs, so select a light crust setting or a sweet bread setting, if available, when making sweet yeast cakes.

Any liquid sweetener can be used instead of sugar, but should be counted as part of the total liquid content of the bread. Adjustments may need to be made.

WHITE SUGARS

Granulated or caster (superfine) sugar can be used for bread making. They are almost pure sucrose and add little flavour to the finished bread. Do not use icing (confectioners') sugar as the anti-caking agent can affect the flavour. Save icing sugar for glazing and dusting.

BROWN SUGARS

Use light or dark brown, refined or unre-fined brown sugar. The darker unrefined sugars will add more flavour, having a higher molasses content. Brown sugars add a touch of colour and also increase the acidity, which can be beneficial.

MALT EXTRACT

An extract from malted wheat or barley, this has a strong flavour, so use sparingly. It is best used in fruit breads.

HONEY AND MAPLE SYRUP

Clear honey can be used as a substitute for sugar, but only use two-thirds of the amount suggested for sugar, as it is sweeter. Maple syrup is the reduced sap of the maple tree; use it in place of honey or sugar. It is slightly sweeter than sugar but not as sweet as honey.

MOLASSES, GOLDEN SYRUP AND TREACLE

All these sweeteners are by-products of sugar refining. Molasses is a thick con-centrated syrup with a sweet, slightly bitter flavour. It adds a golden colour to bread. Golden (light corn) syrup is light and sweet with a slight butterscotch flavour.

Treacle is brownish black and more intensely flavoured, and, like molasses, adds a slight bitter-ness to the bread.

ADDITIONAL INGREDIENTS

MEATS

Meats can be used to flavour bread recipes. The best results often come from using cured meats, such as ham, bacon or salami, and cooked sausages such as pepperoni.

When you use a strongly flavoured meat, it is best to chop it finely and add it to the dough during its final kneading. You don't need much – 25–50g/1–2oz will be quite sufficient to add extra flavour without overpowering the bread.

Ham and bacon are best added as small pieces, late on in the kneading cycle. Dice ham small. Fry or grill (broil) bacon rashers, then crumble them or cut into pieces, or use ready-cut cubes of bacon or pancetta and sauté them first. Make sure the bacon is fully cooked before adding it to the bread dough.

LEFT: Sausages and bacon are a good addition to bread. They should be cooked before adding to a dough.

Thinly sliced preserved meats, such as prosciutto, pastrami, speck, pepperoni and smoked venison can be added as thin strips towards the end of the kneading cycle or incorporated in the dough during shaping, for hand-shaped loaves. Cured and smoked venison marinated in olive oil and herbs gives a basic loaf of bread a wonderful burst of flavour, or you could try adding pastrami to a bread containing rye flour. Strongly flavoured meats will make the most impact, but remember that you need only small amounts.

USING BACON IN THE BREAD MACHINE

1 Cut the bacon into thin strips and grill it, or dry-fry in a non-stick frying pan, until it is crisp.

2 Transfer the cooked bacon to a plate lined with kitchen paper, to blot up excess fat. Leave to cool.

3 Add the strips to the breadmaking machine towards the end of the kneading process or when the machine beeps.

USING MEATS

Some meats are best kept whole or coarsely chopped and used as a filling, as when sausage is layered through a brioche dough, or used as a topping on tray-baked breads and pizzas. There are many different types of salami, flavoured with spices such as peppercorns, coriander or paprika, as well as pepperoni and cooked spicy Continental-style sausages, all of which are suitable.

LEFT: From top to bottom: salami, pepperoni, thinly sliced smoked venison, prosciutto

*RIGHT: From left to right:
cottage cheese, mascarpone,
fromage frais*

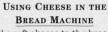

CHEESES

Cheese can be added to a wide variety of breads, to make them more moist and to give them more taste. Some cheeses have powerful flavours that really impact on the bread, while others are much more subtle, and are indistinguishable from the other ingredients except for the richness and tenderness they impart. Soft cheeses such as cottage cheese, mascarpone, fromage frais and ricotta are added in this way as part of the liquid content of the recipe. They contribute little to the overall taste of the bread, but help to create a more tender loaf with a softer crumb.

Grated or chopped hard cheeses can be added at the beginning of kneading so they are totally incorporated in the dough, or else towards the end of kneading, meaning that small amounts can clearly be detected in the bread. Alternatively, the cheese can be sprinkled over the top just before baking, to add colour and texture to the crust, or used as a topping or filling, as in pizzas or calzones.

For maximum cheese flavour, use small amounts of strongly flavoured cheeses such as extra-mature Cheddar, Parmesan, Pecorino, or blue cheeses such as Roquefort, Gorgonzola, Danish Blue or Stilton.

*RIGHT: Selection of cheeses, clockwise
from top left: Cheddar, Emmenthal,
feta, Gorgonzola; centre: mozzarella*

If the cheese is salty, reduce the amount of added salt, or the action of the yeast will be retarded and the bread may taste unacceptably salty.

Machine-made breads incorporating hard cheeses may not rise as high as ones without, due to the increased richness in the dough, but the texture and flavour are likely to be superb.

HERBS AND SPICES

Use herbs and spices as the main flavouring ingredient in bread or to enhance other ingredients.

HERBS

Fresh herbs have the most wonderful aroma, matched only by their flavour in freshly baked breads. Use fresh herbs if possible. Dried herbs that are oily and pungent, such as sage, rosemary and thyme, also work well. Rosemary is especially pungent, so use sparingly. Dried oregano is a fine substitute for fresh. Dried herbs have a more concentrated flavour than fresh; use about a third of the quantity recommended for fresh.

A number of herbs are now available freshly chopped and preserved in oil, which is a good alternative for more delicate herbs such as basil and coriander

LEFT: Clockwise from top: basil, thyme, flat leaf parsley, oregano, coriander, dill

(cilantro) which do not dry well. Add fresh herbs toward the end of the kneading cycle. Dried herbs can be added with the dry ingredients. Avoid using dried parsley; substitute a different herb instead.

BELOW: From left to right: Front row: black onion seeds, saffron, fennel, nutmeg; back row: allspice, cinnamon, cumin, ginger

SPICES

Spices are the dried, intensely aromatic, seeds, pods, stems, bark, buds or roots of plants. As with herbs, the fresher they are the more aromatic they will be; the volatile oils fade with age. Use freshly grated black pepper and nutmeg. Cumin, fennel, caraway and cardamom can be bought as whole seeds, and ground in a spice mill, or a coffee mill kept for the purpose, as needed. If you buy ground spices, use them within 6 months.

Add saffron, nutmeg, cinnamon, anise, allspice and cardamom to sweet or savoury breads. Mixed spice and ginger are sweet spices, while juniper berries, cumin, coriander and black onion seeds provide aromatic flavourings for savoury breads. A number of whole spices can also be used as toppings for breads.

ADDING HERBS AND SPICES

- Frozen chopped herbs are a quick alternative to fresh herbs. Add them to the dough just before the end of the kneading process.
- Add ground spices after the flour, so they do not come into contact with the liquid before mixing.
- Add whole spices along with the dry ingredients if you want them to break down during kneading. If not, add them when the machine beeps, towards the end of kneading.

ABOVE: *Clockwise from top right: pistachio nuts, pecan nuts, pine nuts, walnuts, slivered almonds, macadamia nuts*

NUTS

Nuts make a wonderful addition to home-made breads. Their crunchiness combines equally well with the sweetness of both dried fruits and fresh fruits. They go well with savoury additions such as cheese, herbs and spices and they can be used on their own to make rustic-style breads.

Nuts contain natural oils which turn rancid if stored too warm or for too long. Buy in small quantities, store in an airtight container in a cool place and use them within a few weeks.

Pecan nuts, almonds, macadamia nuts, pistachio nuts and walnuts give wonderful flavour and texture when added to basic breads towards the end of the kneading process. They can be added to teabreads, or used as a decoration on top of sweet breads or yeast cakes. Walnut bread is a rich brown loaf with a soft crunch, perfect with cheeses.

Lightly toast pine nuts, hazelnuts and almonds first to bring out their flavour. Spread the nuts on a baking sheet and place them in an oven preheated to 180°C/350°F/Gas 4 for 5–8 minutes, or grill (broil) until golden. Avoid scorching, and cool before adding them to the bread.

Hazelnuts, almonds and walnuts can be finely ground and used as a nutritious and flavoursome flour substitute. Replace up to 15 per cent of the flour with the ground nuts. If using hazelnuts, remove the skin first, as it is bitter. This will easily rub off if you toast the nuts in the oven.

Use coconut freshly grated or choose desiccated (dry unsweetened shredded), either plain or toasted.

SAVOURY NUT BREAD

These quantities are for a medium loaf. Increase all ingredients by 20 per cent for a large loaf; decrease by 25 per cent for small. Use size setting 1kg/2lb for large or 500g for small.

1 Put 175g/6oz/½ cup unsweetened chestnut purée in a bowl and stir in 250ml/9fl oz/scant 1¼ cups water. Mix well. Place in the bread pan.

2 Sprinkle over 450g/1lb/4 cups white bread flour and 50g/2oz/½ cup whole-meal (whole-wheat) bread flour. Add 30ml/2 tbsp skimmed milk powder (non fat dry milk), 2.5ml/½tsp ground cloves and 5ml/1 tsp grated nutmeg. Place 5ml/1 tsp salt, 15ml/1 tbsp light muscovado (brown) sugar and 40g/1½oz/3 tbsp butter in corners. Make a shallow indent; add 7.5ml/1½tsp easy bake (rapid-rise) dried yeast.

3 Set to white/basic, raisin setting, if available; light crust. Select size large/750g. Press Start. Add 75g/3oz/¾ cup chopped walnuts at the beep or after the first kneading. Cool on a wire rack.

VEGETABLES

Raw, canned, dried and freshly cooked vegetables all make perfect additions to savoury breads. Making bread also provides a good opportunity to use up any leftover cooked vegetables. Vegetable breads are richer than basic breads, the vegetables contributing flavour and texture to the finished loaves. Many vegetable breads are subtly coloured or dotted with attractive flecks.

Fresh vegetables are relatively high in liquid, so if you add them, calculate that about half of their weight will be water

BELOW: Clockwise from top: spinach, green, red and yellow (bell) peppers, courgettes (zucchini), sweet potatoes

LEFT: Clockwise from top right: garlic, spring onions (scallions), chilli peppers, dried sliced onion, onions

and deduct the equivalent amount of liquid from the recipe. Keep an eye on the dough as it mixes and add more flour or liquid as needed.

STARCHY VEGETABLES

Potatoes, sweet potatoes, parsnips, carrots, swede and other varieties of starchy vegetables sweeten the bread and contribute a soft texture. You can use leftover mashed or even instant potato, adding 115g/4oz/1⅓ cups–225g/8oz/2⅔ cups to a basic bread recipe depending on the size of your machine. Adjust the liquid accordingly.

SPINACH

Fresh spinach leaves need to be blanched briefly in boiling water before being used. After blanching, add them whole with the liquid ingredients at the beginning of

---

PREPARING PEPPERS

1 Cut each (bell) pepper into three or four flat pieces. Remove the core and seeds. Place in a grill (broiling) pan or roasting pan and brush the pieces lightly with olive oil or sunflower oil.

2 Grill (broil) until the skins blister and begin to char. Remove each piece as it is cooked and place inside a plastic bag. Seal the bag and leave to cool.

3 Peel off and discard the skin, then chop the peppers and add when the bread machine beeps, or 5 minutes before the kneading cycle ends.

LEFT: Fresh or dried mushrooms work well in breads

the kneading process, and they will mix in and become finely chopped as the cycle progresses. Frozen chopped spinach can be substituted for fresh, but thaw it completely first and reduce the liquid in the recipe to allow for the extra water.

ONIONS, LEEKS AND CHILLIES
These vegetables are best if you sauté them first in a little butter or oil, which brings out their flavour. Caramelized onions will add richness and a light golden colour to the bread. For speed, you can add dried sliced onions instead of fresh onions, but you may need to add an extra 15ml/1 tbsp or so of liquid.

MUSHROOMS
Dried wild mushrooms can be used in the same way as sun-dried tomatoes to produce a very tasty loaf for serving with soups, casseroles and stews. Strain the soaking water, if you intend to use it in a recipe, to remove any grit.

TOMATOES
Tomatoes are very versatile and give bread a delicious flavour. They can be puréed, canned, fresh or sun-dried. Depending on when you add sun-dried tomatoes they will either remain as pieces, making a bread with interesting flecks of colour, or be fully integrated in the dough to provide flavour. To intensify the taste, choose regular sun-dried tomatoes, rather than the ones preserved in oil,

reconstitute them in water, then use the soaking water as the liquid in the recipe. Other tomato products are best added at the beginning of the breadmaking cycle, to ensure a richly coloured, full-bodied loaf with a distinct tomato flavour.

OTHER VEGETABLES
Add vegetables such as corn kernels, chopped olives or chopped spring onions (scallions) towards the end of the kneading cycle to ensure that they remain whole. All will impart flavour, colour and texture.

Frozen vegetables should be thawed completely before using in the machine. You may need to reduce the liquid quantity in the recipe if you use frozen vegetables instead of fresh. Canned vegetables should be well drained.

CHICKPEAS
The starchiness of chickpeas, like that of potatoes, produces a light bread with good keeping qualities. Add cooked drained chickpeas whole; the machine will reduce them to a pulp very effectively. Chickpeas add a pleasant, nutty flavour to breads.

ADDING VEGETABLES TO BREAD
There are several ways of preparing vegetables ready to add to the machine.

• Add grated raw vegetables such as courgettes (zucchini), carrots or beetroot (beet), when you add the water to the pan.

• Sweet potatoes, parsnips, potatoes, winter squashes and pumpkin should be cooked first. Drain, reserving the cooking liquid, and mash them. When cool, add both the cooking liquid and the mashed vegetable to the dough.

• If you want vegetables to remain identifiable in the finished bread add them when the machine beeps for adding extra ingredients or 5 minutes before the end of the kneading cycle, so they stay as slices or small pieces.

FRUIT

Whether you use them fresh, dried or as purées or juices, fruits add complementary flavours to breads and teacakes. The natural sugars help to feed the yeast and improve the leavening process, while fruits with natural pectin will improve the keeping quality of baked goods.

DRIED CAKE FRUITS

The familiar dried cake fruits such as sultanas (golden raisins), currants and raisins can easily be incorporated in basic breads, adding their own distinctive flavours. Sprinkle them in gradually, when the machine beeps or towards the end of the kneading cycle. For added flavour, plump them up in fruit juice or liqueur. You can add up to 50g/2oz/⅓ cup of dried fruit for a small bread machine, 115g/4oz/⅔ cup for a large machine. If you soak the dried

BELOW: Clockwise from top left: candied citrus peel, dried pears, dried cranberries, dried prunes, dried mango, and dried figs

ABOVE: Pears, bananas, apples

fruit first, use the excess as part of the measured liquid. You may need to add a spoonful or so of extra liquid to a basic bread recipe if you do not soak the fruit first.

RIGHT: Goji berries, Strawberries, raspberries, blueberries

DRIED, SEMI-DRIED AND READY-TO-EAT DRIED FRUITS

These are perfect for breads, because their flavours are so concentrated, and there is a vast range to choose from. Use combinations of exotic dried fruits, such as mango, papaya, melon and figs. Some dried fruits, such as cranberries, goji berries, cherries, sultanas and raisins, can be added whole, while larger exotic fruits need to be chopped, as do apricots, pears, dates and peaches. Dried fruits like pitted prunes can be soaked in sherry or a liqueur, like cake fruits.

FRESH FRUITS

Some fruits, such as berries, can be frozen before they are added to dough. This keeps them intact. Spread the fruits out in a single layer on a baking sheet and freeze until they are solid. Add to the dough in the machine just before the end of the kneading cycle. You can also use ready-frozen fruits in this way. When adding juicy fruits, toss them with a little extra flour, to keep the consistency of the bread dough correct. Soft fruits can be added to teabread mixtures too; just fold them in at the end of mixing.

Firm fruits, such as apples or pears, can be added raw, chopped into small chunks. Plums and rhubarb can also be used raw; simply cut them into small pieces. Rhubarb can also be poached first, so that it softens slightly. You can also grate firm fruits, or mash soft ripe fruits such as bananas and pears.

PINEAPPLE AND BANANA BREAD

The quantities given here are for a medium-sized loaf. Increase by 20 per cent for a large loaf; decrease by 25 per cent for small. Use size setting 1kg/2lb for large or 500g for small.

1 Pour 60ml/4 tbsp pineapple juice and 200ml/7fl oz/⅞ cup buttermilk into the bread pan. Add 1 large mashed banana (about 180g/6½oz). Add the dry ingredients first if your machine specifies this.

2 Sprinkle over 450g/1lb/4 cups white bread flour and 50g/2oz/½ cup wholemeal (whole-wheat) bread flour. Place 5ml/1 tsp salt, 45ml/3 tbsp caster (superfine) sugar and 40g/1½oz/3 tbsp butter in corners. Make an indent in the flour; add 5ml/1 tsp easy bake (rapid-rise) dried yeast.

3 Set to white/basic, raisin setting if available, light crust. Select size large/750g. Press Start. Add 75g/3oz/½ cup chopped pineapple chunks at the beep or towards the end of the cycle. Turn out on to a wire rack.

ADDING FRUIT TO BREADS

When you add the fruit and how heavily processed it is will determine whether it remains clearly detectable as whole pieces or blends fully into the dough to impart an even flavour and moistness throughout the bread.

• Add frozen orange concentrate or fruit juice right at the beginning of the mixing process, unless the instructions for your machine state you should add the dry ingredients first.

• Add purées, such as apple, pear or mango, after the water in the recipe has been poured into the bread pan. Alternatively, blend the two together first, then add the mixture to the pan.

BELOW: Fruit juice can replace part of the water quantity in some breads. Left to right: apple juice, pineapple juice, mango juice

• If you wish to add mashed or grated fruits, such as bananas or pears, put them in after the liquids.

• Add fresh or frozen whole fruits, such as berries, when the machine beeps or about 5 minutes before the end of the kneading cycle. Chopped fruits, such as apples and plums, as well as dried fruits, should also be added towards the end of the kneading process.

EQUIPMENT

The accessories required for bread-making are quite simple, the most expensive being the bread machine, which you probably already own. The essential pieces of equipment are largely concerned with accurate measuring; the remaining items are useful for hand-shaped breads.

MEASURING
Items to measure ingredients accurately are vital for making machine-breads.

SCALES
Electronic scales give the most accurate results and are well worth investing in. You can place the bread pan directly on the scales and weigh the ingredients straight into it. The display can be set to zero after each ingredient has been added, which makes additions to the pan easy to perform and absolutely precise.

MEASURING SPOONS
Smaller quantities of dry ingredients, such as sugar, salt and, most importantly, yeast, need to be measured carefully. A set of measuring spoons from 1.5ml/¼ tsp to 15ml/1 tbsp is ideal. Always level off the ingredient in the spoon for an accurate measure.

MEASURING JUGS (CUPS)
Heatproof glass jugs that are clearly marked in metric and imperial units are very useful. Place the measuring jug on a flat surface to ensure accuracy, and check the level of the ingredients by bending down so the measurements are at eye level.

LEFT: Having a range of different-size glass bowls is useful.

LEFT: Bannetons may be used for final proving before the bread is baked.

LEFT: Use scales and measuring jugs, cups and spoons to ensure the correct quantity of ingredients. Accuracy is essential to give good results.

MIXING AND RISING
The bread machine will automatically mix dough and make it rise, but there may be some items of equipment you need for hand-shaped breads.

GLASS BOWLS
While most of the mixing will take place inside the machine, you will still need to mix glazes, add extra ingredients, transfer doughs or batters to a large bowl, or use a large bowl as a cover for hand-shaped bread during the final proving period. Glass bowls give all-round visibility and a selection of sizes will prove universally useful around the kitchen.

BELOW: A French baguette tray will give French loaves their traditional shape.

LEFT: Speciality cake tins such as a kugelhopf tin and small brioche moulds may be worth acquiring.
BELOW: Assorted cake tins (pans), fluted loose-based tart tin

BANNETON
During the final prov-ing, breads are sometimes supported in cloth-lined bas-kets, called bannetons. Place baguettes in long bannetons and round loaves in round baskets. Flour the cloth well to prevent the dough from sticking. When the dough has risen you can up-turn the basket and place the bread directly on a prepared baking sheet.

DISHTOWELS AND CLEAR FILM
Use a clean dishtowel or clear film (plastic wrap) to cover the dough during proving. This prevents a dry crust from forming. Before using, lightly flour the dishtowel or oil the clear film to prevent the dough from sticking to the cover.

TIMER
If your bread machine does not have an audible signal to remind you to add extra ingredients, or you want to remember to check the

dough partway through the cycle, set a kitchen timer. It is also a good idea to set a timer if the beep of your bread machine is not particularly loud and you are unlikely to be in the kitchen when the signal goes off.

BAKING HAND-SHAPED LOAVES
A variety of tins (pans), trays and other equipment will help you bake breads of interesting shapes or with a crispier crust.

BREAD PANS AND MOULDS
Heavy gauge baking tins and moulds are best, because they are less likely to distort in the oven. A number of shapes and sizes are useful. A 1kg or a 2lb loaf tin (pan) measuring 18.5–11.5cm/ 7¼ × 4½in is a good basic size and shape, or try a longer, slightly nar-rower tin about 23–28cm/9–10in long. Both round and square cake tins are used for bread making, to support the dough while it rises. A 15cm/6in deep cake tin is used for baking pannetone.

RIGHT: Baking trays and loaf tins

BELOW: A peel is useful when making pizzas

Springform cake tins (pans) with diameters of 20–25cm/8–10in make the removal of sweet breads and cakes much easier than when a fixed-based cake tin is used. Square and rectangular tins are perfect for both sweet-and-savoury topped breads.

Focaccia or deep-pan pizzas are best cooked in a large, shallow, round cake tin with a diameter of 25–28cm/10–11in. A fluted loose-based tart pan and shallow pizza pan are good investments if you cook those types of bread regularly.

Shaped moulds are often used for baking speciality breads. A fluted mould with sloping sides is the classic shape for both individual and large Brioche. Kugelhopf is made in a deep fluted tin with a central hole, Savarin in a shallow ring mould and Babas in shallow, individual ring moulds.

FRENCH BAGUETTE TRAY
A moulded tray, designed to hold two or three loaves, this has a perforated base to ensure an even heat while baking. The bread is given its final proving in the tray, which is then placed in the oven for baking. Loaves baked in a tray will have small dimples on the base and sides.

BAKING SHEETS
A number of free-form breads need to be transferred to a baking sheet for cooking. A selection of strong, heavy baking sheets is best. Use either totally flat baking sheets, or ones with a lip on one edge only. These make it possible to remove the cooked breads easily.

BAKING STONE
For more rustic bread, sourdoughs, pizza and focaccia, a baking stone or pizza stone helps to ensure a crisp crust.

TERRACOTTA TILES
Unglazed quarry tiles or terracotta tiles can be used instead of a baking stone. The tiles will draw out moisture and help to produce the traditional crisp crust.

PEEL
If you are regularly going to use a baking stone or tiles, a peel (baker's shovel) is a useful piece of equipment. Use it to slide pizzas and bread doughs into the oven, placing them directly on to the preheated surface. Flour the peel generously and place the bread on it for its final proving. Give it a gentle shake just before placing it in the oven to make sure the base of the bread doesn't stick to the peel.

WATER SPRAY BOTTLE
Use a water spray bottle to mist the oven when you wish to achieve a crisp crust. A pump-action plastic bottle with a fine spray-head is ideal.

USEFUL TOOLS
This section includes tools for preparing ingredients and for finishing hand-shaped and machine breads.

CUTTERS
Plain cutters are used to cut dough for muffins and rolls. Metal cutters are best as they are not distorted when pressure is applied. A range of cutters 5–10cm/2–4in in diameter is most useful.

VEGETABLE PEELER
Use a fixed-blade vegetable peeler for peeling vegetables and fruit, or removing strips of citrus peel. A swivel-blade peeler is useful for paring very thin layers of citrus skin.

ZESTER
Many sweet breads and cakes include fresh citrus zest and this handy little tool makes light work of preparing it. The zester has a row of holes with cutting edges which shave off thin strips of zest without including the bitter pith that lies just beneath the coloured citrus peel. You may then wish to chop the strips into smaller pieces with a very sharp knife.

PASTRY BRUSHES
These are used to apply washes and glazes. Avoid nylon brushes, which will melt if used on hot breads. Brushes made from natural fibre are better.

LEFT: A baking stone, terracotta tiles and a water spray all help to produce breads with a crispier crust.

PLASTIC SCRAPER AND SPATULA

Make sure these tools are pliable. Use them to help remove dough that is stuck on the inside of the bread machine pan. The scraper also comes in handy for lifting and turning sticky dough and dividing dough into pieces for shaping into rolls.

KNIVES

You will need a sharp cook's knife for slashing doughs and a smaller paring knife for preparing fruit and vegetables. Use stainless steel for acidic fruits.

SCISSORS AND SCALPEL

Both these items can be used for slashing breads and rolls, to give decorative finishes before baking. A medium-size pair of scissors with thin, pointed blades is perfect. If you use a scalpel, replace the blade regularly, as it must be sharp.

ROLLING PINS

Some breads and buns need to be rolled out for shaping. Cylindrical wooden pins are best. Use a heavy rolling pin about 45cm/18in long for breads and a smaller one for individual rolls, buns and pastries. A child's toy rolling pin can be very useful for fiddly items.

LEFT: Selection of rolling pins

ABOVE: From left to right: spatula, cook's knife, vegetable knife, scalpel and scissors

THERMOMETERS

All ovens cook with slightly different heat intensities. An oven thermometer will enable you to establish how your oven cooks so you can make any necessary adjustments to recipes.

The time-honoured way of testing if a loaf of bread is cooked through is to tap it on the base to determine if it sounds hollow.

A much more scientific method is to insert a thermometer into the centre of a hand-shaped loaf and check the internal temperature. It should be 190–195°C (375–383°F).

SIEVES

A large sieve is essential for sifting flours together, and it will be handy to have one or two small sieves for sifting ingredients such as dried skimmed milk, icing (confectioners') sugar and ground spices. Use a plastic sieve for icing sugar, so as not to discolour it.

COOLING AND SLICING

Cooling a bread properly gives a crispier crust. The bread is then ready to eat.

OVEN GLOVES

A thick pair of oven gloves or mitts is essential for lifting the bread pan from the machine or breads from the oven, because the metal items will be very hot.

WIRE RACK

The hot cooked bread should be turned out on to a wire rack and left to cool before storing or slicing.

BREAD KNIFE AND BOARD

To preserve the delicate crumb structure, bread should be sawn with a sharp knife that has a long serrated blade. Cut the bread on a wooden board to prevent damaging the serrated knife.

ABOVE: Oven gloves, and a wire rack for cooling bread

RECRIPES

With the help of your bread machine you can create a vast array of distinctive breads, both sweet and savoury. The machine-baked breads have three sets of ingredients – for small, medium and large bread machines – as the quantities are crucial for success. Other breads can be mixed in any machine, shaped by hand then baked in an oven. Fresh bread tastes delicious and fills the kitchen with a wonderful aroma; now making it has never been easier.

BASIC BREADS

These recipes are the everyday breads that you will want to make time and again. They are some of the easiest breads to make in your machine; perfect for serving toasted with lashings of butter or for use in sandwiches. The range of breads includes wholemeal, Granary and rye breads, and those flavoured and enriched with milk, buttermilk, eggs, or potato. If you haven't made bread in your machine before, this is the place to start.

RAPID WHITE BREAD

A delicious basic white loaf which can be cooked on the fastest setting.
It is the ideal bread if you are in a hurry.

SMALL
210ml/7½fl oz/scant 1 cup
lukewarm water
22ml/1½ tbsp sunflower oil
375g/13oz/3¼ cups unbleached white
bread flour
15ml/1 tbsp skimmed milk powder
(non fat dry milk)
7.5ml/1½ tsp salt
15ml/1 tbsp granulated sugar
5ml/1 tsp easy bake (rapid-rise)
dried yeast

MEDIUM
315ml/11fl oz/1⅓ cups lukewarm water
30ml/2 tbsp sunflower oil
500g/1lb 2oz/4½ cups unbleached
white bread flour
22ml/1½ tbsp skimmed milk powder
7.5ml/1½ tsp salt
15ml/1 tbsp granulated sugar
5ml/1 tsp easy bake dried yeast

LARGE
385ml/13½fl oz/1⅝ cups
lukewarm water
45ml/3 tbsp sunflower oil
625g/1lb 6 oz/5½ cups unbleached
white bread flour
30ml/2 tbsp skimmed milk powder
10ml/2 tsp salt
22ml/1½ tbsp granulated sugar
10ml/2 tsp easy bake dried yeast

MAKES 1 LOAF

2 Sprinkle over the flour, covering the water. Add the milk powder. Place the salt and sugar in separate corners of the bread pan. Make a shallow indent in the centre of the flour (but not down as far as the liquid) and add the yeast.

3 Set the machine to the white rapid/basic rapid/fastbake setting, medium crust. Size: 500g for small, large/750g for medium or 1kg/2lb for large. Press Start.

4 Remove the bread at the end of the baking cycle. Turn out on to a wire rack.

> **COOK'S TIP**
> On the quick setting the yeast has less time to work, and breads may not rise as high as those cooked on the white/basic setting.
> In cold weather use warm water – one part boiling to two parts cold – to help speed up the action of the yeast.

1 Pour the water and the sunflower oil into the bread machine pan. However, if the instructions for your machine specify that the yeast is to be placed in the pan first, then reverse the order in which you add the liquid and dry ingredients.

Per loaf Energy 1528kcal/6476kJ; Protein 38.6g; Carbohydrate 312.1g, of which sugars 26.3g; Fat 22.6g, of which saturates 3.7g; Cholesterol 6mg; Calcium 653mg; Fibre 11.6g; Sodium 67mg.

MILK LOAF

Adding milk results in a soft, velvety grained loaf with a beautifully browned crust. Milk also improves the keeping quality of the bread.

SMALL
180ml/6½fl oz/generous ¾ cup milk
60ml/2fl oz/¼ cup water
375g/13oz/3¼ cups unbleached white bread flour
7.5ml/1½ tsp salt
10ml/2 tsp granulated sugar
20g/¾oz/1½ tbsp butter
2.5ml/½ tsp easy bake (rapid-rise) dried yeast

MEDIUM
230ml/8fl oz/1 cup milk
100ml/3½fl oz/7 tbsp water
500g/1lb 2oz/4½ cups unbleached white bread flour
7.5ml/1½ tsp salt
10ml/2 tsp granulated sugar
25g/1oz/2 tbsp butter
5ml/1 tsp easy bake dried yeast

LARGE
250ml/9fl oz/generous 1 cup milk
115ml/4fl oz/½ cup water
600g/1lb 5oz/5¼ cups unbleached white bread flour
10ml/2 tsp salt
10ml/2 tsp granulated sugar
25g/1oz/2 tbsp butter
7.5ml/1½ tsp easy bake dried yeast

MAKES 1 LOAF

COOK'S TIP
The milk should be at room temperature, or it will retard the action of the yeast and the bread will not rise properly. Remove the milk from the refrigerator 30 minutes before use. You can use full-cream (whole) or semi-skimmed (low-fat) milk.

1 Pour the milk and water into the bread machine pan. If the instructions for your machine specify that the yeast is to be placed in the pan first, reverse the order in which you add the liquid and dry ingredients.

2 Sprinkle over the flour, ensuring that it covers the water. Add the salt, sugar and butter in separate corners of the bread pan. Make a small indent in the centre of the flour (but not down as far as the liquid) and add the yeast.

3 Set the bread machine to the white/basic setting, medium crust. Size: 500g for small, large/750g for medium or 1kg/2lb for large. Press Start.

4 Remove the bread at the end of the baking cycle and turn out on to a wire rack to cool.

Per loaf Energy 1548kcal/6563kJ; Protein 41.3g; Carbohydrate 310.8g, of which sugars 25.1g; Fat 24.3g, of which saturates 13.4g; Cholesterol 57mg; Calcium 750mg; Fibre 11.6g; Sodium 3208mg.

WHITE BREAD

This simple recipe makes the perfect basis for experimenting. Be prepared to make minor alterations to quantities, to find the right recipe for your machine.

SMALL
230ml/8fl oz/1 cup water
375g/13oz/3¼ cups unbleached
white bread flour
7.5ml/1½ tsp salt
7.5ml/1½ tsp granulated sugar
25g/1oz/2 tbsp butter
5ml/1 tsp easy bake (rapid-rise)
dried yeast

MEDIUM
330ml/scant 12fl oz/1¼ cups
+ 2 tbsp water
500g/1lb 2oz/4½ cups unbleached
white bread flour
7.5ml/1½ tsp salt
10ml/2 tsp granulated sugar
25g/1oz/2 tbsp butter
5ml/1 tsp easy bake
dried yeast

LARGE
370ml/13fl oz/1½ cups
+ 1 tbsp water
600g/1lb 5oz/5¼ cups unbleached
white bread flour
7.5ml/1½ tsp salt
15ml/1 tbsp granulated sugar
40g/1½oz/3 tbsp butter
7.5ml/1½ tsp easy bake
dried yeast

MAKES 1 LOAF

1 Pour the water into the bread machine pan. However, if the instructions for your machine specify that the yeast is to be placed in the pan first, reverse the order in which you add the liquid and dry ingredients.

2 Sprinkle over the flour, ensuring that it covers the water. Add the salt, sugar and butter in separate corners of the bread pan. Make a small indent in the centre of the flour (but not down as far as the liquid) and add the yeast.

COOK'S TIP
To give the crust a richer golden appearance, add skimmed milk powder (non fat dry milk) to the flour. For a small loaf, you will need 15ml/ 1 tbsp; for a medium loaf 22ml/1½ tbsp and for a large loaf 30ml/2 tbsp.

3 Set the bread machine to the white/ basic setting, medium crust. Size: 500g for small, large/750g for medium or 1kg/2lb for large. Press Start.

4 Remove the bread at the end of the baking cycle. Turn out on to a wire rack.

Per loaf Energy 1493kcal/6321kJ; Protein 35.4g; Carbohydrate 299.2g, of which sugars 13.5g; Fat 25.3g, of which saturates 14.3g; Cholesterol 58mg; Calcium 533mg; Fibre 11.6g; Sodium 3147mg.

EGG-ENRICHED WHITE LOAF

Adding egg to a basic white loaf gives a richer flavour and creamier crumb, as well as a wonderfully golden finish to the crust.

1 Put the egg(s) in a measuring jug (cup) and add sufficient water to give 240ml/ 8½fl oz/generous 1 cup, 300ml/10½fl oz/ 1⅓ cups or 385ml/13½fl oz/1⅝ cups, according to the size of loaf selected.

2 Mix lightly and pour into the bread machine pan. If your instructions specify that the yeast is to be placed in the pan first, reverse the order in which you add the liquid and the dry ingredients.

SMALL
1 egg
water, see method
375g/13oz/3¼ cups unbleached white
bread flour
7.5ml/1½ tsp granulated sugar
7.5ml/1½ tsp salt
20g/¾oz/1½ tbsp butter
4ml/¾ tsp easy bake (rapid-rise)
dried yeast

MEDIUM
1 egg plus 1 egg yolk
water, see method
500g/1lb 2oz/4½ cups unbleached
white bread flour
10ml/2 tsp granulated sugar
7.5ml/1½ tsp salt
25g/1oz/2 tbsp butter
5ml/1 tsp easy bake dried yeast

LARGE
2 eggs
water, see method
600g/1lb 5oz/5¼ cups unbleached
white bread flour
10ml/2 tsp granulated sugar
7.5ml/1½ tsp salt
25g/1oz/2 tbsp butter
7.5ml/1½ tsp easy bake dried yeast

MAKES 1 LOAF

3 Sprinkle over the flour, covering the water. In separate corners of the pan, add the sugar, salt and butter. Make an indent in the centre of the flour. Add the yeast.

4 Set the bread machine to the white/ basic setting, medium crust. Size: 500g for small, large/750g for medium or 1kg/2lb for large. Press Start. At the end of the cycle, turn out on to a wire rack.

Per loaf Energy 1529kcal/6476kJ; Protein 41.6g; Carbohydrate 299.2g, of which sugars 13.5g; Fat 26.8g, of which saturates 13.1g; Cholesterol 236mg; Calcium 561mg; Fibre 11.6g; Sodium 3179mg.

BUTTERMILK BREAD

Buttermilk adds a pleasant, slightly sour note to the flavour of this bread. It also gives the bread a light texture and a golden brown crust.

SMALL

230ml/8fl oz/1 cup buttermilk
30ml/2 tbsp water
15ml/1 tbsp clear honey
15ml/1 tbsp sunflower oil
250g/9oz/2¼ cups unbleached white
bread flour
125g/4½oz/generous 1 cup wholemeal
(whole-wheat) bread flour
7.5ml/1½ tsp salt
5ml/1 tsp easy bake (rapid-rise)
dried yeast

MEDIUM

285ml/10fl oz/1¼ cups buttermilk
65ml/4½ tbsp water
22ml/1½ tbsp clear honey
22ml/1½ tbsp sunflower oil
350g/12oz/3 cups unbleached white
bread flour
150g/5½oz/1⅓ cups wholemeal
bread flour
7.5ml/1½ tsp salt
7.5ml/1½ tsp easy bake dried yeast

LARGE

330ml/scant 12fl oz/1¼ cups
+ 2 tbsp buttermilk
70ml/2½fl oz/⅓ cup water
22ml/1⅓ tbsp clear honey
30ml/2 tbsp sunflower oil
425g/15oz/3¾ cups unbleached white
bread flour
175g/6oz/generous 1½ cups wholemeal
bread flour
7.5ml/1½ tsp salt
7.5ml/1½ tsp easy bake dried yeast

MAKES 1 LOAF

COOK'S TIP
Buttermilk is a by-product of butter making and is the fairly thin liquid left after the fat has been made into butter. It is pasteurized and mixed with a special culture which causes it to ferment, resulting in the slightly sour flavour. If you run short of buttermilk, using a low-fat natural (plain) yogurt and 5–10ml/1–2 tsp lemon juice is an acceptable alternative.

1 Pour the buttermilk, water, honey and oil into the bread machine pan. If your instructions specify that the yeast is to be placed in the pan first, reverse the order of the liquid and dry ingredients.

2 Sprinkle over both the white and wholemeal flours, ensuring that the water is completely covered. Add the salt in one corner of the pan. Make a small indent in the centre of the flour (but not down as far as the liquid) and add the yeast.

3 Set the bread machine to the white/basic setting, medium crust. Size: 500g for small, large/750g for medium or 1kg/2lb for large. Press Start.

4 Remove the bread from the pan at the end of the baking cycle and turn out on to a wire rack to cool.

Per loaf Energy 1458kcal/6185kJ; Protein 47g; Carbohydrate 297.1g, of which sugars 29.3g; Fat 17.7g, of which saturates 2.4g; Cholesterol 9mg; Calcium 745mg; Fibre 19g; Sodium 2702mg.

Light Wholemeal Bread

A tasty, light wholemeal loaf, which can be cooked on the quicker basic or normal setting of your bread machine.

Small
280ml/10fl oz/1¼ cups water
250g/9oz/2¼ cups wholemeal
(whole-wheat) bread flour
125g/4½oz/generous 1 cup white
bread flour
15ml/1 tbsp skimmed milk powder
7.5ml/1½ tsp salt
7.5ml/1½ tsp granulated sugar
20g/¾oz/1½ tbsp butter
5ml/1 tsp easy bake (rapid-rise)
dried yeast

Medium
350ml/12fl oz/1½ cups water
350g/12oz/3 cups wholemeal bread flour
150g/5½oz/1¼ cups white bread flour
30ml/2 tbsp skimmed milk powder
7.5ml/1½ tsp salt
10ml/2 tsp granulated sugar
25g/1oz/2 tbsp butter
7.5ml/1½ tsp easy bake dried yeast

Large
400ml/14fl oz/scant 1¾ cups water
425g/15oz/3¾ cups wholemeal
bread flour
175g/6oz/generous 1½ cups white
bread flour
30ml/2 tbsp skimmed milk powder
10ml/2 tsp salt
15ml/1 tbsp granulated sugar
25g/1oz/2 tbsp butter
7.5ml/1½ tsp easy bake dried yeast

Makes 1 Loaf

VARIATION
Another option for a lighter brown bread is to replace the wholemeal bread flour with brown bread flour. This contains less bran and wheatgerm than wholemeal flour, making it lighter.

1 Pour the water into the bread machine pan. If the instructions for your bread machine specify that the yeast is to be placed in the pan first, reverse the order in which you add the liquid and dry ingredients to the pan.

2 Sprinkle over both flours ensuring that the water is completely covered. Add the skimmed milk powder. Add the salt, sugar and butter in separate corners of the bread pan. Make a small indent in the centre of the flour and add the yeast.

3 Set the bread machine to the white/basic setting, medium or light crust. Size: 500g for small, large/750g for medium or 1kg/2lb for large. Press Start.

4 Remove the bread at the end of the baking cycle. Turn out on to a wire rack.

Per loaf Energy 1277kcal/5429kJ; Protein 46.8g; Carbohydrate 260.7g, of which sugars 20g; Fat 8.8g, of which saturates 2g; Cholesterol 6mg; Calcium 395mg; Fibre 26.4g; Sodium 3014mg.

CORN MEAL BREAD

This scrumptious bread has a sweet flavour and crumbly texture. Use a finely ground corn meal (also known as maize meal) from the health-food store. The coarsely ground meal used for polenta makes a good topping.

SMALL

150ml/5fl oz/⅔ cup warm water
85ml/3fl oz/5 tbsp lukewarm milk
15ml/1 tbsp corn oil
275g/10oz/2½ cups unbleached white
bread flour
100g/3½oz/scant 1 cup corn meal
5ml/1 tsp salt
7.5ml/1½ tsp light muscovado
(brown) sugar
5ml/1 tsp easy bake (rapid-rise)
dried yeast
water, for glazing
polenta, for sprinkling

MEDIUM

210ml/7½fl oz/scant 1 cup
warm water
90ml/3fl oz/6 tbsp lukewarm milk
22ml/1½ tbsp corn oil
350g/12½oz/3 cups unbleached white
bread flour
150g/5oz/1¼ cups corn meal
5ml/1 tsp salt
10ml/2 tsp light muscovado sugar
5ml/1 tsp easy bake dried yeast
water, for glazing
polenta, for sprinkling

LARGE

225ml/8fl oz/scant 1 cup warm water
140ml/5fl oz/⅝ cup lukewarm milk
30ml/2 tbsp corn oil
400g/14oz/3½ cups unbleached white
bread flour
200g/7oz/1¾ cups corn meal
7.5ml/1½ tsp salt
10ml/2 tsp light muscovado sugar
7.5ml/1½ tsp easy bake dried yeast
water, for glazing
polenta, for sprinkling

MAKES 1 LOAF

COOK'S TIP

This bread is best cooked on a rapid setting, even though corn meal gives a slightly shallow loaf. If the rapid programme is less than 1 hour 50 minutes use warm milk and water to help the performance of the yeast.

1 Pour the water, milk and corn oil into the pan. Reverse the order in which you add the wet and dry ingredients if the instructions to your machine specify this.

2 Add the flour and the corn meal, covering the water. Place the salt and sugar in separate corners. Make a shallow indent in the flour; add the yeast.

3 Set the bread machine to the white rapid/basic rapid/fastbake setting, medium crust. Size: 500g for small, large/750g for medium or 1kg/2lb for large. Press Start. Just before the baking cycle starts, brush loaf with water and sprinkle with polenta.

4 Remove the bread at the end of the baking cycle. Turn out on to a wire rack.

Per loaf Energy 1473kcal/6226kJ; Protein 38.1g; Carbohydrate 298.9g, of which sugars 16.2g; Fat 19.3g, of which saturates 2.5g; Cholesterol 5mg; Calcium 494mg; Fibre 10.7g; Sodium 2020mg.

ANADAMA BREAD

This traditional New England bread is made with a mixture of white and wholemeal flours and polenta, which is a coarse corn meal. The molasses sweetens the bread and gives it a rich colour.

SMALL
200ml/7fl oz/⅞ cup water
45ml/3 tbsp molasses
5ml/1 tsp lemon juice
275g/10oz/2½ cups unbleached white bread flour
65g/2½oz/generous ½ cup wholemeal (whole-wheat) bread flour
40g/1½oz/⅓ cup polenta
7.5ml/1½ tsp salt
25g/1oz/2 tbsp butter
5ml/1 tsp easy bake (rapid-rise) dried yeast

MEDIUM
240ml/8½fl oz/generous 1 cup water
60ml/4 tbsp molasses
5ml/1 tsp lemon juice
360g/12½oz/generous 3 cups unbleached white bread flour
75g/3oz/¾ cup wholemeal bread flour
65g/2½oz/generous ½ cup polenta
10ml/2 tsp salt
40g/1½oz/3 tbsp butter
5ml/1 tsp easy bake dried yeast

LARGE
250ml/9fl oz/generous 1 cup water
75ml/5 tbsp molasses
10ml/2 tsp lemon juice
450g/1lb/4 cups unbleached white bread flour
75g/3oz/⅔ cup wholemeal bread flour
75g/3oz/⅔ cup polenta
10ml/2 tsp salt
40g/1½oz/3 tbsp butter
7.5ml/1½ tsp easy bake dried yeast

MAKES 1 LOAF

3 Set the machine to the white/basic setting, medium crust. Size: 500g for small, large/750g for medium or 1kg/2lb for large. Press Start.

4 Remove the bread at the end of the baking cycle. Turn out on to a wire rack.

> **COOK'S TIP**
> Check the dough after a few minutes' kneading. If dry, add a little water.

1 Pour the water, molasses and lemon juice into the bread machine pan. If the instructions for your machine specify that the yeast is to be placed in the pan first, reverse the order in which you add the liquid and dry ingredients.

2 Sprinkle over both types of flour, then the polenta, so that the water is completely covered. Add the salt and butter in separate corners of the bread pan. Make a small indent in the centre of the flour and add the yeast.

Per loaf Energy 1586kcal/6711kJ; Protein 38.5g; Carbohydrate 314.7g, of which sugars 35.7g; Fat 26.8g, of which saturates 14.2g; Cholesterol 58mg; Calcium 640mg; Fibre 15.3g; Sodium 3188mg.

SMALL

210ml/7½fl oz/scant 1 cup water
350g/12oz/3 cups unbleached white
bread flour, plus extra for dusting
25g/1oz/¼ cup wholemeal
(whole-wheat) bread flour
15ml/1 tbsp skimmed milk powder
(non fat dry milk)
7.5ml/1½ tsp salt
7.5ml/1½ tsp granulated sugar
15g/½oz/1 tbsp butter
4ml/¾ tsp easy bake (rapid-rise)
dried yeast
water, for glazing

MEDIUM

320ml/11¼fl oz/generous 1⅓ cups water
425g/15oz/3¾ cups unbleached white
bread flour, plus extra for dusting
75g/3oz/¾ cup wholemeal bread flour
22ml/1½ tbsp skimmed milk powder
7.5ml/1½ tsp salt
7.5ml/1½ tsp granulated sugar
25g/1oz/2 tbsp butter
5ml/1 tsp easy bake dried yeast
water, for glazing

LARGE

375ml/13½fl oz/1½ cups + 1 tbsp water
525g/1lb 3oz/4¾ cups unbleached
white bread flour, plus extra
for dusting
75g/3oz/⅔ cup wholemeal bread flour
30ml/2 tbsp skimmed milk powder
10ml/2 tsp salt
10ml/2 tsp granulated sugar
25g/1oz/2 tbsp butter
7.5ml/1½ tsp easy bake dried yeast
water, for glazing

MAKES 1 LOAF

1 Pour the water into the bread pan. If the instructions for your machine specify that the yeast is to be placed in the pan first, reverse the order in which you add the liquid and dry ingredients. Sprinkle over both the flours, covering the water completely. Add the milk powder. Add the salt, sugar and butter in separate corners. Make a small indent in the centre of the flour (but not down as far as the liquid) and add the yeast.

FARMHOUSE LOAF

The flour-dusted split top gives a charmingly rustic look to this tasty wholemeal-enriched white loaf.

2 Set the bread machine to the white/basic setting, medium crust. Size: 500g for small, large/750g for medium or 1kg/2lb for large. Press Start.

3 Ten minutes before the baking time commences, brush the top of the loaf with water and dust with white bread flour. Slash the top with a sharp knife.

4 Remove the bread at the end of the baking cycle and turn out on to a wire rack to cool.

COOK'S TIP
Try this rustic bread using Granary or Malthouse flour instead of wholemeal bread flour for added texture.

Per loaf Energy 1457kcal/6180kJ; Protein 39.5g; Carbohydrate 300.8g, of which sugars 18.6g; Fat 19.1g, of which saturates 9.9g; Cholesterol 40mg; Calcium 626mg; Fibre 13.1g; Sodium 3127mg.

GRANARY BREAD

Granary flour – like Malthouse flour – is a blend, and contains malted wheat grain which gives a crunchy texture to this loaf.

1 Add the water to the bread machine pan. If the instructions for your particular machine specify that the yeast is to be placed in the pan first, simply reverse the order in which you add the liquid and dry ingredients to the bread machine pan.

2 Sprinkle over the flour, ensuring that it covers the water, then add the salt, sugar and butter in separate corners of the bread pan. Make a small indent in the centre of the flour (but not down as far as the liquid) and add the yeast to the indent.

3 Set the machine to the wholewheat setting, medium crust. Size: 500g for small, large/750g for medium or 1kg/2lb for large. Press Start.

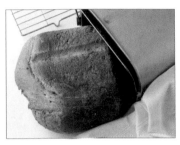

4 Remove the bread at the end of the baking cycle. Turn out on to a wire rack.

COOK'S TIP
You could use Malthouse bread flour instead of Granary. If your loaf collapses slightly before baking, next time add 10–15ml/2–3 tsp lemon juice or a crushed 100mg vitamin C tablet.

SMALL
240ml/8½fl oz/generous 1 cup water
375g/13oz/3¼ cups Granary
(whole-wheat) bread flour
5ml/1 tsp salt
10ml/2 tsp granulated sugar
20g/¾oz/1½ tbsp butter
5ml/1 tsp easy bake (rapid-rise)
dried yeast

MEDIUM
325ml/11½fl oz/generous 1⅓ cups water
500g/1lb 2oz/4½ cups Granary bread flour
7.5ml/1½ tsp salt
15ml/1 tbsp granulated sugar
25g/1oz/2 tbsp butter
7.5ml/1½ tsp easy bake dried yeast

LARGE
375ml/13½fl oz/1½ cups + 1 tbsp water
625g/1lb 6oz/5½ cups Granary
bread flour
10ml/2 tsp salt
15ml/1 tbsp granulated sugar
25g/1oz/2 tbsp butter
7.5ml/1½ tsp easy bake dried yeast

MAKES 1 LOAF

Per loaf Energy 1340kcal/5717kJ; Protein 47.8g; Carbohydrate 250.1g, of which sugars 18.3g; Fat 24.6g, of which saturates 11.9g; Cholesterol 46mg; Calcium 151mg; Fibre 33.8g; Sodium 2127mg.

MALTED LOAF

A malt and sultana loaf makes the perfect breakfast or tea-time treat.
Serve it sliced and generously spread with butter.

SMALL
210ml/7½fl oz/scant 1 cup water
15ml/1 tbsp golden (light corn) syrup
22ml/1½ tbsp malt extract
375g/13oz/3¼ cups unbleached white
bread flour
22ml/1½ tbsp skimmed milk powder
(non fat dry milk)
2.5ml/½ tsp salt
40g/1½oz/3 tbsp butter
2.5ml/½ tsp easy bake (rapid-rise)
dried yeast
75g/3oz/½ cup sultanas (golden raisins)

MEDIUM
280ml/10fl oz/1¼ cups water
22ml/1½ tbsp golden syrup
30ml/2 tbsp malt extract
500g/1lb 2oz/4½ cups unbleached
white bread flour
30ml/2 tbsp skimmed milk powder
5ml/1 tsp salt
50g/2oz/¼ cup butter
5ml/1 tsp easy bake dried yeast
100g/3½oz/generous ½ cup sultanas

LARGE
320ml/11fl oz/generous 1⅓ cups water
30ml/2 tbsp golden syrup
45ml/3 tbsp malt extract
600g/1lb 5oz/5¼ cups unbleached
white bread flour
30ml/2 tbsp skimmed milk powder
5ml/1 tsp salt
50g/2oz/¼ cup butter
7.5ml/1½ tsp easy bake dried yeast
125g/4½oz/generous ⅔ cup sultanas

MAKES 1 LOAF

1 Pour the water, golden syrup and malt extract into the bread machine pan. If the instructions for your machine specify that the yeast is to be placed in the pan first, reverse the order in which you add the liquid and dry ingredients.

2 Sprinkle over the flour so that it covers the liquid. Add the milk powder. Add the salt and butter in separate corners. Make a shallow indent in the centre of the flour and add the yeast.

3 Set the machine to the white/basic setting, raisin setting if available. Select light crust, 500g for small; medium crust, large/750g for medium; or medium crust 1kg/2lb for large. Add the sultanas to the automatic dispenser, if available, or when the machine beeps during the kneading cycle. Press Start.

4 Remove the loaf at the end of the baking cycle and turn out on to a wire rack.

5 Glaze the bread immediately, if you like, by dissolving 15ml/1 tbsp caster (superfine) sugar in 15ml/1 tbsp milk and brushing over the top crust. Allow to cool.

Per loaf Energy 1876kcal/7938kJ; Protein 37.5g; Carbohydrate 368.9g, of which sugars 83.1g; Fat 37.9g, of which saturates 22.4g; Cholesterol 92mg; Calcium 676mg; Fibre 13.1g; Sodium 1401mg.

Light Rye and Caraway Bread

Rye flour adds a distinctive slightly sour flavour to bread. Rye breads can be dense, so the flour is usually mixed with wheat flour to lighten the texture.

1 Add the water, lemon juice and oil to the bread pan. If your instructions specify that the yeast is to be placed in the pan first, reverse the order in which you add the liquid and dry ingredients.

2 Sprinkle over the rye flour and the white bread flour, ensuring they cover the water. Add the skimmed milk powder and caraway seeds. Add the salt and sugar in separate corners of the bread pan. Make a small indent in the centre of the flour, but not down as far as the liquid, and add the yeast.

3 Set the bread machine to the white/basic setting, medium crust. Size: 500g for small, large/750g for medium or 1kg/2lb for large. Press Start.

4 Remove the bread at the end of the cycle and transfer to a wire rack to cool.

SMALL
210ml/7½fl oz/scant 1 cup water
5ml/1 tsp lemon juice
15ml/1 tbsp sunflower oil
85g/3oz/¾ cup rye flour
285g/10oz/2½ cups unbleached white bread flour
15ml/1 tbsp skimmed milk powder (non fat dry milk)
5ml/1 tsp caraway seeds
5ml/1 tsp salt
10ml/2 tsp light muscovado (brown) sugar
3.5ml/¾ tsp easy bake (rapid-rise) dried yeast

MEDIUM
300ml/10½fl oz/1¼ cups water
10ml/2 tsp lemon juice
22ml/1½ tbsp sunflower oil
125g/4½oz/generous 1 cup rye flour
375g/13oz/3¼ cups unbleached white bread flour
22ml/1½ tbsp skimmed milk powder
7.5ml/1½ tsp caraway seeds
7.5ml/1½ tsp salt
15ml/1 tbsp light muscovado sugar
5ml/1 tsp easy bake dried yeast

LARGE
330ml/scant 12fl oz/1¼ cups
+ 2 tbsp water
10ml/2 tsp lemon juice
30ml/2 tbsp sunflower oil
155g/5½oz/1⅓ cups rye flour
450g/1lb/4 cups unbleached white bread flour
30ml/2 tbsp skimmed milk powder
10ml/2 tsp caraway seeds
10ml/2 tsp salt
15ml/1 tbsp light muscovado sugar
7.5ml/1½ tsp easy bake dried yeast

MAKES 1 LOAF

Per loaf Energy 1441kcal/6116kJ; Protein 37.1g; Carbohydrate 301.4g, of which sugars 19.7g; Fat 18.1g, of which saturates 3.1g; Cholesterol 6mg; Calcium 552mg; Fibre 18.8g; Sodium 2030mg.

FRENCH BREAD

French bread traditionally has a crisp crust and light, chewy crumb. Use the special French bread setting on your bread machine to help to achieve this unique texture.

SMALL
MAKES 1 LOAF
150ml/5fl oz/⅔ cup water
225g/8oz/2 cups unbleached white bread flour
5ml/1 tsp salt
7.5ml/1½ tsp easy bake (rapid-rise) dried yeast

MEDIUM
MAKES 2–3 LOAVES
315ml/11fl oz/1⅓ cups water
450g/1lb/4 cups unbleached white bread flour
7.5ml/1½ tsp salt
7.5ml/1½ tsp easy bake dried yeast

LARGE
MAKES 3–4 LOAVES
500ml/17½fl oz/2⅛ cups water
675g/1½lb/6 cups unbleached white bread flour
10ml/2 tsp salt
10ml/2 tsp easy bake dried yeast

1 Add the water to the bread machine pan. If the instructions for your machine specify that the yeast is to be placed in the pan first, reverse the order in which you add the liquid and dry ingredients.

2 Sprinkle the flour over the water. Add the salt in a corner. Make an indent in the centre of the flour and add the yeast. Use the French dough/Artisan dough setting (see Cook's Tip). Press Start.

3 When the dough cycle has finished, remove the dough from the machine, place it on a lightly floured surface and knock it back (punch it down). Divide it into two or three equal portions if using the medium quantities or three or four portions if using the large quantities.

4 On a floured surface shape each piece of dough into a ball, then roll out to a rectangle measuring 18–20 × 7.5cm/ 7–8 × 3in. Fold one-third up lengthways and one-third down, then press. Repeat twice more, leaving the dough to rest between foldings to avoid tearing.

5 Gently roll and stretch each piece to a 28–33cm/11–13in loaf, depending on whether you aim to make smaller or larger loaves. Place each loaf in a floured banneton or between the folds of a floured and pleated dishtowel, so that the French bread shape is maintained during rising.

6 Cover with lighly oiled clear film (plastic wrap) and leave in a warm place for 30–45 minutes. Preheat the oven to 230°C/450°F/Gas 8.

7 Roll the loaf or loaves on to a baking sheet, spaced well part. Slash the tops with a knife. Place at the top of the oven, spray the inside of the oven with water and bake for 15–20 minutes, or until golden. Transfer to a wire rack.

> **COOK'S TIP**
> Use the French bread baking setting if you do not have a French bread dough setting. Remove the dough before the final rising stage and shape as directed.

Per loaf Energy 767kcal/3263kJ; Protein 21.1g; Carbohydrate 174.8g, of which sugars 3.4g; Fat 2.9g, of which saturates 0.5g; Cholesterol 0mg; Calcium 316mg; Fibre 7g; Sodium 1972mg.

ITALIAN BREADSTICKS

These crisp breadsticks will keep for a couple of days if stored in an airtight container. If you like, you can refresh them in a hot oven for a few minutes before serving. The dough can be made in any size of breadmaking machine.

1 Pour the water and olive oil into the bread machine pan. If the instructions for your machine specify that the yeast is to be placed in the pan first, reverse the order in which you add the liquid and dry ingredients.

2 Sprinkle over the flour, ensuring that it covers the water completely. Add the salt in one corner of the pan. Make a small indent in the centre of the flour (but not down as far as the liquid) and add the easy bake dried yeast.

3 Set the bread machine to the dough setting; use basic dough setting (if available). Press Start.

4 Lightly oil two baking sheets. Preheat the oven to 200°C/400°F/Gas 6.

5 When the dough cycle has finished, remove the dough from the machine, place it on a lightly floured surface and knock it back (punch it down). Roll it out to a rectangle measuring 23 × 20cm/9 × 8in.

6 Cut into three 20cm/8in long strips. Cut each strip widthways into ten. Roll and stretch each piece to 30cm/12in.

7 Roll in poppy seeds or sea salt if you like. Space well apart on the baking sheets. Brush lightly with olive oil, cover with clear film (plastic wrap) and leave in a warm place for 10–15 minutes.

8 Bake for 15–20 minutes, or until golden, turning once. Transfer to a wire rack to cool.

200ml/7fl oz/⅞ cup water
45ml/3 tbsp olive oil, plus extra
350g/12oz/3 cups unbleached white
bread flour
7.5ml/1½ tsp salt
7.5ml/1½ tsp easy bake (rapid-rise)
dried yeast
poppy seeds and coarse sea salt,
for coating (optional)

MAKES 30

COOK'S TIP
If you are rolling the breadsticks in sea salt, don't use too much. Crush the sea salt slightly if the crystals are large.

Per breadstick Energy 50kcal/210kJ; Protein 1.1g; Carbohydrate 9.1g, of which sugars 0.2g; Fat 1.3g, of which saturates 0.2g; Cholesterol 0mg; Calcium 16mg; Fibre 0.4g; Sodium 99mg.

CRISPY FRENCH BREAD

This is an easy way to make French bread. The French bread programme will produce a light textured bread with the extra crispy crust that is commonly associated with French bread.

SMALL
300ml/10½fl oz/1¼ cups water
400g/14oz/3½ cups unbleached white bread flour
15g/½oz/1 tbsp butter
5ml/1 tsp salt
5ml/1 tsp easy bake (rapid-rise) dried yeast

MEDIUM
350ml/12fl oz/1½ cups water
500g/1lb 2oz/4½ cups unbleached white bread flour
15g/½oz/1 tbsp butter
7.5ml/1½ tsp salt
7ml/1¼ tsp easy bake dried yeast

LARGE
420ml/15fl oz/1¾ cups water
600g/1lb 5oz/5¼ cups unbleached white bread flour
25g/1oz/2 tbsp butter
10ml/2 tsp salt
7.5ml/1½ tsp easy bake dried yeast

MAKES 1 LOAF

1 Pour the water into the bread machine pan. If the manufacturer's instructions for your particular machine specify that the yeast is to be placed in the pan first, reverse the order in which you add the liquid and the dry ingredients.

2 Sprinkle over the flour, ensuring that it covers the water. Add the butter and salt in two separate corners of the bread pan. Make a small indent in the centre of the flour (but not down as far as the liquid) and add the yeast into the indent.

3 Set the bread machine to the French setting, medium crust. Size: 500g for small, large/750g for medium or 1kg/2lb for large. Press Start.

4 Remove the bread at the end of the baking cycle. Turn out on to a wire rack.

Per loaf Energy 1475kcal/6255kJ; Protein 37.7g; Carbohydrate 310.8g, of which sugars 6g; Fat 17.5g, of which saturates 8.9g; Cholesterol 35mg; Calcium 563mg; Fibre 12.4g; Sodium 2090mg.

POTATO BREAD

This golden crusty loaf has a moist soft centre and is perfect for sandwiches. Use the water in which the potatoes have been cooked to make this bread. If you haven't got enough, make up the remainder with tap water.

1 Pour the water and sunflower oil into the bread machine pan. However, if the instructions for your machine specify that the yeast is to be placed in the pan first, reverse the order in which you add the liquid and dry ingredients.

2 Sprinkle over the flour, ensuring that it covers the water. Add the mashed potato and milk powder. Add the salt and sugar in separate corners of the bread pan. Make a small indent in the centre of the flour (but not down as far as the liquid) and add the yeast.

3 Set the bread machine to the white/basic setting, medium or light crust. Size: 500g for small, large/750g for medium or 1kg/2lb for large. Press Start. To glaze the loaf, brush with the top of the milk halfway through the cooking time.

4 Remove the bread at the end of the baking cycle. Turn out on to a wire rack.

SMALL
200ml/7fl oz/⅞ cup potato cooking water, at room temperature
30ml/2 tbsp sunflower oil
375g/13oz/3¼ cups unbleached white bread flour
125g/4½oz/1½ cups cold mashed potato
15ml/1 tbsp skimmed milk powder (non fat dry milk)
5ml/1 tsp salt
7.5ml/1½ tsp granulated sugar
5ml/1 tsp easy bake (rapid-rise) dried yeast
milk, for glazing

MEDIUM
240ml/8½fl oz/generous 1 cup potato cooking water, at room temperature
30ml/2 tbsp sunflower oil
500g/1lb 2oz/4½ cups unbleached white bread flour
175g/6oz/2 cups cold mashed potato
22ml/1½ tbsp skimmed milk powder
7.5ml/1½ tsp salt
10ml/2 tsp granulated sugar
7.5ml/1½ tsp easy bake dried yeast
milk, for glazing

LARGE
290ml/generous ½ pint/scant 1¼ cups potato cooking water, at room temperature
45ml/3 tbsp sunflower oil
600g/1lb/5¼ cups unbleached white bread flour
200g/7oz/scant 2½ cups cold cooked mashed potato
30ml/2 tbsp skimmed milk powder
7.5ml/1½ tsp salt
15ml/1 tbsp granulated sugar
7.5ml/1½ tsp easy bake dried yeast
milk, for glazing

MAKES 1 LOAF

COOK'S TIP
If using leftover potatoes mashed with milk and butter you may need to reduce the liquid. If making the mashed potato, use 175g/6oz, 200g/7oz or 250g/9oz raw potatoes, depending on machine size.

Per loaf Energy 1643kcal/6953kJ; Protein 38g; Carbohydrate 319.3g, of which sugars 15.5g; Fat 32.5g, of which saturates 7g; Cholesterol 16mg; Calcium 564mg; Fibre 13g; Sodium 2039mg.

GLUTEN-FREE SEED BREAD

Gluten-free breads do not keep as long as wheat-based breads so consume within two days. Alternatively, slice part of the loaf after cooling, wrap it and freeze. Use frozen bread within one month.

SMALL
300ml/10½fl oz/1¼ cups water
15ml/1 tbsp sunflower oil
350g/12½oz/3 cups Juvela gluten-free mix for bread
15ml/1 tbsp pumpkin seeds
15ml/1 tbsp sunflower seeds
15ml/1 tbsp poppy seeds
2.5ml/½ tsp salt
5ml/1 tsp dried yeast, from the gluten-free mix pack

MEDIUM AND LARGE
400ml/14fl oz/scant 1¾ cups water
22ml/1½ tbsp sunflower oil
500g/1lb 2oz/4½ cups Juvela gluten-free mix for bread
22ml/1½ tbsp pumpkin seeds
30ml/2 tbsp sunflower seeds
15ml/1 tbsp poppy seeds
2.5ml/½ tsp salt
7.5ml/1½ tsp dried yeast, from the gluten-free mix pack

MAKES 1 LOAF

COOK'S TIP
Results may vary if a different brand of gluten-free bread mix is used. Gluten-free bread mixes are available at pharmacies and health food stores.

2 Sprinkle over the gluten-free mix, ensuring that it covers the water. Add the pumpkin seeds, sunflower seeds and poppy seeds.

3 Add the salt in one corner of the bread pan. Make a small indent in the centre of the flour (but not down as far as the liquid) and add the yeast, from the Juvela mix.

4 Set the bread machine to the gluten-free setting if available, if not the white/basic setting. Use dark crust on the gluten-free setting, if available, and medium on white/basic setting. Size: 500g for small, 750g for medium or 1kg/2lb for large. The weight setting is not available on some gluten-free cycles. Press Start. You may need to scrape down the mixture after 5 minutes, if it is stuck around the pan. Use a plastic spatula, as metal may damage the surface.

5 Remove the bread at the end of the baking cycle and turn out on to a wire rack to cool. If using a basic setting check the loaf about 10 minutes before the end of the cycle. If it is well risen and brown, remove from the bread machine early and cancel the programme.

1 Pour the water into the bread machine pan. Add the sunflower oil. If the instructions for your machine specify that the yeast is to be placed in the pan first, reverse the order in which you add the liquid and the dry ingredients. Check with your manufacturer's instructions as you may need to add the water first for the gluten-free programme.

Per loaf Energy 1554kcal/6566kJ; Protein 41.8g; Carbohydrate 280.3g, of which sugars 6g; Fat 36.9g, of which saturates 4g; Cholesterol 0mg; Calcium 540mg; Fibre 13.6g; Sodium 994mg.

GLUTEN- AND WHEAT-FREE BREAD

If gluten- and wheat-free bread is part of your dietary requirements, this bread is perfect. Depending on your machine and the length of the gluten-free cycle, this recipe may produce a lighter loaf on the white/basic setting.

SMALL
1 egg
30ml/2 tbsp sunflower oil
5ml/1 tsp cider vinegar
260g/9½oz/2⅓ cups brown rice flour
90g/3¼oz/½ cup potato flour
10ml/2 tsp xanthum gum
45ml/3 tbsp skimmed milk powder
5ml/1 tsp salt
10ml/2 tsp sugar
5ml/1 tsp easy bake (rapid-rise)
dried yeast

MEDIUM
2 eggs
45ml/3 tbsp sunflower oil
5ml/1 tsp cider vinegar
300g/11oz/2½ cups brown rice flour
100g/3½oz/generous ½ cup potato flour
15ml/1 tbsp xanthum gum
75ml/5 tbsp skimmed milk powder
5ml/1 tsp salt
15ml/1 tbsp sugar
5ml/1 tsp easy bake dried yeast

LARGE
3 eggs
60ml/4 tbsp sunflower oil
5ml/1 tsp cider vinegar
375g/13oz/3¼ cups brown rice flour
125g/4½oz/¾ cup potato flour
15ml/1 tbsp xanthum gum
75ml/5 tbsp skimmed milk powder
7.5ml/1½ tsp salt
22.5ml/1½ tbsp sugar
7.5ml/1½ tsp easy bake dried yeast

MAKES 1 LOAF

1 Put the egg(s) in a measuring jug (cup) and add sufficient tepid water to give 460ml/16½fl oz/scant 2 cups, 560ml/1 pint/2⅜ cups, or 660ml/ 23½fl oz/generous 2¾ cups, according to the size of loaf you are making.

2 Mix the egg(s) and water lightly and pour into the bread machine pan. Add the sunflower oil and cider vinegar. If the instructions for your machine specify that the yeast is to be placed in the pan first, reverse the order in which you add the liquid and the dry ingredients. Check your manufacturer's instructions as you may need to add the water first for the gluten-free programme.

3 Sprinkle over the flours, ensuring they cover the water. Add the xanthum gum and skimmed milk powder. Add the salt and sugar in separate corners of the bread pan. Make a small indent in the centre of the flour (but not down as far as the liquid) and add the yeast.

4 Set the bread machine to the gluten-free setting, dark crust, if available, or white/basic setting, medium crust. Size: 500g for small, 750g for medium or 1kg/2lb for large. Weight settings are not available on some gluten-free cycles. You may need to scrape down the mixture after 5 minutes, if it is stuck around the pan. Use a plastic spatula, as metal may damage the surface.

5 Remove the bread at the end of the baking cycle. Turn out on to a wire rack

Per loaf Energy 1641kcal/6856kJ; Protein 33.6g; Carbohydrate 298.3g, of which sugars 17.9g; Fat 30.8g, of which saturates 4.3g; Cholesterol 196mg; Calcium 298mg; Fibre 7g; Sodium 2134mg.

SPECIALITY GRAINS

This selection of recipes includes classic flours from around the world, producing loaves with a variety of textures and flavours. Gluten is an essential part of the structure of bread, to ensure an open, light crumb and texture. Most grains other than wheat have little or no gluten, so millet, buckwheat, barley and rye have been blended with wheat flours to provide rich, nutty flavoured loaves which can be successfully baked in your bread machine.

MUESLI AND DATE BREAD

This makes the perfect breakfast or brunch bread. Use your own favourite unsweetened muesli to ring the changes.

260ml/9fl oz/scant 1⅛ cups water
30ml/2 tbsp sunflower oil
15ml/1 tbsp clear honey
300g/10½oz/2⅔ cups unbleached white bread flour
75g/3oz/¾ cup wholemeal (whole-wheat) bread flour
150g/5½oz/1½ cups unsweetened fruit and nut muesli (granola)
45ml/3 tbsp skimmed milk powder (non fat dry milk)
7.5ml/1½ tsp salt
7.5ml/1½ tsp easy bake (rapid-rise) dried yeast
65g/2½oz/scant ½ cup stoned (pitted) dates, chopped

MAKES 1 LOAF

1 Pour the water, oil and honey into the bread pan. Reverse the order in which you add the wet and dry ingredients if necessary. Sprinkle over the flours, covering the water. Add the muesli and milk powder, then the salt, in a corner.

2 Make a small indent in the flour; add the yeast. Set to the dough setting; use basic raisin dough setting (if available). Press Start. Add the dates at the beep or during the last 5 minutes of kneading. Lightly oil a baking sheet.

3 When the dough cycle has finished, remove from the machine and place it on a surface dusted with wholemeal flour. Knock back (punch down) gently.

4 Shape the dough into a plump round and place it on the prepared baking sheet. Using a sharp knife make three cuts on the top about 1cm/½in deep, to divide the bread into six sections.

5 Cover the loaf with lightly oiled clear film (plastic wrap) and leave for 30–45 minutes, or until almost doubled in size.

6 Preheat the oven to 200°C/400°F/ Gas 6. Bake the loaf for 30–35 minutes until it is golden and hollow sounding. Transfer it to a wire rack to cool.

> **COOK'S TIP**
> The amount of water required may vary with the type of muesli used. Add another 15ml/1 tbsp water if the dough is too firm.

BARLEY-ENRICHED FARMHOUSE LOAF

Barley adds a very distinctive, earthy, slightly nutty flavour to this crusty white loaf.

260ml/9fl oz/1⅛ cups water
45ml/3 tbsp double (heavy) cream
400g/14oz/3½ cups unbleached white bread flour
115g/4oz/1 cup barley flour
10ml/2 tsp granulated sugar
10ml/2 tsp salt
7.5ml/1½ tsp easy bake (rapid-rise) dried yeast
25g/1oz/2 tbsp pumpkin seeds
flour, for dusting

MAKES 1 LOAF

1 Pour the water and cream into the pan. Reverse the order in which you add the liquid and dry ingredients if necessary. Sprinkle over both types of flour, covering the water completely. Add the sugar and salt, placing them in separate corners of the pan. Make a shallow indent in the centre of the flour and add the yeast.

2 Set the bread machine to the dough setting; use basic raisin dough setting (if available). Press Start. Add the pumpkin seeds when the machine beeps or during the last 5 minutes of kneading. Lightly oil a 900g/2lb loaf tin (pan) measuring 18.5 × 12cm/7¼ × 4½in.

3 When the dough cycle has finished, remove the dough from the machine and place on a lightly floured surface. Knock back (punch down) gently. Shape the dough into a rectangle, making the longer side the same length as the tin.

4 Roll the dough up lengthways, and tuck the ends under. Place it in the prepared tin, with the seam underneath. Cover with oiled clear film (plastic wrap) and leave for 30–45 minutes, or until the dough reaches the top of the tin.

5 Dust the loaf with flour then make a deep lengthways cut along the top. Leave to rest for 10 minutes. Preheat the oven to 220°C/425°F/Gas 7.

6 Bake the loaf for 15 minutes, then reduce the oven temperature to 200°C/ 400°F/Gas 6 and bake for 20–25 minutes more, or until the bread is golden and sounds hollow when tapped on the base. Transfer it to a wire rack to cool.

Per loaf Energy 2852kcal/12101kJ; Protein 65.9g; Carbohydrate 587.6g, of which sugars 197.4g; Fat 42.6g, of which saturates 7.4g; Cholesterol 9mg; Calcium 807mg; Fibre 31.6g; Sodium 3136mg.
Per loaf Energy 2143kcal/9070kJ; Protein 54.2g; Carbohydrate 416.5g, of which sugars 19.8g; Fat 42.7g, of which saturates 15.7g; Cholesterol 59mg; Calcium 777mg; Fibre 17.5g; Sodium 3963mg.

BRAN AND YOGURT BREAD

This soft-textured yogurt bread is enriched with bran. It is high in fibre and makes wonderful toast.

SMALL

150ml/5fl oz/⅔ cup water
125ml/4½fl oz/generous ½ cup
natural (plain) yogurt
15ml/1 tbsp sunflower oil
15ml/1 tbsp molasses
200g/7oz/1¾ cups unbleached white
bread flour
150g/5½oz/1⅓ cups wholemeal
(whole-wheat) bread flour
25g/1oz/⅛ cup wheat bran
5ml/1 tsp salt
4ml/¾ tsp easy bake (rapid-rise)
dried yeast

MEDIUM

185ml/6½fl oz/generous ¾ cup water
175ml/6fl oz/¾ cup natural yogurt
22ml/1½ tbsp sunflower oil
30ml/2 tbsp molasses
260g/generous 9oz/2⅓ cups
unbleached white bread flour
200g/7oz/1¾ cups wholemeal
bread flour
40g/1½oz/½ cup wheat bran
7.5ml/1½ tsp salt
5ml/1 tsp easy bake dried yeast

LARGE

200ml/7fl oz/⅞ cup water
190ml/6¾fl oz/scant ⅞ cup
natural yogurt
30ml/2 tbsp sunflower oil
30ml/2 tbsp molasses
340g/12oz/3 cups unbleached white
bread flour
225g/8oz/2 cups wholemeal
bread flour
40g/½oz/⅔ cup wheat bran
10ml/2 tsp salt
7.5ml/1½ tsp easy bake dried yeast

MAKES 1 LOAF

COOK'S TIP
Molasses is added to this bread to give
added flavour and colour. You can use
treacle or golden (light corn) syrup
instead, to intensify or lessen the
flavour respectively, if desired.

1 Pour the water, yogurt, oil and molasses into the bread machine pan. If the instructions for your machine specify that the yeast is to be placed in the pan first, reverse the order in which you add the liquid and dry ingredients.

2 Sprinkle over both the white and the wholemeal flours, ensuring that the liquid mixture is completely covered. Add the wheat bran and salt, then make a small indent in the centre of the dry ingredients (but not down as far as the liquid) and add the easy bake dried yeast.

3 Set the bread machine to the white/basic setting, medium crust. Size: 500g for small, large/750g for medium or 1kg/2lb for large. Press Start.

4 Remove the bread from the pan at the end of the baking cycle and turn out on to a wire rack to cool. Serve when still just warm, if you like.

Per loaf Energy 1406kcal/5961kJ; Protein 47.9g; Carbohydrate 277.4g, of which sugars 26.6g; Fat 19.5g, of which saturates 3g; Cholesterol 2mg; Calcium 678mg; Fibre 28.8g; Sodium 2101mg.

WHOLEMEAL BREAD

This is a hearty bread with a full nutty flavour and coarse texture from the wheatgerm and bran found in the wholemeal flour.

SMALL
280ml/10fl oz/1 cup + 3 tbsp water
10ml/2 tsp lemon juice
385g/13½ oz/3⅜ cups wholemeal
(whole-wheat) bread flour
20g/¾ oz/1½ tbsp butter
7.5ml/1½ tsp salt
7.5ml/1½ tsp sugar
5ml/1 tsp easy bake (rapid-rise)
dried yeast

MEDIUM
350ml/12fl oz/1½ cups water
10ml/2 tsp lemon juice
500g/1lb 2oz/ 4½ cups wholemeal
bread flour
25g/1oz/2 tbsp butter
10ml/2 tsp salt
10ml/2 tsp sugar
5ml/1 tsp easy bake dried yeast

LARGE
380ml/13½fl oz/1⅝ cups water
15ml/1 tbsp lemon juice
600g/1lb 5oz/5¼ cups wholemeal
bread flour
25g/1oz/2 tbsp butter
10ml/2 tsp salt
15ml/1 tbsp sugar
6.5ml/1⅓ tsp easy bake dried yeast

MAKES 1 LOAF

3 Set the bread machine to the whole wheat setting, medium crust, if available. Size: 500g for small, large/750g for medium or 1kg/2lb for large. Press Start.

4 Remove the bread from the bread pan at the end of the baking cycle, then turn it out on to a wire rack to cool.

COOK'S TIP
Depending on the gluten strength of the flour, some bread machines work better if vitamin C is added to the dough. If your loaf over-rises and collapses slightly, try adding 1 x 100mg vitamin C tablet, crushed, to the flour in step 2.

1 Pour the water into the bread machine pan. Add the lemon juice. If the instructions for your machine specify that the yeast is to be placed in the pan first, reverse the order in which you add the liquid and the dry ingredients.

2 Sprinkle over the flour, ensuring that it covers the water. Add the butter, salt and sugar in separate corners of the bread pan. Make a small indent in the centre of the flour (but not down as far as the liquid) and add the yeast.

Per loaf Energy 1370kcal/5807kJ; Protein 49g; Carbohydrate 253.9g, of which sugars 15.0g, Fat 24.8g, of which saturates 12g; Cholesterol 46mg; Calcium 154mg; Fibre 34.6g; Sodium 3110mg.

TOASTED MILLET AND RYE BREAD

*The dough for this delectable loaf is made in the bread machine, but it is
shaped by hand before being baked in the oven.*

300ml/10½fl oz/1¼ cups water
50g/2oz/½ cup rye flour
450g/1lb/4 cups unbleached white
bread flour
25g/1oz/¼ cup millet flakes
15ml/1 tbsp light muscovado
(brown) sugar
5ml/1 tsp salt
25g/1oz/2 tbsp butter
5ml/1 tsp easy bake (rapid-rise)
dried yeast
50g/2oz/⅓ cup millet seeds
millet flour, for dusting

MAKES 1 LOAF

COOK'S TIP
Toast the millet seeds under a grill
(broiler) to enhance their flavour.

1 Pour the water into the bread pan. If
the instructions for your bread machine
specify that the yeast is to be placed in
the pan first, reverse the order in which
you add the liquid and dry ingredients.

2 Sprinkle over both types of flour, then
add the millet flakes, ensuring that the
water is completely covered. Add the
sugar, salt and butter, placing them in
separate corners. Make an indent in the
centre of the flour (but not down as far
as the liquid) and add the yeast.

3 Set the bread machine to the dough
setting; use basic raisin dough setting
(if available). Press Start. Add the millet
seeds when the machine beeps or
during the last 5 minutes of kneading.
Lightly flour a baking sheet.

4 When the dough cycle has finished,
knock the dough back (punch it down)
gently on a lightly floured surface.

5 Shape the dough into a rectangle.
Roll it up lengthways, then shape it into a
thick baton with square ends. Place it on
the prepared baking sheet, making sure
that the seam is underneath. Cover it with
lightly oiled clear film (plastic wrap) and
leave in a warm place for 30–45 minutes,
or until almost doubled in size.

6 Remove the clear film and dust the
top of the loaf with the millet flour.
Using a sharp knife, make slanting cuts
in alternate directions along the top of
the loaf. Leave it to stand for about
10 minutes. Meanwhile, preheat the
oven to 220°C/425°F/Gas 7.

7 Bake the loaf for 25–30 minutes,
or until golden and hollow-sounding.
Turn out on to a wire rack to cool.

Per loaf Energy 2211kcal/9360kJ; Protein 50.9g; Carbohydrate 459.8g, of which sugars 22.4g; Fat 28.6g, of which saturates 14.6g; Cholesterol 58mg; Calcium 688mg; Fibre 19.8g; Sodium 2183mg.

BUCKWHEAT AND WALNUT BREAD

Buckwheat flour has a distinctive earthy taste, perfectly mellowed when blended with white flour and walnuts in this compact bread, flavoured with molasses.

1 Pour the water, molasses and walnut or olive oil into the bread pan. If the instructions for your machine specify that the yeast is to be placed in the pan first, reverse the order in which you add the liquid and dry ingredients.

2 Sprinkle over the flours, covering the liquid. Add the milk powder. Place the salt and sugar in separate corners. Make a small indent in the centre of the flour (but not down as far as the liquid) and add the easy bake dried yeast.

SMALL

210ml/7½fl oz/scant 1 cup water
10ml/2 tsp molasses
30ml/2 tbsp walnut or olive oil
325g/11½oz/scant 3 cups unbleached white bread flour
50g/2oz/½ cup buckwheat flour
15ml/1 tbsp skimmed milk powder (non fat dry milk)
5ml/1 tsp salt
2.5ml/½ tsp granulated sugar
5ml/1 tsp easy bake (rapid-rise) dried yeast
40g/1½oz/⅓ cup walnut pieces

MEDIUM

315ml/11fl oz/1⅓ cups water
15ml/3 tsp molasses
30ml/2 tbsp walnut or olive oil
425g/15oz/3¾ cups unbleached white bread flour
75g/3oz/¾ cup buckwheat flour
22ml/1½ tbsp skimmed milk powder
7.5ml/1½ tsp salt
4ml/¾ tsp granulated sugar
5ml/1 tsp easy bake dried yeast
50g/2oz/½ cup walnut pieces

LARGE

360ml/12¼fl oz/generous 1½ cups water
20ml/4 tsp molasses
45ml/3 tbsp walnut or olive oil
500g/1lb 2oz/4½ cups unbleached white bread flour
100g/3½oz/scant 1 cup buckwheat flour
30ml/2 tbsp skimmed milk powder
10ml/2 tsp salt
5ml/1 tsp granulated sugar
7.5ml/1½ tsp easy bake dried yeast
65g/2½oz/⅝ cup walnut pieces

MAKES 1 LOAF

3 Set the machine to white/basic, raisin setting (if available), medium crust. Size: 500g for small, large/750g for medium or 1kg/2lb for large. Add the walnuts to the automatic dispenser, if available. Press Start. If adding manually, do so when the machine beeps during the kneading cycle, or after the first kneading. Remove the bread at the end of the baking cycle and turn on to a wire rack to cool.

Per loaf Energy 1825kcal/7690kJ; Protein 45.2g; Carbohydrate 310.3g, of which sugars 22.4g; Fat 53.5g, of which saturates 6.6g; Cholesterol 6mg; Calcium 488mg; Fibre 2.5g; Sodium 2082mg.

WILD RICE, OAT AND POLENTA BREAD

*Coarse-textured polenta, rolled oats and nutty-tasting wild rice blend
perfectly to make this delightful, nourishing bread.
The dark, slender grains of wild rice add beautiful flecks of colour which
are revealed when this bread is split open.*

50g/2oz/¼ cup wild rice
300ml/10½fl oz/1¼ cups water
30ml/2 tbsp sunflower oil
*325g/11½oz/scant 3 cups unbleached
white bread flour*
*50g/2oz/½ cup strong wholemeal
(whole-wheat) flour*
50g/2oz/½ cup polenta
50g/2oz/½ cup rolled oats
*30ml/2 tbsp skimmed milk powder
(non fat dry milk)*
30ml/2 tbsp golden (light corn) syrup
10ml/2 tsp salt
*5ml/1 tsp easy bake (rapid-rise)
dried yeast*

MAKES 1 LOAF

3 Sprinkle over the white bread flour
and the strong wholemeal flour, then
add the polenta, rolled oats and
skimmed milk powder, ensuring that the
water is completely covered.

4 Add the golden syrup and the salt,
placing them in separate corners of the
bread pan. Make a shallow indent in
the centre of the flour mixture (but not
down as far as the liquid) and add the
easy bake dried yeast.

5 Set the bread machine to the dough
setting; use basic raisin dough setting
(if available). Press Start.

6 Add the cooked wild rice when the
machine beeps or during the last
5 minutes of kneading. Lightly oil a
23 × 13cm/9 × 5in loaf tin (pan).

8 Divide the dough into six equal pieces.
In turn, shape each piece of dough into
an oblong mini loaf, about 13cm/5in in
length. Then place the six dough shapes
widthways, side by side, in the prepared
loaf tin.

9 Cover the dough with lightly oiled
clear film (plastic wrap) and leave
to rise in a warm place for about
30–45 minutes, or until the dough
almost reaches the top of the tin.
Meanwhile preheat the oven to
220°C/425°F/Gas 7.

10 Bake the loaf for 30–35 minutes,
or until it is golden and sounds hollow
when tapped on the base. Turn out on
to a wire rack to cool.

1 Cook the wild rice in boiling salted
water according to the instructions on
the packet.

2 Pour the water and the sunflower oil
into the bread machine pan. If the
instructions for your machine specify
that the yeast is to be placed in the pan
first, reverse the order in which you add
the liquid and dry ingredients.

7 When the dough cycle has finished,
remove the dough from the bread
machine pan and place it on a surface
that has been lightly floured. Knock the
dough back (punch it down) gently.

VARIATIONS
This bread can also be made with
other varieties of rice. Long grain
brown rice and white rice are both
good, and they are also much faster to
cook than wild rice.
If you like, use the wild or red
Camargue rice. This variety takes
about an hour to cook, but the vivid
red colour of the rice will give unusual
and very attractive flecks of colour
in the bread.

Per loaf Energy 2170kcal/9169kJ; Protein 55.6g; Carbohydrate 427g, of which sugars 35.6g; Fat 35.6g, of which saturates 4.6g; Cholesterol 7mg; Calcium 665mg; Fibre 19.1g; Sodium 4105mg.

FOUR SEED BREAD

280ml/10fl oz/1¼ cups water
30ml/2 tbsp extra virgin olive oil
400g/14oz/3½ cups unbleached white
bread flour
50g/2oz/½ cup millet flour
50g/2oz/½ cup wholemeal
(whole-wheat) bread flour
15ml/1 tbsp granulated sugar
10ml/2 tsp salt
5ml/1 tsp easy bake (rapid-rise)
dried yeast
30ml/2 tbsp pumpkin seeds
30ml/2 tbsp sunflower seeds
22ml/1½ tbsp linseeds
22ml/1½ tbsp sesame seeds,
lightly toasted
15ml/1 tbsp milk
30ml/2 tbsp golden linseeds

MAKES 1 LOAF

1 Pour the water and oil into the bread pan. Reverse the order in which you add the wet and dry ingredients if your machine specifies this.

2 Sprinkle over all three types of flour, ensuring that the water is completely covered. Add the sugar and salt in separate corners of the bread pan.

3 Make a shallow indent in the centre of the flour and add the yeast. Set the bread machine to the dough setting; use basic raisin dough setting (if available). Press Start. Add the seeds when the machine beeps to add extra ingredients or during the last 5 minutes of kneading.

4 When the dough cycle has finished, place the dough on a lightly floured surface and knock back (punch down) gently.

This light bread contains a variety of seeds, all available from health-food stores.

5 Lightly oil a baking sheet. Shape the dough into a round flat loaf. Make a hole in the centre with your finger. Gradually enlarge the cavity, turning the dough, until you have a ring. Place the ring on the baking sheet. Cover it with lightly oiled clear film (plastic wrap) and leave in a warm place for 30–45 minutes, or until the dough has doubled in size.

6 Meanwhile, preheat the oven to 200°C/400°F/Gas 6. Brush the top of the bread with milk and sprinkle it with the golden linseeds. Make slashes around the loaf, radiating outwards.

7 Bake for 30–35 minutes, or until golden and hollow-sounding. Turn out on to a wire rack to cool.

Per loaf Energy 2657kcal/11186kJ; Protein 71.2g; Carbohydrate 419.2g, of which sugars 25.5g; Fat 86.4g, of which saturates 9.6g; Cholesterol 1mg; Calcium 758mg; Fibre 24.1g; Sodium 3967mg.

HAZELNUT AND FIG BREAD

This healthy, high-fibre bread is flavoured with figs and hazelnuts.

1 Pour the water and the lemon juice into the bread machine pan. If the instructions for your machine specify that the yeast is to be placed in the pan first, reverse the order in which you add the liquid and dry ingredients.

2 Sprinkle the flours over, then the wheatgerm, covering the water. Add the milk powder. Add the salt, sugar and butter in separate corners. Make an indent in the flour; add the yeast. Coarsely chop the figs.

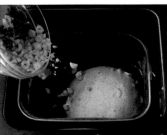

3 Set the bread machine to white/basic, raisin setting (if available), medium crust. Size: 500g for small, large/750g for medium or 1kg/2lb for large. Add the hazelnuts and figs to the automatic dispenser, if available. Press Start. If adding manually, do so when the machine beeps during the kneading cycle, or after the first kneading.

4 Remove the bread at the end of the baking cycle and turn out on to a wire rack to allow to cool.

SMALL
230ml/8fl oz/1 cup water
5ml/1 tsp lemon juice
280g/10oz/2½ cups unbleached white bread flour
75g/3oz/¾ cup brown bread flour
45ml/3 tbsp toasted wheatgerm
15ml/1 tbsp skimmed milk powder (non fat dry milk)
5ml/1 tsp salt
10ml/2 tsp granulated sugar
20g/¾oz/1½ tbsp butter
5ml/1 tsp easy bake (rapid-rise) dried yeast
25g/1oz/3 tbsp skinned hazelnuts, roasted and chopped
25g/1oz/3 tbsp ready-to-eat dried figs

MEDIUM
280ml/10fl oz/1¼ cups water
7.5ml/1½ tsp lemon juice
350g/12oz/3 cups unbleached white bread flour
100g/3½oz/scant 1 cup brown bread flour
60ml/4 tbsp toasted wheatgerm
30ml/2 tbsp skimmed milk powder
7.5ml/1½ tsp salt
15ml/1 tbsp granulated sugar
25g/1oz/2 tbsp butter
7.5ml/1½ tsp easy bake dried yeast
40g/1½oz/⅓ cup skinned hazelnuts, roasted and chopped
40g/1½oz/¼ cup ready-to-eat dried figs

LARGE
390ml/14fl oz/1⅔ cups water
10ml/2 tsp lemon juice
435g/15½oz/3⅞ cups unbleached white bread flour
100g/3½oz/scant 1 cup brown bread flour
65ml/4½ tbsp toasted wheatgerm
45ml/3 tbsp skimmed milk powder
10ml/2 tsp salt
20ml/4 tsp granulated sugar
40g/1½oz/3 tbsp butter
7.5ml/1½ tsp easy bake dried yeast
50g/2oz/½ cup skinned hazelnuts, roasted and chopped
50g/2oz/⅓ cup ready-to-eat dried figs

MAKES 1 LOAF

Per loaf Energy 1799kcal/7610kJ; Protein 54.1g, Carbohydrate 318.1g, of which sugars 36.9g; Fat 43.4g, of which saturates 14.4g; Cholesterol 52mg; Calcium 793mg; Fibre 44.1g; Sodium 254mg.

RUSSIAN BLACK BREAD

European rye breads often include cocoa and coffee to add colour to this dark traditionally dense, chewy bread. Try it as the basis of an open sandwich.

SMALL

240ml/8½ fl oz/generous 1 cup water
30ml/2 tbsp sunflower oil
22ml/1½ tbsp molasses
115g/4oz/1 cup rye flour
50g/2oz/½ cup wholemeal
(whole-wheat) bread flour
175g/6oz/1½ cups unbleached white
bread flour
25g/1oz/2 tbsp oat bran
50g/2oz/½ cup dried breadcrumbs
15ml/1 tbsp cocoa powder (unsweetened)
22ml/1½ tbsp instant coffee granules
7.5ml/1½ tsp caraway seeds
5ml/1 tsp salt
5ml/1 tsp easy bake (rapid-rise)
dried yeast

1 Pour the water, sunflower oil and molasses into the bread machine pan. If the instructions for your machine specify that the yeast is to be placed in the bread pan first, then simply reverse the order in which you add the liquid and dry ingredients.

2 Sprinkle over the rye, wholemeal and white flours, then the oat bran and breadcrumbs, ensuring that the water is completely covered. Add the cocoa powder, coffee granules, caraway seeds and salt. Make a small indent in the centre of the flour (but not down as far as the liquid) and add the easy bake dried yeast.

3 Set the bread machine to the whole wheat setting, medium crust. Size: 500g for small, large/750g for medium or 1kg/2lb for large. Press Start.

4 Remove the bread at the end of the baking cycle. Turn out on to a wire rack.

MEDIUM

360ml/12½fl oz/generous 1½ cups water
30ml/2 tbsp sunflower oil
40ml/2½ tbsp molasses
155g/5½oz/1⅛ cups rye flour
90g/3¼oz/¾ cup wholemeal bread flour
250g/9oz/2¼ cups unbleached white
bread flour
40g/1½oz/3 tbsp oat bran
75g/3oz/¾ cup dried breadcrumbs
22ml/1½ tbsp cocoa powder
30ml/2 tbsp instant coffee granules
7.5ml/1½ tsp caraway seeds
7.5ml/1½ tsp salt
7.5ml/1½ tsp easy bake dried yeast

LARGE

400ml/14fl oz/scant 1¾ cups water
45ml/3 tbsp sunflower oil
40ml/2½ tbsp molasses
190g/6½oz/1⅝ cups rye flour
90g/3¼oz/¾ cup wholemeal bread flour
280g/10oz/2½ cups unbleached white
bread flour
50g/2oz/4 tbsp oat bran
100g/3½oz/scant 1 cup dried breadcrumbs
30ml/2 tbsp cocoa powder
30ml/2 tbsp instant coffee granules
7.5ml/1½ tsp caraway seeds
10ml/2 tsp salt
10ml/2 tsp easy bake dried yeast

MAKES 1 LOAF

Per loaf Energy 1746kcal/7397kJ; Protein 44.7g; Carbohydrate 335.6g, of which sugars 21.2g; Fat 34.4g, of which saturates 5.4g; Cholesterol 0mg; Calcium 503mg; Fibre 27.8g; Sodium 2345mg.

APPLE AND CIDER SEEDED BREAD

*This bread is perfect served with a selection of cold meats, paté or cheese
for a delicious lunchtime spread.*

SMALL
*200ml/7fl oz/⅞ cup medium sweet
cider, left to become flat
15ml/1 tbsp sunflower oil
115g/4oz/¾ cup finely chopped green
eating apple
400g/14oz/3½ cups seeded white
bread flour
15ml/1 tbsp skimmed milk powder
(non fat dry milk)
5ml/1 tsp salt
7.5ml/1½ tsp sugar
5ml/1 tsp easy bake (rapid-rise)
dried yeast*

MEDIUM
*260ml/9fl oz/1⅛ cups medium sweet
cider, left to become flat
30ml/2 tbsp sunflower oil
125g/4½oz/1 cup finely chopped green
eating apple
525g/1lb 3oz/4¾ cups seeded white
bread flour
22ml/1½ tbsp skimmed milk powder
7.5ml/1½ tsp salt
7.5ml/1½ tsp sugar
5ml/1 tsp easy bake dried yeast*

LARGE
*320ml/11½fl oz/1⅓ cups medium
sweet cider, left to become flat
30ml/2 tbsp sunflower oil
150g/5oz/generous 1 cup finely
chopped green eating apple
625g/1lb 5oz/5½ cups seeded white
bread flour
30ml/2 tbsp skimmed milk powder
7.5ml/1½ tsp salt
10ml/2 tsp sugar
7.5ml/1½ tsp easy bake dried yeast*

MAKES 1 LOAF

1 Pour the cider into the bread machine pan. Add the sunflower oil and chopped apple. If the instructions for your machine specify that the yeast is to be placed in the pan first, reverse the order in which you add the liquid and the dry ingredients.

2 Sprinkle over the flour, ensuring that it covers the water. Add the skimmed milk powder, salt and sugar in separate corners of the bread pan. Make a small indent in the centre of the flour (but not down as far as the liquid) and add the yeast.

3 Set the bread machine to the white/basic setting, light crust. Size: 500g for small, large/750g for medium or 1kg/2lb for large. Press Start.

4 Remove the bread at the end of the baking cycle. Turn out on to a wire rack.

Per loaf Energy 1663kcal/7053kJ; Protein 41.3g; Carbohydrate 342.5g, of which sugars 37.7g; Fat 18g, of which saturates 3.1g; Cholesterol 6mg; Calcium 705mg; Fibre 14.2g; Sodium 2049mg.

For the Milk Rolls
145ml/5fl oz/scant ⅔ cup milk
225g/8oz/2 cups unbleached white
bread flour
7.5ml/1½ tsp granulated sugar
5ml/1 tsp salt
15g/½oz/1 tbsp butter
2.5ml/½ tsp easy bake (rapid-rise)
dried yeast

For the Wholemeal Rolls
175ml/6fl oz/¾ cup water
175g/6oz/1½ cups wholemeal
(whole-wheat) bread flour
75g/3oz/¾ cup unbleached white
bread flour
7.5ml/1½ tsp granulated sugar
5ml/1 tsp salt
25g/1oz/2 tbsp butter
2.5ml/½ tsp easy bake dried yeast

For the Topping
1 egg yolk, mixed with 15ml/1 tbsp
cold water
15ml/1 tbsp rolled oats or cracked wheat
15ml/1 tbsp poppy seeds

MAKES 19 ROLLS

1 Pour the milk for making the milk rolls into the bread machine pan. However, if the instructions for your bread machine specify that the yeast is to be placed in the pan first, simply reverse the order in which you add the liquid and dry ingredients.

2 Sprinkle over the white bread flour, making sure that it covers the milk completely. Add the sugar, salt and butter, placing them in separate corners of the bread pan.

3 Make a small indent in the centre of the flour (but not down as far as the liquid underneath) and add the easy bake dried yeast.

4 Set the bread machine to the dough setting; use basic dough setting (if available). Press Start.

PARTYBROT

These traditional Swiss-German rolls are baked as one, in a round tin.
As the name suggests, partybrot is perfect for entertaining.

5 Lightly oil a 25cm/10in springform or loose-based cake tin (pan), and a large mixing bowl. When the dough cycle has finished, remove the dough from the machine and place it in the mixing bowl.

6 Cover the dough with oiled clear film (plastic wrap) and chill while you make the wholemeal dough. Follow the instructions for the milk roll dough, but use water instead of milk.

7 Remove the milk roll dough from the refrigerator 20 minutes before the end of the wholemeal dough cycle. When the wholemeal dough is ready, remove it from the machine and place on a lightly floured surface. Knock it back (punch down) gently. Do the same with the milk roll dough.

8 Divide the milk roll dough into nine pieces and the wholemeal dough into 10. Shape each piece of dough into a small round ball.

9 Place 12 balls, equally spaced, around the outer edge of the prepared cake tin, alternating milk dough with wholemeal.

10 Add an inner circle with six more balls and place the remaining ball of wholemeal dough in the centre.

11 Cover the tin with lightly oiled clear film and leave the rolls to rise in a warm place for 30–45 minutes, or until they have doubled in size. Meanwhile, preheat the oven to 200°C/400°F/Gas 6.

12 Brush the wholemeal rolls with the egg yolk and water glaze. Sprinkle with rolled oats or cracked wheat. Glaze the white rolls and sprinkle with poppy seeds. Bake for 35–40 minutes, until the partybrot is golden. Leave for 5 minutes to cool in the tin, then turn out on to a wire rack to cool. Serve warm or cold.

Per roll Energy 104kcal/441kJ; Protein 2.9g; Carbohydrate 19.4g, of which sugars 1.7g; Fat 2.2g, of which saturates 1.3g; Cholesterol 5mg; Calcium 33mg; Fibre 1.2g; Sodium 228mg.

FLATBREADS AND PIZZAS

Flatbreads are fun to bake and make delicious meal accompaniments. Naan, often flavoured with coriander or black onion seeds, is typical of Indian flatbread, whilst Lavash, Pitta and Pide are traditional Middle Eastern specialities. Italy is famous for Focaccia, pizzas and Calzone, while the French version of pizza is the Pissaladière. All of these breads can be made in your machine using the "dough only" setting and then hand-shaped and oven-baked.

GARLIC AND CORIANDER NAAN

100ml/3½ fl oz/7 tbsp water
60ml/4 tbsp natural (plain) yogurt
280g/10oz/2½ cups unbleached white
bread flour
1 garlic clove, finely chopped
5ml/1 tsp black onion seeds
5ml/1 tsp ground coriander
5ml/1 tsp salt
10ml/2 tsp clear honey
15ml/1 tbsp melted ghee or butter,
plus 30–45ml/2–3 tbsp
5ml/1 tsp easy bake (rapid-rise)
dried yeast
15ml/1 tbsp chopped fresh
coriander (cilantro)

MAKES 3

VARIATION
For a basic naan omit the coriander,
garlic and black onion seeds. Include
a little ground black pepper or chilli
powder for a slightly piquant note.

*Indian restaurants the world over have introduced us to several
differently flavoured examples of this leavened flatbread, and this version
is particularly tasty and will become a great favourite. The bread is
traditionally made in a tandoor oven, but this method has been developed
to give almost identical results.*

1 Pour the water and natural yogurt
into the bread machine pan. If the
instructions for your bread machine
specify that the easy bake dried yeast is
to be placed in the pan first, then simply
reverse the order in which you add the
liquid and dry ingredients.

2 Sprinkle over the flour, ensuring that
it covers the liquid completely. Add the
garlic, black onion seeds and ground
coriander. Add the salt, honey and the
15ml/1 tbsp melted ghee or butter in
separate corners of the bread pan. Make
a small indent in the centre of the flour
(but not down as far as the liquid) and
add the easy bake dried yeast.

3 Set the bread machine to the dough
setting; use basic or pizza dough setting
(if available). Press Start.

4 When the dough cycle has finished,
preheat the oven to its highest setting.
Place three baking sheets in the oven to
heat. Remove the dough from the
breadmaking machine and place it on
a lightly floured surface.

5 Knock the naan dough back (punch
it down) gently and then knead in the
chopped fresh coriander. Divide the
dough into three equal pieces.

6 Shape each piece into a ball and cover
two of the pieces with oiled clear film
(plastic wrap). Roll out the remaining
piece of dough into a large teardrop
shape, making it about 5–8mm/¼–⅜in
thick. Cover with oiled clear film while
you roll out the remaining two pieces of
dough to make two more naan.

7 Preheat the grill (broiler) to its
highest setting. Place the naan on the
preheated baking sheets and then bake
them for 4–5 minutes, until puffed up.
Remove the baking sheets from the oven
and place them under the hot grill for a
few seconds, until the naan start to
brown and blister.

8 Brush the naan with melted ghee or
butter and serve warm.

Per naan Energy 374kcal/1585kJ; Protein 10.4g; Carbohydrate 74.2g, of which sugars 2.9g; Fat 6.1g, of which saturates 3g; Cholesterol 11mg; Calcium 176mg; Fibre 2.8g; Sodium 706mg.

CARTA DI MUSICA

This crunchy, crisp bread looks like sheets of music manuscript paper, which is how it came by its name. It originated in Sardinia and can be found throughout southern Italy, where it is eaten not only as a bread, but as a substitute for pasta in lasagne. It also makes a good pizza base.

280ml/10fl oz/1¼ cups water
450g/1lb/4 cups unbleached white
bread flour
7.5ml/1½ tsp salt
5ml/1 tsp granulated sugar
5ml/1 tsp easy bake (rapid-rise)
dried yeast

MAKES 8

COOK'S TIP
Cutting the partially cooked breads in half is quite tricky. You may find it easier to divide the dough into six or eight pieces, and roll these as thinly as possible before baking. The cutting stage can then be avoided.

5 Now roll out the other three pieces. If the dough starts to tear, cover it with oiled clear film (plastic wrap) and leave it to rest for 2–3 minutes.

6 When all the dough has been rolled out, cover with oiled clear film and leave to rest on the floured surface for 10–15 minutes. Preheat the oven to 230°C/450°F/Gas 8. Place two baking sheets in the oven to heat.

7 Keeping the other dough rounds covered, place one round on each baking sheet. Bake for 5 minutes, or until puffed up.

1 Pour the water into the bread machine pan. If the instructions specify that the yeast should be placed in the pan first, simply reverse the order in which you add the liquid and dry ingredients to the pan.

2 Sprinkle over the white bread flour, ensuring that it covers the water. Add the salt in one corner of the bread pan and the sugar in another corner. Make a small indent in the centre of the flour (but not down as far as the liquid) and add the easy bake dried yeast.

3 Set the bread machine to the dough setting; use basic dough setting (if available). Press Start.

4 When the dough cycle has finished, remove the dough from the machine and place it on a lightly floured surface. Knock it back (punch it down) gently and divide it into four equal pieces. Shape each piece of dough into a ball, then roll a piece out until about 3mm/⅛in thick.

8 Remove from the oven and cut each round in half horizontally to make two thinner breads. Place these cut side up on the baking sheets, return them to the oven and bake for 5–8 minutes more, until crisp. Turn out on to a wire rack and cook the remaining breads.

Per bread Energy 194kcal/824kJ; Protein 5.3g; Carbohydrate 44.2g, of which sugars 1.4g; Fat 0 7g, of which saturates 0.1g; Cholesterol 0mg; Calcium 79mg; Fibre 1.7g; Sodium 370mg.

*250ml/generous 8½fl oz/generous
1 cup water
45ml/3 tbsp natural (plain) yogurt
350g/12oz/3 cups unbleached white
bread flour
115g/4oz/1 cup wholemeal
(whole-wheat) bread flour
5ml/1 tsp salt
5ml/1 tsp easy bake (rapid-rise)
dried yeast*

*FOR THE TOPPING
30ml/2 tbsp milk
30ml/2 tbsp millet seeds*

MAKES 10

VARIATION
Instead of making individual lavash
you could divide the dough into five
or six pieces and make large lavash.
Serve these on a platter in the centre
of the table and invite guests to break
off pieces as required.

LAVASH

*These Middle Eastern flatbreads puff up slightly during cooking, to make a
bread which is crispy, but not as dry and crisp as a cracker. Serve warm
straight from the oven or cold, with a little butter, if wished.*

1 Pour the water and yogurt into the
bread machine pan. If the instructions
for your machine specify that the yeast
is to be placed in the pan first, reverse
the order in which you add the liquid
and dry ingredients.

2 Sprinkle over both types of flour,
ensuring that the liquid is completely
covered. Add the salt in one corner of
the bread pan. Make an indent in the
centre of the flour; add the yeast.

3 Set the bread machine to the dough
setting; use basic or pizza dough setting
(if available). Press Start.

4 When the dough cycle has finished,
place the dough on a lightly floured
surface. Knock it back gently (punch it
down) and divide it into 10 equal pieces.

5 Shape each piece into a ball, then
flatten into a disc with your hand. Cover
with oiled clear film (plastic wrap);
leave to rest for 5 minutes. Preheat the
oven to 230°C/450°F/Gas 8. Place three
or four baking sheets in the oven.

6 Roll each ball of dough out very thinly,
then stretch it over the backs of your
hands, to make the lavash. If the dough
starts to tear, leave it to rest for a few
minutes after rolling. Stack the lavash
between layers of oiled clear film and
cover to keep moist.

7 Place as many lavash as will fit
comfortably on each baking sheet, brush
with milk and sprinkle with millet seeds.
Bake for 5–8 minutes, or until puffed
and starting to brown. Transfer to a wire
rack and cook the remaining lavash.

PITTA BREADS

*These well-known flatbreads are easy to make and extremely versatile.
Serve them warm with dips or soups, or split them in half and stuff the
pockets with your favourite vegetable, meat or cheese filling.*

*210ml/7½fl oz/scant 1 cup water
15ml/1 tbsp olive oil
350g/12oz/3 cups unbleached white
bread flour, plus extra for sprinkling
7.5ml/1½ tsp salt
5ml/1 tsp granulated sugar
5ml/1 tsp easy bake (rapid-rise)
dried yeast*

MAKES 6–10

1 Pour the water and oil into the bread
machine pan. If your instructions specify
that the yeast is to be placed in the pan
first, reverse the order in which you add
the liquid and dry ingredients. Add the
flour, ensuring it covers the water.

2 Add the salt and sugar in separate
corners. Make a shallow indent in the
centre of the flour and add the yeast.
Set to the dough setting; use basic or
pizza dough setting (if available). Start.

3 When the dough cycle has finished,
remove the dough from the machine.
Place it on a lightly floured surface and
knock it back (punch it down) gently.

4 Divide the dough into six or ten equal-
size pieces, depending on whether you
want large or small pitta breads. Shape
each piece into a ball.

5 Cover the balls of dough with oiled
clear film (plastic wrap) and leave them
to rest for about 10 minutes. Preheat
the oven to 230°C/450°F/Gas 8. Place
three baking sheets in the oven to heat.

6 Flatten each piece of dough slightly,
and then roll out into an oval or round,
about 5mm/¼in thick.

7 Lightly sprinkle each pitta with flour.
Cover with oiled clear film and leave to
rest for 10 minutes.

8 Place the pittas on the baking sheets
and bake for 5–6 minutes, or until they
are puffed up and lightly browned.
Transfer the pitta breads on to wire
racks to cool.

Per lavash Energy 151kcal/644kJ; Protein 5.1g; Carbohydrate 33g, of which sugars 1.2g; Fat 0.8g, of which saturates 0.1g; Cholesterol 0mg; Calcium 57mg; Fibre 2.4g; Sodium 203mg.
Per pitta Energy 150kcal/638kJ; Protein 3.9g; Carbohydrate 32.4g, of which sugars 0.6g; Fat 1.5g, of which saturates 0.2g; Cholesterol 0mg; Calcium 58mg; Fibre 1.3g; Sodium 492mg.

MOROCCAN KSRA

200ml/7fl oz/⅞ cup water
250g/9oz/2¼ cups unbleached white
bread flour
75g/3oz/¾ cup semolina
5ml/1 tsp aniseed
7.5ml/1½ tsp salt
2.5ml/½ tsp granulated sugar
5ml/1 tsp easy bake (rapid-rise)
dried yeast
olive oil, for brushing
sesame seeds, for sprinkling

MAKES 2

1 Pour the water into the machine pan. Reverse the order in which you add the wet and dry ingredients if necessary. Add the flour, semolina and aniseed, covering the water. Place the salt and sugar in separate corners. Make an indent in the flour; add the yeast. Set the machine to the dough setting; use the basic dough setting if available.

This leavened flatbread is made with semolina and spiced with aniseed. It is the traditional accompaniment to tagine, a spicy Moroccan stew, but is equally good with salad, cheeses or dips. It can be served warm or cold.

2 Press Start on your bread machine, then lightly flour two baking sheets. When the cycle has finished, place the dough on a lightly floured surface.

3 Knock the dough back (punch it down) gently, shape into two balls, then flatten into 2cm/¾in thick discs. Place each dough disc on a baking sheet.

4 Cover the dough discs with oiled clear film (plastic wrap) and leave to rise for 30 minutes, or until doubled in bulk.

5 Preheat the oven to 200°C/400°F/Gas 6. Brush the top of each piece of dough with olive oil and sprinkle with sesame seeds. Prick the surface with a skewer.

6 Bake for about 20–25 minutes, or until the ksra are golden and sound hollow when tapped underneath. Turn out on to a wire rack to cool.

VARIATION
Replace up to half the white bread flour with wholemeal (whole-wheat) bread flour for a nuttier flavour.

PIDE

240ml/8½fl oz/generous 1 cup water
30ml/2 tbsp olive oil
450g/1lb/4 cups unbleached white
bread flour
5ml/1 tsp salt
5ml/1 tsp sugar
5ml/1 tsp easy bake (rapid-rise)
dried yeast
1 egg yolk mixed with 10ml/2 tsp
water, for glazing
nigella or poppy seeds, for sprinkling

MAKES 3

1 Pour the water and oil into the machine pan. If the instructions for your machine specify that the yeast is to be added first, reverse the order in which you add the liquid and dry ingredients.

2 Sprinkle over the flour, ensuring that it covers the liquid. Add the salt in one corner of the bread pan and the sugar in another corner. Make a small indent in the centre of the flour; add the yeast.

A traditional Turkish ridged flatbread, this is often baked plain, but can also be sprinkled with aromatic black nigella seeds, which taste rather like oregano. If you can't find nigella seeds, use poppy seeds.

3 Set the bread machine to the dough setting; use basic dough setting (if available). Press Start.

4 When the dough cycle has finished, remove the pide dough from the bread machine and place it on a surface lightly dusted with flour. Knock the dough back (punch it down) gently and divide it into three equal-size pieces. Shape each piece of dough into a ball.

5 Roll each ball of dough into a round, about 15cm/6in in diameter. Cover with oiled clear film (plastic wrap) and leave for 20 minutes. Meanwhile, preheat the oven to 230°C/450°F/Gas 8.

6 Using your fingers, ridge the bread, while enlarging it until it is 5mm/¼in thick. Start from the top of the round, pressing your fingers down and away from you, into the bread. Repeat a second row beneath the first row, and continue down the bread.

7 Turn the bread by 90 degrees and repeat the pressing to give a criss-cross ridged effect. Place the pide on floured baking sheets, brush with egg glaze and sprinkle with nigella or poppy seeds. Bake for 9–10 minutes, or until puffy and golden. Serve immediately.

Per ksra Energy 563kcal/2392kJ; Protein 15.8g; Carbohydrate 127.5g, of which sugars 3.2g; Fat 2.3g, of which saturates 0.3g; Cholesterol 0mg; Calcium 183mg; Fibre 4.7g; Sodium 1482mg.
Per pide Energy 603kcal/2553kJ; Protein 15.1g; Carbohydrate 117.9g, of which sugars 3.6g; Fat 11.1g, of which saturates 1.8g; Cholesterol 67mg; Calcium 219mg; Fibre 4.6g; Sodium 663mg.

OLIVE FOUGASSE

210ml/7½fl oz/scant 1 cup water
15ml/1 tbsp olive oil, plus extra
for brushing
350g/12oz/3 cups unbleached white
bread flour
5ml/1 tsp salt
5ml/1 tsp granulated sugar
5ml/1 tsp easy bake (rapid-rise)
dried yeast
50g/2oz/½ cup pitted black
olives, chopped

MAKES 1 FOUGASSE

A French hearth bread, fougasse is traditionally baked on the floor of the hot bread oven, just after the fire has been raked out. It can be left plain or flavoured with olives, herbs, nuts or cheese.

1 Pour the water and the oil into the machine pan. Reverse the order in which you add wet and dry ingredients if necessary. Sprinkle over the flour, ensuring that it covers the liquid. Add the salt in one corner of the bread pan and the sugar in another corner. Make a small indent in the centre of the flour (but not down as far as the liquid) and add the yeast.

2 Set the bread machine to the dough setting; use basic or pizza dough setting (if available). Press Start. When the cycle has finished, remove the dough from the machine and place it on a lightly floured surface.

3 Knock the dough back (punch it down) gently and flatten it slightly. Sprinkle over the olives and fold over the dough two or three times to incorporate them.

4 Flatten the dough and roll it into an oblong, about 30cm/12in long. With a sharp knife make four or five parallel cuts diagonally through the body of the dough, but leaving the edges intact. Gently stretch the fougasse dough so that it resembles a ladder.

5 Lightly oil a baking sheet, then place the shaped dough on it. Cover with oiled clear film (plastic wrap) and leave in a warm place for about 30 minutes, or until the dough has doubled in bulk.

6 Preheat the oven to 220°C/425°F/ Gas 7. Brush the top of the fougasse with olive oil, place in the oven and bake about for 20–25 minutes, or until the bread is golden. Turn out on to a wire rack to cool.

Per fougasse Energy 1360kcal/5760kJ; Protein 33.4g; Carbohydrate 276.1g, of which sugars 9.4g; Fat 21g, of which saturates 3.1g; Cholesterol 0mg; Calcium 523mg; Fibre 12.3g; Sodium 3101mg.

ONION FOCACCIA

Focaccia, with its characteristic texture and dimpled surface, has become hugely popular in recent years. This version has a delectable red onion and fresh sage topping.

210ml/7½fl oz/scant 1 cup water
15ml/1 tbsp olive oil
350g/12oz/3 cups unbleached white bread flour
2.5ml/½ tsp salt
5ml/1 tsp granulated sugar
5ml/1 tsp easy bake (rapid-rise) dried yeast
15ml/1 tbsp chopped fresh sage
15ml/1 tbsp chopped red onion

FOR THE TOPPING
30ml/2 tbsp olive oil
½ red onion, thinly sliced
5 fresh sage leaves
10ml/2 tsp coarse sea salt
coarsely ground black pepper

MAKES 1 FOCACCIA

6 Meanwhile, preheat the oven to 200°C/400°F/Gas 6. Uncover the focaccia, and, using your fingertips, poke the dough to make deep dimples over the surface. Cover and leave to rise for 10–15 minutes, or until the dough has doubled in bulk.

7 Drizzle over the olive oil and sprinkle with the onion, sage leaves, sea salt and black pepper. Bake for 20–25 minutes, or until golden. Turn out on to a wire rack to cool slightly. Serve warm.

1 Pour the water and oil into the bread pan. Reverse the order in which you add the wet and dry ingredients if necessary.

2 Sprinkle over the flour, ensuring that it covers the liquid. Add the salt and sugar in separate corners. Make a small indent in the flour and add the yeast.

3 Set the bread machine to the dough setting. If your machine has a choice of settings use the basic or pizza dough setting. Press Start.

4 Lightly oil a 25–28cm/10–11in shallow round cake tin or pizza pan. When the cycle has finished, remove the dough from the pan and place it on a surface lightly dusted with flour.

5 Knock the dough back (punch it down) and flatten it slightly. Sprinkle over the sage and red onion and knead gently to incorporate. Shape the dough into a ball, flatten it, then roll it into a round of about 25–28cm/10–11in. Place in the prepared tin. Cover with oiled clear film (plastic wrap) and leave to rise in a warm place for 20 minutes.

Per focaccia Energy 1508kcal/6362kJ; Protein 32.1g; Carbohydrate 264.6g, of which sugars 6.7g; Fat 42.9g, of which saturates 6.2g; Cholesterol 0mg; Calcium 481mg; Fibre 10.9g; Sodium 2959mg.

TOMATO AND PROSCIUTTO PIZZA

This combination of fresh plum tomatoes, sun-dried tomatoes, garlic and prosciutto with three cheeses is truly mouthwatering. Pizzas provide the perfect opportunity for exercising your individuality, so experiment with different topping ingredients if you prefer.

SMALL AND MEDIUM
MAKES ONE 30CM/12IN PIZZA
140ml/5fl oz/⅔ cup water
15ml/1 tbsp extra virgin olive oil
225g/8oz/2 cups unbleached white bread flour
5ml/1 tsp salt
2.5ml/½ tsp granulated sugar
2.5ml/½ tsp easy bake (rapid-rise) dried yeast

FOR THE FILLING
45ml/3 tbsp sun-dried tomato paste
150g/5½oz mozzarella cheese, sliced
4 fresh plum tomatoes, about 400g/14oz, roughly chopped
1 small yellow (bell) pepper, halved, seeded and cut into thin strips
50g/2oz prosciutto, torn into pieces
8 fresh basil leaves
4 large garlic cloves, halved
50g/2oz feta cheese, crumbled
30ml/2 tbsp extra virgin olive oil
30ml/2 tbsp freshly grated Parmesan cheese
salt and freshly ground black pepper

LARGE
MAKES TWO 30CM/12IN PIZZAS
280ml/10fl oz/1¼ cups water
30ml/2 tbsp extra virgin olive oil
450g/1lb/4 cups unbleached white bread flour
7.5ml/1½ tsp salt
2.5ml/½tsp granulated sugar
5ml/1 tsp easy bake dried yeast

FOR THE FILLING
90ml/6 tbsp sun-dried tomato paste
300g/11oz mozzarella cheese, sliced
8 fresh plum tomatoes, about 800g/1¾lb, roughly chopped
1 large yellow (bell) pepper, halved, seeded and cut into thin strips
115g/4oz prosciutto, torn into pieces
16 fresh basil leaves
8 large garlic cloves, halved
115g/4oz feta cheese, crumbled
45ml/3 tbsp extra virgin olive oil
60ml/4 tbsp freshly grated Parmesan cheese
salt and freshly ground black pepper

1 Pour the water and olive oil into the bread machine pan. If the instructions for your machine specify that the yeast is to be placed in the pan first, reverse the order in which you add the liquid and dry ingredients.

2 Sprinkle over the flour, ensuring that it covers the liquid. Add the salt in one corner of the bread pan and the sugar in another corner. Make a small indent in the centre of the flour, then add the yeast.

3 Set the bread machine to the dough setting; use basic or pizza dough setting (if available). Press Start. Lightly oil one or two pizza pans or baking sheets.

4 When the dough cycle has finished, remove the dough from the machine and place it on a lightly floured surface. Knock it back (punch it down) gently. If making the larger quantity divide the dough into two equal pieces. Preheat the oven to 220°C/425°F/Gas 7.

5 Roll out the pizza dough into one or two 30cm/12in rounds. Place in the prepared pan(s) or on the baking sheet(s). Spread the sun-dried tomato paste over the pizza base(s) and arrange two-thirds of the mozzarella slices on top.

6 Scatter with the chopped tomatoes, pepper strips, prosciutto, whole basil leaves, garlic, remaining mozzarella and feta. Drizzle over the olive oil and sprinkle with the Parmesan. Season with salt and pepper. Bake the pizza for 15–20 minutes, or until golden and sizzling. Serve immediately.

VARIATION
This topping lends itself particularly well to the nutty flavour of a wholemeal pizza base. Replace half the unbleached white bread flour with wholemeal (whole-wheat) bread flour. You may need to add a little more water as wholemeal flour absorbs more liquid.

Per pizza Energy 1928kcal/8090kJ; Protein 84.5g; Carbohydrate 208.1g, of which sugars 36g; Fat 89.9g, of which saturates 39.8g; Cholesterol 181mg; Calcium 1467mg; Fibre 15g; Sodium 4362mg.

CALZONE

Calzone is an enclosed pizza, with the filling inside. It originates from Naples and was originally made from a rectangular piece of pizza dough, unlike the modern version, which looks like a large Cornish pasty.

130ml/4½fl oz/generous ½ cup water
30ml/2 tbsp extra virgin olive oil,
plus extra for brushing
225g/8oz/2 cups unbleached white
bread flour
5ml/1 tsp salt
2.5ml/½ tsp granulated sugar
5ml/1 tsp easy bake (rapid-rise)
dried yeast

FOR THE FILLING
75g/3oz salami, in one piece
50g/2oz/½ cup drained sun-dried
tomatoes in olive oil, chopped
100g/4oz/⅔ cup mozzarella cheese,
cut into small cubes
50g/2oz/⅔ cup freshly grated
Parmesan cheese
50g/2oz Gorgonzola cheese, cubed
75g/3oz/scant ½ cup ricotta cheese
30ml/3 tbsp chopped fresh basil
2 egg yolks
salt and freshly ground black pepper

MAKES 2

1 Pour the water and olive oil into the bread pan. Reverse the order in which this is necessary for your machine. Sprinkle over the white bread flour, ensuring that it covers the liquid.

VARIATIONS
The ingredients for the filling can be varied, depending on what you have in the refrigerator, and to suit personal tastes. Replace the salami with ham or sautéed mushrooms. Add a freshly chopped chilli for a more piquant version. Make four individual calzones instead of two large ones.

2 Add the salt and sugar in separate corners of the bread pan. Make a small indent in the centre of the flour (but not down as far as the liquid) and add the easy bake dried yeast.

3 Set the bread machine to the dough setting; use basic or pizza dough setting (if available). Press Start.

4 To make the topping, cut the salami into 5mm/¼in dice. Put the dice in a bowl and add the sun-dried tomatoes, mozzarella, Parmesan, Gorgonzola and ricotta cheeses, basil and egg yolks. Mix well and season to taste with salt and plenty of ground black pepper. Lightly oil a large baking sheet.

5 When the cycle has finished, remove the calzone dough from the bread pan and place it on a lightly floured surface. Knock it back (punch it down) gently then divide the dough into two equal pieces. Roll out each piece of dough into a flat round, about 5mm/¼in thick. Preheat the oven to 220°C/425°F/Gas 7.

COOK'S TIP
Calzone can be made in advance, ready for baking. Make the dough, then transfer to a bowl, cover with oiled clear film and store in the refrigerator for up to 4 hours. Knock back if the dough starts to rise to the top of the bowl. Bring back to room temperature, then continue with the shaping and filling. If preferred, shape and fill up to 2 hours before baking. Place the calzone in the refrigerator until you are ready to bake them.

6 Divide the filling between the two pieces of dough, placing it on one half only, in each case. Leave a 1.5cm/½in border of the dough all round.

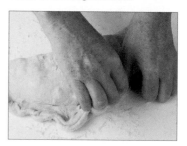

7 Dampen the edges of each dough round with water, fold the remaining dough over the filling and then crimp the edges of each calzone with your fingers to seal securely.

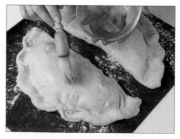

8 Place the calzone on the baking sheet, brush with olive oil and bake for 20 minutes, or until golden and well risen.

Per calzone Energy 625kcal/2626kJ; Protein 22.5g; Carbohydrate 75.1g, of which sugars 7.3g; Fat 28.2g, of which saturates 9.8g; Cholesterol 39mg; Calcium 305mg; Fibre 4g; Sodium 1053mg.

SOURDOUGHS AND STARTER DOUGH BREADS

Breads made with starters acquire their wonderful textures and flavours from the multiple ferments and starter doughs. The bread machine provides the perfect environment to nurture these doughs. This section also includes a recipe for bread made with fresh yeast.

FRESH YEAST BREAD

15g/½oz fresh yeast
5ml/1 tsp granulated sugar
260ml/9fl oz/1⅛ cups water
30ml/2 tbsp sunflower oil
450g/1lb/4 cups unbleached white
bread flour
30ml/2 tbsp skimmed milk powder
(non fat dry milk)
10ml/2 tsp salt
75ml/5 tbsp sunflower seeds, for coating

MAKES 1 LOAF

Bread machine manufacturers do not recommend using fresh yeast for bread baked in their appliances, but if the bread is to be baked in the oven, the machine can be used to prepare the dough.

5 Sprinkle the sunflower seeds on a clean area of work surface and roll the bread in them until evenly coated. Place on the prepared baking sheet. Cover with lightly oiled clear film (plastic wrap) or a large inverted bowl and leave to rise in a warm place for 30–45 minutes, or until doubled in size.

6 Meanwhile, preheat the oven to 230°C/450°F/Gas 8. Cut two slashes, one on each side of the loaf, then cut two slashes at right angles to the first to make a noughts and crosses grid.

7 Bake the loaf for 15 minutes, then reduce the oven temperature to 200°C/400°F/Gas 6. Bake for 20 minutes more, or until the bread sounds hollow when tapped on the base. Turn out on to a wire rack to cool.

> **COOK'S TIP**
> This makes a basic fresh yeast bread which you can shape or flavour to suit yourself. Leave out the sunflower seeds, if you like.

1 In a small bowl, cream the fresh yeast with the sugar and 30ml/2 tbsp of the water. Leave to stand for 5 minutes then scrape the mixture into the bread machine pan. Add the remaining water and the sunflower oil. However, if the instructions for your bread machine specify that the yeast is to be placed in the pan first, simply reverse the order in which you add the liquid and dry ingredients to the pan.

2 Sprinkle over the flour, ensuring that it covers the water completely. Add the skimmed milk powder and salt to the bread pan.

3 Set the bread machine to the dough setting; use basic dough setting (if available). Press Start, then lightly oil a baking sheet.

4 When the dough cycle has finished, remove the dough from the machine and place it on a lightly floured surface. Knock it back (punch it down) gently, and then knead for 2–3 minutes. Roll the dough into a ball and pat it into a plump round cushion shape.

Per loaf Energy 1757kcal/7444kJ; Protein 43g; Carbohydrate 354.8g, of which sugars 11.9g; Fat 28.2g, of which saturates 3.7g; Cholesterol 1mg; Calcium 657mg; Fibre 13.9g; Sodium 3955mg.

SCHIACCIATA CON UVA

This Tuscan bread is baked throughout the region to celebrate the grape harvest each year. The fresh grapes on top are the new crop while the raisins inside symbolize last year's gathering-in.

FOR THE STARTER
200ml/7fl oz/⅞ cup water
175g/6oz/1½ cups organic white
bread flour
1.5ml/¼ tsp easy bake (rapid-rise)
dried yeast

FOR THE SCHIACCIATA DOUGH
200g/7oz/generous 1 cup raisins
150ml/5fl oz/⅔ cup Italian red wine
45ml/3 tbsp extra virgin olive oil
45ml/3 tbsp water
280g/10oz/2½ cups unbleached white
bread flour
50g/2oz/¼ cup granulated sugar
7.5ml/1½ tsp salt
5ml/1 tsp easy bake dried yeast

FOR THE TOPPING
280g/10oz small black seedless grapes
30ml/2 tbsp demerara (raw) sugar

MAKES 1 LOAF

1 Pour the water for the starter into the bread machine pan. If the instructions for your machine specify that the yeast is to be placed in the pan first, reverse the order in which you add the liquid and dry ingredients.

2 Sprinkle over the organic flour, ensuring that it completely covers the water. Make a small indent in the centre of the flour (but not down as far as the liquid) and add the easy bake dried yeast. Set the bread machine to the dough setting; use basic dough setting (if available). Press Start. Mix for 5 minutes, then switch off the machine and set aside.

3 Leave the starter to ferment inside the machine for 24 hours. Do not lift the lid. If you need the machine, transfer the starter to a bowl, cover it with a damp dishtowel and leave it to stand at room temperature.

4 Place the raisins for the dough in a small pan. Add the wine and heat gently until warm. Cover and set aside.

5 Remove the bread pan from the machine. Return the starter to the pan, if necessary, and pour in the oil and water. Sprinkle over the flour. Add the sugar and salt in separate corners. Make a shallow indent in the centre of the flour and add the yeast.

6 Set the bread machine to the dough setting. If your machine has a choice of settings, use the basic dough setting. Press Start. Lightly oil a baking sheet.

7 When the dough cycle has finished, remove the dough from the machine and place it on a lightly floured surface. Knock it back (punch it down) gently, then divide it in half. Roll each piece of dough out into a circle, about 1cm/½in thick. Place one circle on the prepared baking sheet.

8 Spread the raisins over the dough. Place the remaining piece of dough on top and pinch the edges together to seal. Cover with lightly oiled clear film (plastic wrap) and leave to rise in a warm place for 30–45 minutes, or until it is almost doubled in size.

9 Meanwhile, preheat the oven to 190°C/375°F/Gas 5. Cover the schiacciata with the fresh black grapes, pressing them lightly into the dough. Sprinkle with the sugar.

10 Bake for 40 minutes, or until the bread is golden and sounds hollow when tapped on the base. Turn out on to a wire rack to cool slightly before serving.

Per loaf Energy 2977kcal/12625kJ; Protein 48.8g; Carbohydrate 619.3g, of which sugars 272.6g; Fat 40g, of which saturates 5.5g; Cholesterol 0mg; Calcium 818mg; Fibre 20.1g; Sodium 159mg.

FRENCH COURONNE

This crown-shaped loaf is made with a chef starter, which is fermented for at least 2 days and up to a week; the longer it is left the more it will develop the characteristic sourdough flavour.

FOR THE CHEF
0.6ml/⅛ tsp easy bake (rapid-rise)
dried yeast
50g/2oz/½ cup organic white bread flour
45ml/3 tbsp water

FOR THE 1ST REFRESHMENT
65ml/4½ tbsp water
115g/4oz/1 cup organic white
bread flour

FOR THE LEVAIN
115ml/4fl oz/½ cup water
115g/4oz/1 cup unbleached white
bread flour

FOR THE COURONNE DOUGH
240ml/8½fl oz/generous 1 cup
cold water
325g/11½oz/scant 3 cups unbleached
white bread flour, plus extra
for dusting
7.5ml/1½ tsp salt
5ml/1 tsp granulated sugar
2.5ml/½ tsp easy bake dried yeast

MAKES 1 LOAF

1 Mix the yeast and organic white bread flour for the chef in a small bowl. Add the water and gradually mix to a stiff dough with a metal spoon. Cover the bowl with oiled clear film (plastic wrap) and set aside in a warm place for 2–3 days.

2 Break open the crust on the chef – the middle should be aerated and sweet smelling. Mix in the water and flour for the first refreshment, stirring to form a fairly stiff dough. Replace the clear film cover and set aside for a further 2 days in a warm place.

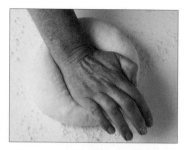

3 Transfer the chef to the machine pan. If the instructions for your machine specify that the yeast is to be placed in the pan first, reverse the order in which you add the liquid and dry ingredients.

4 Add the water for the levain. Sprinkle over the flour, ensuring that it covers the water. Set the bread machine to the dough setting; use basic dough setting (if available). Press Start.

5 When the dough cycle has finished, switch the machine off, leaving the levain inside. Do not lift the lid. Leave the levain for 8 hours. If you need the machine, transfer the levain to a bowl, cover it with a damp dishtowel and leave it at room temperature.

6 Take the bread pan out of the machine. Remove about half of the levain from the pan. If the levain is in a bowl, put 200g/7oz/scant 1 cup of it back in the pan. Reserve the spare levain to replenish and use for your next loaf of bread. Meanwhile pour the water for the dough into the bread pan. Sprinkle over the flour. Add the salt and sugar, placing them in separate corners of the bread pan. Make a small indent in the centre of the flour and add the yeast.

7 Set the bread machine to the dough setting; use basic dough setting (if available). Press Start. Lightly oil a baking sheet.

8 When the dough cycle has finished, remove the dough from the machine and place it on a lightly floured surface. Knock it back (punch it down) gently, then shape it into a ball and make a hole in the centre with the heel of your hand. Gradually enlarge this cavity, using your fingertips and turning the dough, then use both hands to stretch the dough gently into a large doughnut shape. The cavity should measure 13–15cm/5–6in across.

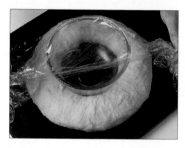

9 Place the shaped dough on the prepared baking sheet. Fit a small bowl into the centre to prevent the dough from filling in the hole when it rises. Cover it with lightly oiled clear film and leave it in a warm place for an hour, or until almost doubled in size.

10 Preheat the oven to 230°C/450°F/ Gas 8. Dust the loaf with flour and make four slashes at equal intervals around the couronne. Bake for 35–40 minutes, or until the bread is golden and sounds hollow when tapped on its base. Turn out on to a wire rack to cool.

Per loaf Energy 1465kcal/6230kJ; Protein 40g; Carbohydrate 334.4g, of which sugars 10.6g; Fat 5.5g, of which saturates 0.8g; Cholesterol 0mg; Calcium 598mg; Fibre 13.2g; Sodium 2960mg.

PAIN DE SEIGLE

For the Chef
200ml/7fl oz/⅞ cup water
175g/6oz/1½ cups rye flour
1.5ml/¼ tsp easy bake (rapid-rise)
dried yeast

For the 1st Refreshment
70ml/2½fl oz/¼ cup + 1 tbsp water
50g/2oz/½ cup plain (all-purpose) flour

For the 2nd Refreshment
15ml/1 tbsp water
50g/2oz/½ cup plain (all-purpose) flour

For the Bread Dough
15ml/1 tbsp water
225g/8oz/2 cups unbleached white
bread flour
10ml/2 tsp salt
5ml/1 tsp clear honey
2.5ml/½ tsp easy bake dried yeast
unbleached white bread flour,
for dusting

MAKES 1 LOAF

Based on a rye starter, this is typical of the breads eaten in the Pyrenees. Serve it thickly buttered – it makes the perfect accompaniment for shellfish.

1 Pour the water for the chef into the machine pan. If the instructions for your machine specify that the yeast is to be added first, reverse the order in which you add the liquid and dry ingredients.

2 Sprinkle over the rye flour, ensuring that it covers the water completely. Make a small indent in the centre of the flour (but not down as far as the liquid) and add the easy bake dried yeast. Set the bread machine to the dough setting; use basic dough setting (if available). Press Start. Mix the dough for about 10 minutes, and then switch off the bread machine.

3 Leave the chef to ferment in the machine, with the lid closed, for about 24 hours. If you need the machine, transfer the chef to a bowl, cover it with a damp dishtowel and then set aside at room temperature.

4 Remove the bread pan from the machine. Return the chef to the bread pan, if necessary, and add the water and flour for the first refreshment. Set the bread machine to the dough setting, press Start and mix for 10 minutes. Switch off the machine and leave the dough inside for a further 24 hours.

5 Add the water and flour for the second refreshment. Mix as for the first refreshment, but this time leave the dough in the machine for only 8 hours.

6 Add the water for the bread dough to the mixture in the bread machine pan. Sprinkle over the flour. Place the salt and honey in separate corners of the bread pan. Make a small indent in the centre of the flour and add the yeast. Set the bread machine to the dough setting; use basic dough setting (if available). Press Start. Lightly flour a baking sheet.

> **COOK'S TIP**
> When shaping the loaf into a twist make sure that you continue to twist it in the same direction after you have turned the dough round to finish shaping the loaf.

7 When the dough cycle has finished, place the dough on a lightly floured surface. Knock it back (punch it down) gently, then divide the dough into two equal pieces. Roll each piece of dough into a rope about 45cm/18in long.

8 Place the two ropes side by side. Starting at the centre, place one piece of dough over the other. Continue twisting in this fashion until you reach the end of the rope. Turn the dough around and twist the other ends. Dampen the ends with water; tuck them under to seal.

9 Place the twist on the baking sheet, cover with oiled clear film (plastic wrap) and leave in a warm place for 45 minutes, or until almost doubled in size.

10 Preheat the oven to 220°C/425°F/ Gas 7. Dust the top of the loaf lightly with flour and bake for 40 minutes, or until the bread is golden and sounds hollow when tapped on the base. Switch off the oven, but leave the loaf inside, with the door slightly ajar, for 5 minutes. Turn out on to a wire rack to cool.

Per loaf Energy 1718kcal/7310kJ; Protein 44.9g; Carbohydrate 391.5g, of which sugars 11g; Fat 7.7g, of which saturates 1.2g; Cholesterol 0mg; Calcium 512mg; Fibre 30.5g; Sodium 3942mg.

FOR THE STARTER
25g/1oz/¼ cup organic plain
(all-purpose) flour
15–30ml/1–2 tbsp warm water

1ST REFRESHMENT FOR THE STARTER
30ml/2 tbsp water
15ml/1 tbsp milk
50g/2oz/½ cup organic plain flour

2ND REFRESHMENT FOR THE STARTER
90ml/6 tbsp water
15–30ml/1–2 tbsp milk
175g/6oz/1½ cups organic white
bread flour

FOR THE DOUGH
100ml/3½fl oz/7 tbsp water
175g/6oz/1½ cups organic white
bread flour

1ST REFRESHMENT FOR THE DOUGH
100ml/3½fl oz/7 tbsp water
175g/6oz/1½ cups organic white
bread flour
50g/2oz/½ cup organic wholemeal
(whole-wheat) bread flour
7.5ml/1½ tsp salt
5ml/1 tsp granulated sugar
unbleached white bread flour, for
dusting

MAKES 1 LOAF

1 Place the flour in a bowl and stir in enough water for the starter to make a firm, moist dough. Knead for 5 minutes. Cover with a damp cloth. Leave for 2–3 days until a crust forms and the dough inflates with tiny bubbles. Remove the hardened crust and place the moist centre in a clean bowl. Add the water and milk for the 1st refreshment.

SAN FRANCISCO-STYLE SOURDOUGH

This tangy, chewy bread originated in San Francisco, but the flavour of the sourdough will actually be unique to wherever it is baked. The bread is made without the use of baker's yeast, and instead uses airborne yeast spores to ferment a flour and water paste.

2 Gradually add the flour and mix to a firm but moist dough. Cover and leave for 1–2 days as before. Then repeat as for 1st refreshment using the ingredients for the 2nd refreshment. Leave for 8–12 hours in a warm place until well risen.

3 Pour the water for the dough into the pan. Add 200g/7oz/scant 1 cup of starter. If necessary for your machine, add the dry ingredients first. Sprinkle over the flour, covering the water. Set the machine to the dough setting; use basic dough setting (if available). Press Start.

4 Mix for 10 minutes then turn off the machine. Leave the dough in the machine for 8 hours. Add the water for the 1st dough refreshment to the pan, then sprinkle over the flours.

5 Add the salt and sugar in separate corners. Set the machine as before. Press Start. Lightly flour a baking sheet.

6 When the dough cycle ends put the dough on a floured surface. Knock it back (punch it down) gently; shape into a plump ball. Place on the baking sheet; cover with oiled clear film (plastic wrap). Leave for 2 hours, or until almost doubled in bulk.

7 Meanwhile, preheat the oven to 230°C/450°F/Gas 8. Dust the loaf with flour and slash the top in a star shape. Bake for 25 minutes, spraying the oven with water three times in the first 5 minutes. Reduce the oven temperature to 200°C/400°F/Gas 6. Bake the loaf for 10 minutes more or until golden and hollow-sounding. Cool on a wire rack.

Per loaf Energy 1748kcal/7435kJ; Protein 48.2g; Carbohydrate 398.4g, of which sugars 7.7g; Fat 6.7g, of which saturates 1g; Cholesterol 0mg; Calcium 718mg; Fibre 15.9g; Sodium 1490mg.

CHALLAH

*The flavour of this traditional Jewish festival bread is enhanced by the use of a
sponge starter, which is left to develop for 8–10 hours before the final dough is
made. The dough is often braided, but can also be shaped into a coil. This shape
is used for Jewish New Year celebrations, symbolizing continuity and eternity.*

For the Sponge
200ml/7fl oz/⅞ cup water
225g/8oz/2 cups unbleached white
bread flour
15ml/1 tbsp granulated sugar
5ml/1 tsp salt
7.5ml/1½ tsp easy bake (rapid-rise)
dried yeast

For the Dough
2 eggs
225g/8oz/2 cups unbleached white
bread flour
15ml/1 tbsp granulated sugar
5ml/1 tsp salt
50g/2oz/¼ cup butter, melted

For the Topping
1 egg yolk
15ml/1 tbsp water
poppy seeds

Makes 1 Loaf

1 Pour the water for the sponge into
the bread machine pan. Reverse the
order in which you add the wet and dry
ingredients if necessary.

2 Sprinkle over the flour ensuring that it
covers the water. Add the sugar and salt
in separate corners. Make an indent in
the centre of the flour and add the yeast.

3 Set the bread machine to the dough
setting; use basic dough setting (if
available). Press Start.

4 When the dough cycle has finished,
switch the machine off, leaving the
sponge inside. Do not lift the lid. Leave
the sponge in the machine for 8 hours.
If necessary, transfer to a bowl, cover
with a damp dishtowel and set aside.

5 Remove the bread pan from the
machine and replace the sponge (if
necessary). Add the eggs for the dough
to the sponge. Sprinkle over the flour.
Place the sugar, salt and melted butter
in separate corners of the bread pan. Set
the bread machine to the dough setting;
use basic dough setting (if available).
Press Start. Lightly oil a baking sheet.

6 When the dough cycle has finished,
remove the dough from the machine and
place it on a lightly floured surface. Knock
it back (punch it down) gently, then
flatten the dough until it is about 2.5cm/
1in thick. Fold both sides to the centre,
fold the dough over again and press to seal.

7 Using your palms, gradually roll the
dough into a rope with tapered ends. It
should be about 50cm/20in long. Coil
the rope into a spiral shape, sealing the
final end by tucking it under the loaf.
Place the coil on the prepared baking
sheet. Cover it with a large glass bowl or
lightly oiled clear film (plastic wrap) and
leave in a warm place for 45–60 minutes,
or until almost doubled in size.

8 Preheat the oven to 190°C/375°F/
Gas 5. In a small bowl, beat the egg yolk
with the water for the topping. Brush
the mixture over the challah. Sprinkle
evenly with the poppy seeds and bake
for 35–40 minutes, or until the bread is
a deep golden brown and sounds hollow
when tapped on the base. Transfer it to
a wire rack to cool before slicing.

Per loaf Energy 2235kcal/9460kJ; Protein 63.1g; Carbohydrate 428.3g, of which sugars 24.6g; Fat 41.9g, of which saturates 7.1g; Cholesterol 403mg; Calcium 811mg; Fibre 16.4g; Sodium 165mg.

SAVOURY BREADS

Adding flavourings to a basic dough provides many new ideas. Herbs, such as tarragon, dill and sage, along with garlic and onion will fill the kitchen with delicious scents. Mozzarella and feta cheese give loaves a subtle flavour, while Gorgonzola, Parmesan and mascarpone are combined with chives to give a rich loaf with a wonderful aroma. Sausages, smoked venison, salami and pancetta are just a few of the meats you can add to savoury breads.

210ml/7½fl oz/scant 1 cup water
350g/12oz/3 cups unbleached white
bread flour
25g/1oz/¼ cup wholemeal
(whole-wheat) bread flour
15ml/1 tbsp skimmed milk powder
(non fat dry milk)
5ml/1 tsp salt
7.5ml/1½ tsp granulated sugar
5ml/1 tsp easy bake (rapid-rise)
dried yeast
40g/1½oz/scant ½ cup well drained,
pitted black olives, chopped
50g/2oz feta cheese, crumbled
15ml/1 tbsp olive oil, for brushing

MAKES 1 LOAF

COOK'S TIP
Depending on the moisture content of
the olives and cheese you may need
to add a tablespoon or two of flour to
the bread dough when adding these
extra ingredients.

FETA CHEESE AND BLACK OLIVE LOAF

Conjuring up memories of holidays in Greece, this bread has a delicious
flavour, thanks to the Mediterranean ingredients.

1 Pour the water into the bread pan. If
necessary, reverse the order in which
you add the liquid and dry ingredients.
Sprinkle over the flours, covering the
water completely. Add the skimmed
milk powder. Place the salt and sugar in
separate corners of the bread pan. Make
an indent in the flour; add the yeast.

2 Set the bread machine to the dough
setting; use basic raisin dough setting
(if available). Press Start. Lightly oil a
18–20cm/7–8in deep round cake tin (pan).

3 Add the olives and feta cheese when
the bread machine beeps or 5 minutes
before the end of the kneading cycle.
Once the dough cycle has finished, place
the dough on a lightly floured surface
and knock back (punch it down) gently.

4 Shape into a plump ball, the same
diameter as the tin. Place in the tin,
cover with oiled clear film (plastic wrap)
and leave to rise for 30–45 minutes.
Preheat the oven to 200°C/400°F/Gas 6.

5 Remove the clear film and brush the
olive oil over the top of the loaf. Bake
for 35–40 minutes, or until golden. Turn
the bread out on to a wire rack to cool.

LEEK AND PANCETTA TRAY BREAD

Serve this bread sliced, with a simple salad of dressed leaves, for a tasty
supper or lunchtime snack.

90ml/6 tbsp water
1 egg
225g/8oz/2 cups unbleached white
bread flour
5ml/1 tsp salt
25g/1oz butter
5ml/1 tsp easy bake (rapid-rise)
dried yeast

FOR THE FILLING
575g/1¼lb/4–5 leeks
30ml/2 tbsp sunflower oil
75g/3oz sliced pancetta or streaky
(fatty) bacon, cut into strips
140ml/5fl oz/⅔ cup sour cream
70ml/2½fl oz/5 tbsp milk
2 eggs, lightly beaten
15ml/1 tbsp chopped fresh basil leaves
salt and freshly ground black pepper

MAKES 1 LOAF

1 Pour the water and egg into the bread
machine pan. Reverse wet and dry
ingredients if necessary. Sprinkle over
the flour, ensuring that it covers the
liquid. Place the salt and butter in
separate corners. Make a shallow indent
in the centre of the flour (but not down
as far as the liquid) and add the yeast.

2 Set the bread machine to the dough
setting; use basic or pizza dough setting
(if available). Press Start. Then lightly
oil a 20 × 30cm/8 × 12in Swiss (jelly) roll
tin (pan) that is about 1cm/½in deep.

3 Slice the leeks thinly. Heat the
sunflower oil in a large frying pan and
cook the leeks over a low heat for about
5 minutes, until they have softened
slightly but not browned. Set them
aside to cool.

4 When the dough cycle has finished,
place the dough on a lightly floured
surface. Knock it back (punch it down)
gently, then roll it out to a rectangle
measuring about 23 × 33 cm/9 × 13in.
Place in the prepared tin and press the
edges outwards and upwards, so that the
dough covers the base and sides evenly.
Preheat the oven to 190°C/375°F/Gas 5.

5 Sprinkle the leeks over the dough.
Arrange the pancetta slices on top.
Mix the sour cream, milk and eggs
together. Add the basil and season with
salt and ground black pepper. Pour the
mixture over the leeks.

6 Bake for 30–35 minutes, or until the
filling has set and the base is golden
around the edges. Serve the bread hot
or warm.

Per loaf Energy 1582kcal/6693kJ; Protein 47.5g; Carbohydrate 293.7g, of which sugars 11.5g; Fat 32.3g, of which saturates 10.8g; Cholesterol 41mg; Calcium 824mg; Fibre 14.3g; Sodium 3651mg.
Per loaf Energy 2022kcal/8462kJ; Protein 67.4g; Carbohydrate 200.3g, of which sugars 24.8g; Fat 111.6g, of which saturates 46.2g; Cholesterol 765mg; Calcium 761mg; Fibre 19.6g; Sodium 3422mg.

STROMBOLI

This variation on Italian Focaccia takes its name from the volcanic island of Stromboli, near Sicily. The dough is pierced to allow the filling to "erupt" through the holes during baking. This bread can be served warm or cold.

200ml/7fl oz/⅞ cup water
350g/12oz/3 cups unbleached white bread flour
2.5ml/½ tsp granulated sugar
5ml/1 tsp salt
5ml/1 tsp easy bake (rapid-rise) dried yeast

FOR THE FILLING
175g/6oz mozzarella cheese, grated or finely chopped
75g/3oz/1 cup freshly grated Parmesan cheese
15ml/1 tbsp chopped fresh parsley
30ml/2 tbsp fresh basil leaves
5ml/1 tsp freshly ground black pepper
1 garlic clove, finely chopped

FOR THE TOPPING
15ml/1 tbsp extra virgin olive oil
4–5 small fresh rosemary sprigs, woody stems removed

MAKES 1 LOAF

1 Pour the water into the machine pan. Reverse the order in which you add the wet and dry ingredients if necessary. Sprinkle over the flour, ensuring that it covers the water. Add the sugar and salt in separate corners of the pan. Make a shallow indent in the centre of the flour and add the yeast.

2 Set the bread machine to the dough setting; use basic dough setting (if available). Press Start.

3 Lightly oil a baking sheet. When the dough cycle has ended, remove the dough and place on a lightly floured surface. Knock it back (punch it down) gently. Roll out into a rectangle 30 × 23cm/12 × 9in. Cover with oiled clear film (plastic wrap) and leave to rest for 5 minutes.

4 Sprinkle over the cheeses leaving a 1cm/½in clear border along each edge. Add the parsley, basil, pepper and garlic.

5 Starting from a shorter side, roll up the dough, Swiss roll fashion, tucking the side edges under to seal. Place the roll, seam down, on the baking sheet. Cover with lightly oiled clear film and leave in a warm place for 30 minutes, or until the dough roll has almost doubled in size.

6 Preheat the oven to 200°C/400°F/ Gas 6. Brush the top of the bread with olive oil, then use a skewer to prick holes in the bread, from the top right through to the base. Sprinkle the rosemary over the bread. Bake for 30–35 minutes, or until the bread is golden. Transfer it to a wire rack.

THREE CHEESES BREAD

A tempting trio of Italian cheeses – mascarpone, Gorgonzola and Parmesan – are responsible for the marvellous flavour of this round loaf.

180ml/6½fl oz/generous ¾ cup water
1 egg
100g/3½oz/5 tbsp mascarpone cheese
400g/14oz/3½ cups unbleached white bread flour
50g/2oz/½ cup Granary (whole-wheat) flour
10ml/2 tsp granulated sugar
5ml/1 tsp salt
7.5ml/1½ tsp easy bake (rapid-rise) dried yeast
75g/3oz Mountain Gorgonzola cheese, cut into small dice
75g/3oz/1 cup freshly grated Parmesan cheese
45ml/3 tbsp chopped fresh chives

FOR THE TOPPING
1 egg yolk
15ml/1 tbsp water
15ml/1 tbsp wheat flakes

MAKES 1 LOAF

1 Add the water, egg and mascarpone to the pan. Reverse the order in which you add the wet and dry ingredients if necessary. Sprinkle over both types of flour, covering the water completely. Add the sugar and salt in separate corners. Make a small indent in the flour; add the yeast. Set the machine to the dough setting; use basic raisin dough setting (if available). Press Start.

2 Add the Gorgonzola, Parmesan and chives as the machine beeps or during the last 5 minutes of kneading. Lightly oil a baking sheet.

3 When the dough cycle has finished, place the dough on a floured surface. Knock back (punch down) gently, then shape it into a round loaf, about 20cm/ 8in in diameter.

4 Cover with oiled clear film (plastic wrap); leave in a warm place for 30–45 minutes. Preheat the oven to 200°C/400°F/Gas 6.

5 Mix the egg yolk and water together and brush this glaze over the top of the bread. Sprinkle with wheat flakes. Score the top of the bread into eight equal segments. Bake for 30–35 minutes, or until golden and hollow-sounding. Turn out on to a wire rack to cool.

Per stromboli Energy 2108kcal/8871kJ; Protein 96.5g; Carbohydrate 275.9g, of which sugars 9g; Fat 76.2g, of which saturates 41.7g; Cholesterol 177mg; Calcium 2125mg; Fibre 13.4g; Sodium 1536mg.
Per loaf Energy 2425kcal/10227kJ; Protein 105.4g; Carbohydrate 357.5g, of which sugars 21.6g; Fat 73.7g, of which saturates 40.8g; Cholesterol 364mg; Calcium 1978mg; Fibre 19.1g; Sodium 3826mg.

VENISON TORDU

This pretty twisted bread is punctuated with strips of smoked venison, black pepper and crushed juniper berries. It tastes delicious on its own, perhaps with a glass of red wine. Alternatively, cut the bread into thick slices and serve it with olives and nuts as a precursor to an Italian meal.

230ml/8fl oz/1 cup water
350g/12oz/3 cups unbleached white bread flour
5ml/1 tsp granulated sugar
5ml/1 tsp salt
5ml/1 tsp easy bake (rapid-rise) dried yeast
40g/1½oz smoked venison, cut into strips
5ml/1 tsp freshly ground black pepper
5ml/1 tsp juniper berries, crushed
unbleached white bread flour, for dusting

MAKES 1 LOAF

1 Pour the water into the bread machine pan. If the instructions for your bread machine specify that the yeast is to be placed in the pan first, simply reverse the order in which you add the liquid and dry ingredients to the pan.

2 Sprinkle over the white bread flour, ensuring that it completely covers the water. Add the sugar and salt, placing them in separate corners of the bread pan. Make a shallow indent in the centre of the flour (but not down as far as the liquid) and add the easy bake dried yeast.

3 Set the bread machine to the dough setting; use basic dough setting (if available). Press Start. Meanwhile, lightly oil a baking sheet.

4 When the dough cycle has finished, remove the dough from the bread machine pan and place it on a lightly floured surface. Knock it back (punch it down) gently. Shape the dough into a ball and flatten the top slightly.

5 Roll the dough out to a round, about 2cm/¾in thick. Sprinkle the top of the dough with venison strips, black pepper and juniper berries. Leave a 1cm/½in clear border around the edge.

6 Fold one side of the dough to the centre, then repeat on the other side.

7 Press the folds gently with a rolling pin to seal them, then fold again along the centre line.

> **COOK'S TIP**
> Try using cured and smoked venison, marinated in olive oil and herbs, for this recipe. The olive oil and herbs add an extra flavour which beautifully complements this bread. Alternatively, sprinkle 5ml/1 tsp of dried herbs such as rosemary, thyme, sage or oregano over the dough in step 4.

8 Press the seam gently to seal, then roll the dough backwards and forwards to make a loaf about 65cm/26in long.

9 Using the side of your hand, press across the centre of the loaf to make an indentation. Bring both ends towards each other to make an upside down "U" shape and twist together.

10 Place the venison tordu on the prepared baking sheet. Cover the loaf with lightly oiled clear film (plastic wrap) and leave to rise in a warm place for 30 minutes, or until it has almost doubled in size. Meanwhile, preheat the oven to 220°C/425°F/Gas 7. Remove the clear film and dust the top of the twisted loaf with white bread flour.

11 Bake for 25–30 minutes, or until the bread is golden and sounds hollow when tapped on the base. Turn out on to a wire rack to cool. Serve freshly baked, while the bread is still slightly warm.

Per loaf Energy 1265kcal/5377kJ; Protein 42.5g; Carbohydrate 277.9g, of which sugars 9.4g; Fat 6.1g, of which saturates 1.1g; Cholesterol 20mg; Calcium 504mg; Fibre 10.9g; Sodium 1999mg.

CAJUN SPICED BRAID

The traditional Deep South flavours of tomatoes, garlic, spices and hot seasonings make this piquant, spicy loaf irresistible.

300ml/10½fl oz/1¼ cups water
30ml/2 tbsp vegetable oil
15ml/1 tbsp tomato purée (paste)
500g/1lb 2oz/4½ cups unbleached
white bread flour
7.5ml/1½ tsp paprika
5ml/1 tsp cayenne pepper
5ml/1 tsp dried oregano
2.5ml/½ tsp freshly ground
black pepper
1 garlic clove, crushed
7.5ml/1½ tsp salt
2.5ml/½ tsp sugar
7.5ml/1½ tsp easy bake (rapid-rise)
dried yeast

FOR THE GLAZE
1 egg yolk
15ml/1 tbsp water

MAKES 1 LOAF

1 Pour the water and vegetable oil into the bread machine pan, then add the tomato purée. If the instructions for your machine specify that the yeast is to be placed in the pan first, reverse the order in which you add the liquid and dry ingredients.

2 Sprinkle over the flour, ensuring that it covers the liquid. Add the paprika, cayenne, oregano, black pepper and crushed garlic. Place the salt and sugar in separate corners of the bread pan. Make a small indent in the centre of the flour (but not down as far as the liquid) and add the yeast.

3 Set the bread machine to the dough setting; use basic dough setting (if available). Press Start. Lightly oil a baking sheet.

4 Once the dough cycle has finished, place the dough on a floured surface. Knock it back (punch it down) and divide into three.

5 Roll the pieces into equal ropes. Put next to each other. From the centre, braid from left to right, working towards you. Press the ends together and tuck under.

6 Turn the dough around and braid the remaining ropes. Place on the prepared baking sheet, cover with oiled clear film (plastic wrap) and leave in a warm place to rise for 30–45 minutes. Meanwhile, preheat the oven to 200°C/400°F/Gas 6.

7 Mix the egg yolk and water for the glaze together. Remove the clear film and brush the glaze over the braid. Bake for 30–35 minutes, or until golden.

SALAMI AND PEPPERCORN BREAD

This loaf marbled with salami and black pepper makes a great accompaniment to hot soup. For a quick snack, try it toasted with a cheese topping.

210ml/7½fl oz/scant 1 cup water
15ml/1 tbsp olive oil
350g/12oz/3 cups unbleached
white flour
50g/2oz/½ cup grated mature
(sharp) Cheddar cheese
2.5ml/½ tsp salt
5ml/1 tsp granulated sugar
5ml/1 tsp easy bake (rapid-rise) dried
yeast
5ml/1 tsp black peppercorns,
coarsely crushed
50g/2oz salami, chopped
milk, for brushing

MAKES 1 LOAF

1 Pour the water and oil into the bread machine pan. If the instructions for your bread machine specify that the yeast is to be placed in the pan first, then simply reverse the order in which you add the liquid and dry ingredients.

2 Sprinkle over the flour, ensuring that it covers the liquid. Add half the cheese. Add the salt in one corner of the bread pan and the sugar in another corner. Make a small indent in the centre of the flour (but not down as far as the liquid) and add the yeast.

3 Set the bread machine to the dough setting; use basic or pizza dough setting (if available). Press Start. Then lightly oil a baking sheet.

4 Once the dough cycle has finished, remove the dough from the machine and place it on a lightly floured surface. Knock it back (punch it down) gently and flatten it slightly. Sprinkle over the peppercorns and salami and knead gently until both are evenly incorporated.

5 Shape into a round loaf; place on the baking sheet. Cover with an oiled bowl and leave in a warm place for 30 minutes. Preheat the oven to 200°C/400°F/Gas 6.

6 Uncover the bread, brush it with milk and sprinkle with the remaining cheese. Bake for about 30–35 minutes, or until golden. Turn out on to a wire rack to cool.

Per braid Energy 1945kcal/8239kJ; Protein 48.8g; Carbohydrate 395.7g, of which sugars 12g; Fat 29.5g, of which saturates 3.4g; Cholesterol 0mg; Calcium 723mg; Fibre 15.9g; Sodium 3001mg.
Per loaf Energy 1762kcal/7427kJ; Protein 55.3g; Carbohydrate 277.1g, of which sugars 9.5g; Fat 54.5g, of which saturates 13.1g; Cholesterol 88mg; Calcium 867mg; Fibre 10.9g; Sodium 2280mg.

140ml/5fl oz/⅝ cup milk
150ml/5fl oz/scant ⅔ cup water
30ml/2 tbsp extra virgin olive oil
450g/1lb/4 cups unbleached white
bread flour
7.5ml/1½ tsp granulated sugar
7.5ml/1½ tsp salt
7.5ml/1½ tsp easy bake (rapid-rise)
dried yeast
100g/3½oz/7 tbsp ready-made
pesto sauce

FOR THE TOPPING
15ml/1 tbsp extra virgin olive oil
10ml/2 tsp coarse sea salt

MAKES 1 LOAF

1 Remove the milk from the refrigerator 30 minutes before using, to bring it to room temperature. Pour the water, milk and extra virgin olive oil into the bread machine pan. If the instructions for your bread machine specify that the yeast is to be placed in the pan first, then simply reverse the order in which you add the liquid and dry ingredients.

2 Sprinkle over the flour, ensuring that it covers the liquid mixture completely. Add the sugar and salt, placing them in separate corners of the bread pan.

MARBLED PESTO BREAD

Using ready-made pesto sauce means that this scrumptious bread is very easy to make. Use a good-quality sauce – or, if you have the time, make your own – so that the flavours of garlic, basil, pine nuts and Parmesan cheese can be clearly discerned.

3 Make a small indent in the centre of the flour (but do not go down as far as the liquid) and pour the dried yeast into the hollow.

4 Set the bread machine to the dough setting. If your machine has a choice of settings use the basic dough setting. Press Start. Lightly oil a 25 × 10cm/ 10 × 4in loaf tin (pan).

5 When the dough cycle has finished, remove the dough from the machine and place it on a lightly floured surface. Knock it back (punch it down) gently, then roll it out to a rectangle about 2cm/ ¾in thick and 25cm/10in long. Cover with oiled clear film (plastic wrap) and leave to relax for a few minutes, if the dough proves difficult to roll out.

6 Spread the pesto sauce over the dough. Leave a clear border of 1cm/½in along one long edge. Roll up the dough lengthways, Swiss (jelly) roll fashion, tuck the ends under and place seam down in the prepared tin.

7 Cover with oiled clear film and set aside in a warm place to rise for 45 minutes or until the dough has more than doubled in size and reaches the top of the loaf tin. Meanwhile, preheat the oven to 220°C/425°F/Gas 7.

8 Remove the clear film and brush the olive oil over the top of the loaf. Use a sharp knife to score the top with four diagonal cuts. Repeat the cuts in the opposite direction to make a criss-cross pattern. Sprinkle with the sea salt.

9 Bake for 25–30 minutes, or until the bread is golden and sounds hollow when tapped on the base. Turn out on to a wire rack to cool.

COOK'S TIP
For a really luxurious twist to this bread, make your own pesto filling. Put 75g/3oz basil leaves, 1 clove garlic, 30ml/2 tbsp pine nuts, salt and pepper, and 90ml/3fl oz olive oil in a mortar and crush to a paste with a pestle, or alternatively, place in a blender and blend until creamy. Work in 50g/2oz freshly grated Parmesan cheese. Any leftover pesto can be kept for up to 2 weeks in the refrigerator.

Per loaf Energy 2316kcal/9754kJ; Protein 57.4g; Carbohydrate 359.3g, of which sugars 14.9g; Fat 82.2g, of which saturates 14.8g; Cholesterol 26mg; Calcium 1066mg; Fibre 15.7g; Sodium 3205mg.

SUN-DRIED TOMATO BREAD

The dense texture and highly concentrated flavour of sun-dried tomatoes makes them perfect for flavouring bread dough, and when Parmesan cheese is added, the result is an exceptionally tasty loaf.

SMALL

15g/½oz/¼ cup sun-dried tomatoes
130ml/4½fl oz/½ cup + 1 tbsp water
70ml/2½fl oz/¼ cup + 1 tbsp milk
15ml/1 tbsp extra virgin olive oil
325g/11½oz/scant 3 cups unbleached white bread flour
50g/2oz/½ cup wholemeal (whole-wheat) bread flour
40g/1½oz/½ cup freshly grated Parmesan cheese
5ml/1 tsp salt
5ml/1 tsp granulated sugar
4ml/¾ tsp easy bake (rapid-rise) dried yeast

MEDIUM

25g/1oz/½ cup sun-dried tomatoes
190ml/6¾fl oz/scant ⅞ cup water
115ml/4fl oz/½ cup milk
30ml/2 tbsp extra virgin olive oil
425g/15oz/3¾ cups unbleached white bread flour
75g/3oz/¾ cup wholemeal bread flour
50g/2oz/⅔ cup freshly grated Parmesan cheese
7.5ml/1½ tsp salt
10ml/2 tsp granulated sugar
5ml/1 tsp easy bake dried yeast

LARGE

35g/1½oz/¾ cup sun-dried tomatoes
210ml/7½fl oz/⅞ cup water
140ml/5fl oz/⅝ cup milk
30ml/2 tbsp extra virgin olive oil
500g/1lb 2oz/4½ cups unbleached white bread flour
100g/4oz/1 cup wholemeal bread flour
65g/2½oz/⅞ cup freshly grated Parmesan cheese
7.5ml/1½ tsp salt
10ml/2 tsp granulated sugar
7.5ml/1½ tsp easy bake dried yeast

MAKES 1 LOAF

1 Place the sun-dried tomatoes in a small bowl and pour over enough warm water to cover them. Leave to soak for 15 minutes, then tip into a sieve placed over a bowl. Allow to drain thoroughly, then chop finely.

2 Check the quantity of tomato water against the amount of water required for the loaf, and add more water if this is necessary. Pour it into the bread machine pan, then add the milk and olive oil. If the instructions for your machine specify that the yeast is to be placed in the pan first, then simply reverse the order in which you add the liquid and dry ingredients.

3 Sprinkle over both types of flour, ensuring that the liquid is completely covered. Sprinkle over the Parmesan, then add the salt and sugar, placing them in separate corners of the bread pan. Make a small indent in the centre of the flour (but not down as far as the liquid) and add the yeast.

4 Set the machine to white/basic; use the raisin setting (if available), medium crust. Size: 500g for small, large/750g for medium or 1kg/2lb for large. Press Start. Add the tomatoes when the machine beeps during the kneading cycle, or after the first kneading. Remove the bread at the end of the baking cycle. Turn on to a wire rack.

Per loaf Energy 1469kcal/6185kJ; Protein 31.2g; Carbohydrate 228.1g, of which sugars 23.6g; Fat 54.3g, of which saturates 9.1g; Cholesterol 9mg; Calcium 576mg; Fibre 8.8g; Sodium 1656mg.

GARLIC AND HERB WALNUT BREAD

Walnut bread is very popular in France. This variation includes both garlic and basil for additional flavour.

SMALL
150ml/5fl oz/⅔ cup milk
60ml/2fl oz/4 tbsp water
30ml/2 tbsp extra virgin olive oil
325g/11½oz/scant 3 cups unbleached white bread flour
40g/1½oz/scant ⅓ cup rolled oats
40g/1½oz/⅓ cup chopped walnuts
1 garlic clove, finely chopped
5ml/1 tsp dried oregano
5ml/1 tsp chopped fresh basil
5ml/1 tsp salt
7.5ml/1½ tsp granulated sugar
2.5ml/½ tsp easy bake (rapid-rise) dried yeast

MEDIUM
185ml/6½fl oz/generous ¾ cup milk
105ml/7 tbsp water
45ml/3 tbsp extra virgin olive oil
450g/1lb/4 cups unbleached white bread flour
50g/2oz/½ cup rolled oats
50g/2oz/½ cup chopped walnuts
1½ garlic cloves, finely chopped
7.5ml/1½ tsp dried oregano
10ml/2 tsp chopped fresh basil
7.5ml/1½ tsp salt
10ml/2 tsp granulated sugar
5ml/1 tsp easy bake dried yeast

LARGE
180ml/6½fl oz/generous ¾ cup milk
130ml/4½fl oz/½ cup + 1 tbsp water
45ml/3 tbsp extra virgin olive oil
550g/1lb 4oz/5 cups unbleached white bread flour
65g/2½oz/generous ½ cup rolled oats
50g/2oz/½ cup chopped walnuts
2 garlic cloves, finely chopped
7.5ml/1½ tsp dried oregano
10ml/2 tsp chopped fresh basil
10ml/2 tsp salt
10ml/2 tsp granulated sugar
7.5ml/1½ tsp easy bake dried yeast

MAKES 1 LOAF

1 Pour the milk, water and olive oil into the bread machine pan. If the instructions for your machine specify that the yeast is to be placed in the pan first, reverse the order in which you add the liquid and dry ingredients.

2 Sprinkle over the flour and rolled oats, ensuring that they completely cover the liquid mixture. Add the chopped walnuts, garlic, oregano and basil. Place the salt and sugar in separate corners of the bread machine pan. Make a small indent in the centre of the flour (but do not go down as far as the liquid) and add the easy bake dried yeast.

3 Set the machine to white/basic, medium crust. Size: 500g for small, large/750g for medium or 1kg/2lb for large. Press Start.

4 Remove the bread at the end of the baking cycle and turn out on to a wire rack to cool.

Per loaf Energy 1836kcal/7739kJ; Protein 46g; Carbohydrate 297.8g, of which sugars 20.8g; Fat 59.5g, of which saturates 7.4g; Cholesterol 8mg; Calcium 687mg; Fibre 14.2g; Sodium 2068mg.

280ml/10fl oz/1¼ cups water
30ml/2 tbsp extra virgin olive oil
100g/3½oz/scant 1 cup rye flour
350g/12½oz/generous 3 cups
unbleached white bread flour, plus
extra for dusting
30ml/2 tbsp skimmed milk powder
(non fat dry milk)
10ml/2 tsp light muscovado
(brown) sugar
5ml/1 tsp salt
5ml/1 tsp easy bake (rapid-rise)
dried yeast
15ml/1 tbsp dried dill
15ml/1 tbsp dill seeds
30ml/2 tbsp dried onion slices

MAKES 2 LOAVES

1 Pour the water and oil into the bread pan. Reverse the order in which you add the wet and dry ingredients if necessary. Sprinkle both types of flour over the water. Add the milk powder. Place the sugar and salt in separate corners.

DILL, ONION AND RYE BREAD

These crusty loaves are perfect partners for your favourite sandwich filling, or can be served solo with pasta, salads and soups.

2 Make a shallow indent in the centre of the flour; add the yeast. Set the machine to the dough setting; use basic raisin dough setting (if available). Press Start.

3 Add the dried dill, dill seeds and dried onion as the machine beeps or during the last 5 minutes of kneading. Lightly oil a baking sheet.

4 When the dough cycle has finished, remove the dough from the machine and place it on a lightly floured surface. Knock it back (punch it down) gently.

5 Divide the dough into two equal pieces. Roll out each piece to a disc, about 2.5cm/1in thick. Fold one side to the centre and press gently with the rolling pin to seal. Repeat with the other side, then fold again along the centre line.

6 Press gently along the seam to seal it, then roll backwards and forwards to make a loaf about 30cm/12in in length. Make a second loaf with the remaining dough.

7 Place the loaves on the baking sheet, leaving plenty of room for rising. Cover with lightly oiled clear film (plastic wrap) and leave in a warm place for 30–45 minutes, or until almost doubled in size.

8 Remove the clear film and dust the tops of the loaves with flour. Using a sharp knife, make slashes along the top of both of them. Leave to stand for 10 minutes. Meanwhile, preheat the oven to 220°C/425°F/Gas 7.

9 Bake the loaves for 20 minutes, or until they sound hollow when tapped on the base. Transfer to a wire rack to cool.

SAGE AND SAUSAGE LOAF

When this tasty loaf is sliced, the sausage filling is revealed. It is perfect for picnics, parties or as a lunchtime meal with salad.

15ml/1 tbsp sunflower oil
200g/7oz spicy Mediterranean sausages
3 eggs
30ml/2 tbsp water
350g/12½oz/generous 3 cups
unbleached white bread flour
30ml/2 tbsp skimmed milk powder
(non fat dry milk)
10ml/2 tsp granulated sugar
7.5ml/1½ tsp salt
50g/2oz/¼ cup butter, melted
5ml/1 tsp easy bake (rapid-rise)
dried yeast
5ml/1 tsp dried sage
1 egg yolk, to glaze
15ml/1 tbsp water, to glaze

MAKES 1 LOAF

1 Heat the oil in a heavy frying pan. Add the sausages. Fry them over a medium heat for 7–10 minutes or until cooked, turning frequently. Cool.

2 Add the eggs and water to the bread pan. Reverse the order in which you add the wet and dry ingredients if necessary.

3 Sprinkle over the flour, covering the liquid. Add the milk powder. Place the sugar, salt and butter in separate corners of the pan. Make a small indent in the centre of the flour; add the yeast.

4 Set the bread machine to the dough setting; use basic raisin dough setting (if available). Press Start. Add the sage when the machine beeps or during the last 5 minutes of kneading. Lightly oil a 23 × 13cm/9 × 5in loaf tin (pan).

5 When the dough cycle has finished, place the dough on a floured surface. Knock back (punch down) gently. Roll into a rectangle 2.5cm/1in × 23cm/9in.

6 Place the sausages down the centre and roll the dough tightly around them. Place in the tin. Cover with lightly oiled clear film (plastic wrap) and leave to rise in a warm place for 30–45 minutes.

7 Preheat the oven to 190°C/375°F/Gas 5. To glaze, mix the yolk and water; brush over the bread and bake for 30–35 minutes, or until golden. Turn out on to a wire rack to cool.

Per bread Energy 928kcal/3931kJ; Protein 23.4g; Carbohydrate 184.3g, of which sugars 10.4g; Fat 16.1g, of which saturates 2.7g; Cholesterol 3mg; Calcium 338mg; Fibre 11.3g; Sodium 1019mg.
Per loaf Energy 2701kcal/11318kJ; Protein 76.5g; Carbohydrate 306.4g, of which sugars 23.5g; Fat 138.9g, of which saturates 59.1g; Cholesterol 786mg; Calcium 791mg; Fibre 11.9g; Sodium 4136mg.

Mixed Herb Cottage Loaf

300ml/10½fl oz/1¼ cups water
450g/1lb/4 cups unbleached white
bread flour, plus extra for dusting
7.5ml/1½ tsp granulated sugar
7.5ml/1½ tsp salt
7.5ml/1½ tsp easy bake (rapid-rise)
dried yeast
15ml/1 tbsp chopped fresh chives
10ml/2 tsp chopped fresh thyme
15ml/1 tbsp chopped fresh tarragon
30ml/2 tbsp chopped fresh parsley
5ml/1 tsp salt, to glaze
15ml/1 tbsp water, to glaze

MAKES 1 LOAF

There's something very satisfying about the shape of a cottage loaf, and the flavour of fresh herbs – chives, thyme, tarragon and parsley – adds to the appeal. This loaf makes the perfect centrepiece for the table, for guests to help themselves.

3 Set the bread machine to the dough setting; use basic raisin dough setting (if available). Press Start.

4 Add the chives, thyme, tarragon and parsley when the machine beeps to add extra ingredients, or during the final 5 minutes of kneading. Lightly flour two baking sheets.

5 When the dough cycle has finished, remove the dough from the machine. Place it on a surface that has been lightly floured. Knock the dough back (punch it down) gently and then divide it into two pieces, making one piece twice as large as the other.

6 Take each piece of dough in turn and shape it into a plump ball. Place the balls of dough on the prepared baking sheets and cover each with a lightly oiled mixing bowl.

7 Leave in a warm place for about 20–30 minutes, or until the dough has almost doubled in size.

8 Cut a cross, about 4cm/1½in across, in the top of the larger piece of dough. Brush the surface with water and place the smaller round on top.

9 Carefully press the handle of a wooden spoon through the centre of both pieces of dough. Cover the loaf with oiled clear film (plastic wrap) and leave it to rise for 10 minutes.

10 Meanwhile, preheat the oven to 220°C/425°F/Gas 7. Mix the salt and water for the glaze in a bowl, then brush the mixture over the top of the bread.

11 Using a sharp knife, make eight long slashes around the top of the bread and 12 small slashes around the base. Dust the top of the bread lightly with white bread flour.

12 Bake for 30–35 minutes, or until the bread is golden and sounds hollow when tapped on the base. Turn the loaf out on to a wire rack to cool.

VARIATION
Vary the combination of fresh herbs you use, according to availability and taste. You should aim for just under 75ml/5 tbsp in all, but use more pungent herbs sparingly, so they do not become too overpowering.

1 Pour the water into the bread machine pan. If the operating instructions for your bread machine specify that the yeast is to be placed in the pan first, then simply reverse the order in which you add the water and dry ingredients.

2 Sprinkle over the flour, ensuring that it covers the water completely. Add the granulated sugar and the salt, placing them in separate corners of the bread machine pan. Make a small indent in the centre of the flour (but do not go down as far as the water) and add the easy bake dried yeast.

Per loaf Energy 1581kcal/6722kJ; Protein 43.8g; Carbohydrate 358.8g, of which sugars 15.7g; Fat 6.5g, of which saturates 0.9g; Cholesterol 0mg; Calcium 734mg; Fibre 16.4g; Sodium 1995mg.

VEGETABLE BREADS

The subtle orange hue from pumpkin or carrot, the orangey-red crumb from tomatoes and the amazing colours of spinach or beetroot bread are only part of the story. Vegetables – grated, puréed, mashed or chopped – can be incorporated into bread doughs to provide wonderfully flavoured and coloured loaves. Almost any vegetable can be used, often in conjunction with spices, as in Carrot and Fennel Bread, or fresh herbs, as in Fresh Tomato and Basil Loaf.

15ml/1 tbsp olive oil
1 onion, chopped
115g/4oz fresh young spinach leaves
120ml/generous 4fl oz/½ cup water
1 egg
450g/1lb/4 cups unbleached white
bread flour
2.5ml/½ tsp freshly grated nutmeg
50g/2oz/⅔ cup freshly grated
Parmesan cheese
7.5ml/1½ tsp salt
5ml/1 tsp granulated sugar
7.5ml/1½ tsp easy bake (rapid-rise)
dried yeast
30ml/2 tbsp pine nuts

MAKES 1 LOAF

1 Heat the olive oil in a frying pan, add the chopped onion and sauté until a light golden colour. Add the spinach, stir well to combine and cover the pan very tightly. Remove from the heat and leave to stand for 5 minutes. Then stir again and leave the pan uncovered, to cool.

2 Tip the spinach mixture into the bread machine pan. Add the water and egg. If the instructions for your machine specify that the yeast is to be placed in the pan first, then simply reverse the order in which you add the liquid mixture and dry ingredients.

SPINACH AND PARMESAN BLOOMER

This pretty pale green loaf is flavoured with spinach, onion and Parmesan cheese. Whole pine nut kernels are dispersed through the dough of this perfect summertime bread.

3 Sprinkle over the white bread flour, ensuring that it completely covers the liquid mixture in the bread pan. Sprinkle the grated nutmeg and the Parmesan cheese over the flour.

4 Place the salt and sugar in separate corners of the bread pan. Make a small indent in the centre of the flour (but not down as far as the liquid) and add the easy bake dried yeast.

5 Set the bread machine to the dough setting; use basic raisin dough setting (if available). Press Start. Lightly flour two baking sheets.

6 Add the pine nuts to the dough when the machine beeps or during the last 5 minutes of the kneading process.

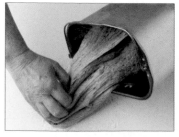

7 When the dough cycle has finished, remove the dough from the machine and place it on a surface that has been lightly floured. Gently knock the dough back (punch it down), then carefully roll it out to a rectangle about 2.5cm/1in thick.

8 Roll up the rectangle of dough from one long side to form a thick baton shape, with a square end.

9 Place the baton on the prepared baking sheet, seam side up, cover it with lightly oiled clear film (plastic wrap) and leave to rest for 15 minutes.

10 Turn the bread over and place on the second baking sheet. Plump up the dough by tucking the ends and sides under. Cover it with lightly oiled clear film again and leave it to rise in a warm place for 30 minutes. Meanwhile preheat the oven to 220°C/425°F/Gas 7.

11 Using a sharp knife, slash the top of the bloomer with five diagonal slashes. Bake it for 30–35 minutes, or until it is golden and the bottom sounds hollow when tapped. Turn the bread out on to a wire rack to cool.

VARIATION
Use Swiss chard instead of spinach, if you prefer. Choose young leaves, stripping them off the ribs. If fresh spinach is unavailable you could replace it with defrosted frozen spinach. Make sure any excess water has been squeezed out first, before placing in the bread machine. It may be worth holding a little of the water back and checking the dough as it starts to mix in step 5.

Per loaf Energy 2205kcal/9305kJ; Protein 76.4g; Carbohydrate 361.6g, of which sugars 17.2g; Fat 60.4g, of which saturates 15.7g; Cholesterol 240mg; Calcium 1475mg; Fibre 17.8g; Sodium 3739mg.

CHICKPEA AND PEPPERCORN BREAD

Bread may be a basic food, but it certainly isn't boring, as this exciting combination proves. Chickpeas help to keep the dough light, while pink and green peppercorns add colour and "explosions" of flavour.

SMALL
200ml/7fl oz/⅞ cup water
15ml/1 tbsp extra virgin olive oil
125g/4½oz/generous ⅔ cup canned
chickpeas
375g/13oz/3¼ cups unbleached white
bread flour
7.5ml/1½ tsp drained fresh pink
peppercorns in brine
7.5ml/1½ tsp drained fresh green
peppercorns in brine
15ml/1 tbsp skimmed milk powder
(non fat dry milk)
5ml/1 tsp salt
7.5ml/1½ tsp granulated sugar
5ml/1 tsp easy bake (rapid-rise)
dried yeast
milk, for brushing (optional)

MEDIUM
265ml/9½fl oz/1⅛ cup water
30ml/2 tbsp extra virgin olive oil
175g/6oz/1 cup canned chickpeas
500g/1lb 2oz/4½ cups unbleached
white bread flour
10ml/2 tsp drained fresh pink
peppercorns in brine
10ml/2 tsp drained fresh green
peppercorns in brine
22ml/1½ tbsp skimmed milk powder
7.5ml/1½ tsp salt
10ml/2 tsp granulated sugar
7.5ml/1½ tsp easy bake dried yeast
milk, for brushing (optional)

LARGE
315ml/11fl oz/1⅓ cups water
45ml/3 tbsp extra virgin olive oil
200g/7oz/1 cup canned chickpeas
600g/1lb 5oz/5¼ cups unbleached
white bread flour
10ml/2 tsp drained fresh pink
peppercorns in brine
15ml/1 tbsp drained fresh green
peppercorns in brine
30ml/2 tbsp skimmed milk powder
10ml/2 tsp salt
10ml/2 tsp granulated sugar
7.5ml/1½ tsp easy bake dried yeast
milk, for brushing (optional)

MAKES 1 LOAF

1 Pour the water and extra virgin olive oil into the bread machine pan. Add the well-drained chickpeas. If the instructions for your bread machine specify that the yeast is to be placed in the pan first, then simply reverse the order in which you add the liquid and dry ingredients to the bread pan.

2 Sprinkle over the flour, ensuring that it covers the ingredients already placed in the pan. Add the pink and green peppercorns and milk powder.

3 Place the salt and sugar in separate corners of the pan. Make a small indent in the centre of the flour (but not down as far as the liquid) and add the yeast.

4 Set the machine to white/basic. Select light crust, 500g for small; medium crust, large/750g for medium; or medium crust, 1kg/2lb for large. Press Start. Brush the top of the loaf with milk just before it starts to bake, if you like.

5 Remove the bread at the end of the baking cycle. Turn out on to a wire rack.

Per loaf Energy 1597kcal/6774kJ; Protein 47.6g; Carbohydrate 324.3g, of which sugars 19g; Fat 21.2g, of which saturates 3.7g; Cholesterol 6mg; Calcium 703mg; Fibre 16.8g; Sodium 2307mg.

CARROT AND FENNEL BREAD

The distinctive flavour of fennel is the perfect foil for the more subtle carrot taste in this unusual bread. It looks pretty when sliced, thanks to the attractive orange flecks of carrot.

SMALL
180ml/6½fl oz/generous ¾ cup water
15ml/1 tbsp sunflower oil
5ml/1 tsp clear honey
140g/5oz/1 cup grated carrot
375g/13oz/3¼ cups unbleached white
bread flour
15ml/1 tbsp skimmed milk powder
(non fat dry milk)
5ml/1 tsp fennel seeds
5ml/1 tsp salt
5ml/1 tsp easy bake (rapid-rise)
dried yeast

MEDIUM
210ml/7½fl oz/scant 1 cup water
30ml/2 tbsp sunflower oil
10ml/2 tsp clear honey
200g/7oz/scant 1½ cups grated carrot
500g/1lb 2oz/4½ cups unbleached
white bread flour
30ml/2 tbsp skimmed milk powder
7.5ml/1½ tsp fennel seeds
7.5ml/1½ tsp salt
5ml/1 tsp easy bake dried yeast

LARGE
260ml/9fl oz/1⅛ cups water
30ml/2 tbsp sunflower oil
15ml/1 tbsp clear honey
250g/9oz/scant 2 cups grated carrot
600g/1lb 5oz/5¼ cups unbleached
white bread flour
30ml/2 tbsp skimmed milk powder
10ml/2 tsp fennel seeds
10ml/2 tsp salt
7.5ml/1½ tsp easy bake dried yeast

MAKES 1 LOAF

3 Set the machine to white/basic, medium crust. Size: 500g for small, large/750g for medium or 1kg/2lb for large. Press Start.

4 Remove at the end of the baking cycle and turn out on to a wire rack to cool.

> **COOK'S TIP**
> When adding the grated carrot, sprinkle it over lightly and evenly, to avoid clumps.

1 Pour the water, oil and honey into the bread machine pan. Sprinkle over the grated carrot. If the instructions for your machine specify that the yeast is to be placed in the pan first, reverse the order in which you add the liquid and dry ingredients.

2 Sprinkle over the flour, ensuring that it covers the water. Add the milk powder and fennel seeds. Add the salt in one corner of the bread pan. Make a small indent in the centre of the flour (but not down as far as the liquid) and add the yeast.

Per loaf Energy 1510kcal/6402kJ; Protein 40.2g; Carbohydrate 315.3g, of which sugars 27.1g; Fat 18.6g, of which saturates 3.3g; Cholesterol 6mg; Calcium 690mg; Fibre 15g; Sodium 2069mg.

15ml/1 tbsp extra virgin olive oil
1 small onion, chopped
3 plum tomatoes, about 200g/7oz,
peeled, seeded and chopped
500g/1lb 2oz/4½ cups unbleached
white bread flour
2.5ml/½ tsp freshly ground black pepper
7.5ml/1½ tsp salt
10ml/2 tsp granulated sugar
5ml/1 tsp easy bake (rapid-rise) dried
yeast
15ml/1 tbsp chopped fresh basil

FOR THE GLAZE
1 egg yolk
15ml/1 tbsp water

MAKES 1 LOAF

1 Heat the extra virgin olive oil in a small frying pan or pan. Add the chopped onion and fry over a moderate heat for 3–4 minutes, until the onion is light golden in colour.

2 Add the plum tomatoes and cook for 2–3 minutes, until slightly softened. Drain through a sieve placed over a measuring jug (cup) or bowl, pressing the mixture gently with the back of a spoon to extract the juices.

3 Set the tomato and onion mixture aside. Make the cooking juices up to 280ml/10fl oz/1¼ cups with water (but see Variation). Set aside. When the liquid is cold, pour it into the bread machine pan. If the instructions for your machine specify that the yeast is to be placed in the pan first, reverse the order in which you add the liquid and dry ingredients.

FRESH TOMATO AND BASIL LOAF

Here are some classic Mediterranean flavours incorporated into a bread. Sweet plum tomatoes, onions and fresh basil complement each other in this attractively shaped loaf. Serve to accompany lunch either with butter or with individual bowls of best quality extra virgin olive oil for dipping.

4 Sprinkle over the flour, ensuring that it covers the tomato and onion liquid. Add the ground black pepper, then place the salt and sugar in separate corners of the bread machine pan.

5 Make a small indent in the centre of the flour (but not down as far as the liquid) and add the yeast.

6 Set the bread machine to the dough setting; use basic dough setting (if available). Press Start. Then lightly oil a 23 × 13cm/9 × 5in bread tin (pan).

7 When the dough cycle has finished, remove the dough from the bread machine and place it on a lightly floured surface. Knock it back (punch it down) gently.

8 Knead in the reserved tomato and onion mixture and the chopped fresh basil. You may need to add a little extra flour if the dough becomes too moist when you have incorporated the vegetable mixture.

9 Flatten the dough and shape it into a 2.5cm/1in thick rectangle. Fold the sides to the middle and press down the edge to seal. Make a hollow along the centre and fold in half again. Gently roll it into a loaf about 40cm/16in long.

10 Shape into an "S" shape and place in the prepared tin. Cover with oiled clear film (plastic wrap) and leave in a warm place for 30–45 minutes. Meanwhile preheat the oven to 200°C/400°F/Gas 6.

11 Make the glaze by mixing the egg yolk and water together. Remove the clear film and brush the glaze over the bread. Bake in the preheated oven for 35–40 minutes, or until golden.

VARIATION
To intensify the tomato flavour of the loaf, substitute 15ml/1 tbsp sun-dried tomato purée (paste) for 15ml/1 tbsp of water when you are topping up the cooking juices in step 3.

Per loaf Energy 1904kcal/8082kJ; Protein 49.6g; Carbohydrate 410.3g, of which sugars 27.9g; Fat 18.4g, of which saturates 2.7g; Cholesterol 0mg; Calcium 764mg; Fibre 19.1g; Sodium 40mg.

CHILLI BREAD

There's a warm surprise waiting for anyone who bites into this tasty wholemeal bread: fresh chillies are speckled throughout the crumb.

SMALL
15ml/1 tbsp sunflower oil
1–2 fresh chillies, chopped
210ml/7½fl oz/scant 1 cup water
250g/9oz/2¼ cups unbleached white bread flour
125g/4½oz/generous 1 cup wholemeal (whole-wheat) bread flour
7.5ml/1½ tsp salt
7.5ml/1½ tsp granulated sugar
25g/1oz/2 tbsp butter
5ml/1 tsp easy bake (rapid-rise) dried yeast

MEDIUM
15ml/1 tbsp sunflower oil
2–3 fresh chillies, chopped
320ml/11fl oz/generous 1⅓ cups water
350g/12oz/3 cups unbleached white bread flour
150g/5½oz/1⅓ cups wholemeal bread flour
10ml/2 tsp salt
10ml/2 tsp granulated sugar
25g/1oz/2 tbsp butter
5ml/1 tsp easy bake dried yeast

LARGE
30ml/2 tbsp sunflower oil
2–3 fresh chillies, chopped
375ml/13½fl oz/1½ cups + 1 tbsp water
425g/15oz/3¾ cups unbleached white bread flour
175g/6oz/generous 1½ cups wholemeal bread flour
10ml/2 tsp salt
10ml/2 tsp granulated sugar
25g/1oz/2 tbsp butter
7.5ml/1½ tsp easy bake dried yeast

MAKES 1 LOAF

VARIATION
Use chilli flakes instead of fresh chillies, if you prefer. You will need 10–20 ml/2–4 tsp, depending on the size of the loaf and how hot you wish to make the bread.

1 Heat the oil in a small frying pan. Add the chillies and sauté them over a moderate heat for 3–4 minutes until softened. Set aside to cool.

2 Tip the chillies and their oil into the bread machine pan. Pour in the water. Reverse the order in which you add the wet and dry ingredients if necessary.

3 Sprinkle over both types of flour, ensuring that the liquid is covered. Place the salt, sugar and butter in separate corners of the bread machine pan. Make an indent in the flour (but not down as far as the liquid) and add the yeast.

4 Set the machine to white/basic. Select light crust, 500g for small; medium crust, large/750g for medium; or medium crust, 1kg/2lb for large. Press Start.

5 Remove the bread at the end of the baking cycle. Turn out on to a wire rack.

Per loaf Energy 1525kcal/6445kJ; Protein 39.8g; Carbohydrate 274.2g, of which sugars 6.4g; Fat 37.5g, of which saturates 15.7g; Cholesterol 58mg; Calcium 405mg; Fibre 19g; Sodium 3147mg.

RYE BREAD WITH ROASTED VEGETABLES

The roasted peppers and onion add a sweetness to this loaf, which complements the rich, slightly sour flavour of the rye flour.

1 Chop the peppers and onion into 1cm/½ inch pieces.

2 Mix the peppers and onion with the oil and place in a shallow roasting pan. Roast them in a preheated oven at 210°C/425°F/Gas 7 for 20 minutes or until starting to brown at the edges. Cool for 10 minutes.

3 Add the water and vegetables, with any remaining oil to the bread pan. Add the oregano. If the instructions for your machine specify that the yeast is to be added first, reverse the order in which you add the liquid and the dry ingredients.

4 Sprinkle over the flours, ensuring they cover the water and vegetables. Add the salt and sugar in separate corners of the bread pan. Make a small indent in the centre of the flour (but not down as far as the liquid), and add the yeast.

5 Set the machine to white/basic, medium crust. Size: 500g for small, large/750g for medium or 1kg/2lb for large. Press Start.

6 Remove the bread at the end of the baking cycle. Turn out on to a wire rack.

SMALL
½ red (bell) pepper, seeded
½ onion
30ml/2 tbsp olive oil
225ml/8fl oz/scant 1 cup water
5ml/1 tsp dried oregano
100g/3½ oz/scant 1 cup rye flour
280g/10oz/2½ cups unbleached white bread flour
5ml/1 tsp salt
10ml/2 tsp sugar
5ml/1 tsp easy bake (rapid-rise) dried yeast

MEDIUM
½ red pepper, seeded
½ yellow pepper, seeded
1 small onion
45ml/3 tbsp olive oil
280ml/10fl oz/1 cup + 3 tbsp water
5ml/1 tsp dried oregano
150g/5½ oz/1⅓ cups rye flour
350g/12½oz/3 cups unbleached white bread flour
7.5ml/1½ tsp salt
15ml/1 tbsp sugar
6.5ml/1⅓ tsp easy bake dried yeast

LARGE
1 small red pepper, seeded
1 small yellow pepper, seeded
1 onion
45ml/3 tbsp olive oil
310ml/11fl oz/scant 1⅓ cups water
7.5ml/1½ tsp dried oregano
175g/6oz/generous 1½ cups rye flour
425g/15oz/3¾ cups unbleached white bread flour
10ml/2 tsp salt
15ml/1 tbsp sugar
7.5ml/1½ tsp easy bake dried yeast

MAKES 1 LOAF

COOK'S TIP
Instead of roasting the peppers and onions, you could sauté them with the oil, in a frying pan, for 5–6 minutes, or until starting to brown.

Per loaf Energy 1581kcal/6693kJ; Protein 36.3g; Carbohydrate 315.1g, of which sugars 24.1g; Fat 28.1g, of which saturates 4g; Cholesterol 0mg; Calcium 453mg; Fibre 22.8g; Sodium 1981mg.

SWEET POTATO BREAD

Adding sweet potato to the dough creates a loaf with a rich golden crust and the crumb is beautifully moist. Make sure you use the deep yellow sweet potatoes, in preference to the white variety of sweet potatoes, to give the bread a lovely colour.

SMALL

175g/6oz sweet potatoes, peeled
190ml/6¾fl oz/scant ⅞ cup water
350g/12oz/3 cups unbleached white bread flour
30ml/2 tbsp rolled oats
22ml/1½ tbsp skimmed milk powder (non fat dry milk)
5ml/1 tsp salt
15ml/1 tbsp muscovado (molasses) sugar
25g/1oz/2 tbsp butter
5ml/1 tsp easy bake (rapid-rise) dried yeast
FOR THE TOPPING
10ml/2 tsp water
5ml/1 tsp rolled oats
5ml/1 tsp wheat grain

MEDIUM

225g/8oz sweet potatoes, peeled
210ml/7½fl oz/scant 1 cup water
500g/1lb 2oz/4½ cups unbleached white bread flour
45ml/3 tbsp rolled oats
30ml/2 tbsp skimmed milk powder
7.5ml/1½ tsp salt
22ml/1½ tbsp muscovado sugar
40g/1½oz/3 tbsp butter
7.5ml/1½ tsp easy bake dried yeast
FOR THE TOPPING
15ml/1 tbsp water
10ml/2 tsp rolled oats
10ml/2 tsp wheat grain

LARGE

310g/11oz sweet potatoes, peeled
285ml/10fl oz/scant 1¼ cups water
600g/1lb 5oz/5¼ cups unbleached white bread flour
45ml/3 tbsp rolled oats
30ml/2 tbsp skimmed milk powder
7.5ml/1½ tsp salt
15ml/1 tbsp muscovado sugar
40g/1½oz/3 tbsp butter
7.5ml/1½ tsp easy bake dried yeast
FOR THE TOPPING
15ml/1 tbsp water
15ml/1 tbsp rolled oats
10ml/2 tsp wheat grain

MAKES 1 LOAF

1 Cook the sweet potato in plenty of boiling water for 40 minutes or until very tender. Drain, and when cool enough to handle, peel off the skin. Place the sweet potato in a large bowl and mash well, but do not add any butter or milk.

2 Pour the water into the bread machine pan. However, if the instructions for your bread machine specify that the yeast is to be placed in the bread pan first, simply reverse the order in which you add the liquid and dry ingredients.

VARIATION

This bread is a good opportunity to use up any leftover sweet potato. If the potato has been mashed with milk and butter you may need to reduce the quantity of liquid a little. Use the following quantities of cooked, mashed sweet potatoes:
small machine: 125g/4½oz/1½ cups
medium machine: 175g/6oz/2 cups
large machine: 200g/7oz/2⅓ cups

COOK'S TIP

Rolled oats add a chewy texture and nutty taste to this loaf of bread. Make sure you use the traditional old-fashioned rolled oats, rather than "quick cook" oats.

3 Sprinkle the white bread flour, rolled oats and skimmed milk powder over the water, covering it completely. Weigh or measure the cooked sweet potatoes to ensure the quantity matches the amount given in the variation. Then add the potatoes to the bread pan.

4 Place the salt, sugar and butter in three separate corners of the bread machine pan. Make a shallow indent in the flour (but not down as far as the liquid underneath) and add the easy bake dried yeast.

5 Set the bread machine to the white/ basic setting, medium crust. Size: 500g for small, large/750g for medium or 1kg/2lb for large. Press Start.

6 When the rising cycle is almost complete, just before the bread begins to bake, add the topping: brush the top of the loaf with the water and sprinkle the rolled oats and wheat grain over the top of the bread.

7 Remove the bread at the end of the baking cycle. Turn out on to a wire rack.

Per loaf Energy 1816kcal/7695kJ; Protein 44.1g; Carbohydrate 362.7g, of which sugars 35.9g; Fat 31.1g, of which saturates 15.4g; Cholesterol 63mg; Calcium 689mg; Fibre 18.1g; Sodium 2304mg.

BUBBLE CORN BREAD

85ml/3fl oz/⅜ cup milk
120ml/4fl oz/½ cup water
1 egg
*400g/14oz/3½ cups unbleached white
bread flour*
100g/3½oz/scant 1 cup yellow corn meal
5ml/1 tsp granulated sugar
5ml/1 tsp salt
*7.5ml/1½ tsp easy bake (rapid-rise)
dried yeast*
15ml/1 tbsp chopped fresh green chilli
*115g/4oz/⅔ cup drained canned
corn kernels*
25g/1oz/2 tbsp butter

MAKES 1 LOAF

1 Pour the milk and water into the
bread pan. Add the egg. Reverse the
order in which you add the liquid and
dry ingredients, if necessary. Sprinkle
over the flour and corn meal, covering
the liquid. Add the sugar and salt in
separate corners. Make a small indent in
the flour; add the yeast.

*This recipe brings together two traditional American breads – corn bread and
bubble loaf. It has the flavour of corn and is spiked with hot chilli. Chunks or
"bubbles" of bread can easily be pulled from the bread for easy eating.*

2 Set the bread machine to the dough
setting; use basic raisin dough setting
(if available). Press Start. Add the chilli
and corn when the machine beeps or
during the last 5 minutes of kneading.
Lightly oil a baking sheet.

3 When the dough cycle has finished,
remove the dough and gently knock it
back (punch it down), then cut it into
20 equal pieces. Shape into balls.

4 Arrange half of the dough balls in
the base of a 22cm/8½in non-stick
springform cake tin (pan), spacing
them slightly apart. Place the remaining
balls of dough on top so that they cover
the spaces.

5 Cover the tin with oiled clear film
(plastic wrap) and leave to rise in a
warm place for about 30–45 minutes,
or until the dough has almost doubled
in bulk. Meanwhile preheat the oven to
200°C/400°F/Gas 6.

6 Melt the butter in a small pan. Drizzle
it over the top of the risen loaf.

7 Bake the bread for 30–35 minutes,
or until golden and well risen. Turn the
bread out on to a wire rack to cool.
Serve warm or cold.

MIXED PEPPER BREAD

½ red (bell) pepper, cored and seeded
½ green (bell) pepper, cored and seeded
½ yellow (bell) pepper, cored and seeded
200ml/7fl oz/⅞ cup milk
120ml/generous 4fl oz/½ cup water
*500g/1lb 2oz/4½ cups unbleached
white bread flour*
10ml/2 tsp granulated sugar
7.5ml/1½ tsp salt
*7.5ml/1½ tsp easy bake (rapid-rise)
dried yeast*
milk, for brushing
5ml/1 tsp cumin seeds

MAKES 1 LOAF

1 Cut the peppers into fine dice. Pour
the milk and water into the bread pan.
Reverse the order in which you add the
wet and dry ingredients if necessary.
Sprinkle over the flour, ensuring that it
covers the liquid. Add the sugar and salt
in separate corners of the pan.

*Colourful and full of flavour, this bread looks good when sliced, as the pretty
pepper studs can be seen to advantage. Add orange pepper too, if you like.*

2 Make a small indent in the centre of
the flour and add the yeast. Set the
bread machine to the dough setting;
use basic raisin dough setting (if
available). Press Start. Lightly oil a
baking sheet.

3 Add the mixed peppers when the
machine beeps or during the last
5 minutes of kneading.

4 When the dough cycle has finished,
remove the dough from the machine and
place it on a lightly floured surface.
Gently knock it back (punch it down)
and shape it into a plump ball. Roll
gently into an oval. Place on the
prepared baking sheet, cover with oiled
clear film (plastic wrap) and leave for
30–45 minutes, or until doubled in bulk.

5 Preheat the oven to 200°C/400°F/
Gas 6. Brush the loaf top with the milk
and sprinkle with the cumin seeds. Use
a sharp knife to cut a lengthways slash.

6 Bake for 35–40 minutes, or until the
bread is golden and the bottom sounds
hollow when tapped. Turn the bread out
on to a wire rack to cool.

Per corn bread Energy 2074kcal/8760kJ; Protein 60g; Carbohydrate 394.7g, of which sugars 16.1g; Fat 36.5g, of which saturates 16.7g; Cholesterol 253mg; Calcium 714mg; Fibre 16.3g; Sodium 3594mg.
Per pepper bread Energy 1994kcal/8470kJ; Protein 60.4g; Carbohydrate 436.3g, of which sugars 54.3g; Fat 13g, of which saturates 4.3g; Cholesterol 18mg; Calcium 1093mg; Fibre 21.1g; Sodium 3142mg.

POTATO AND SAFFRON BREAD

A dough that includes potato produces a moist loaf with a springy texture and good keeping qualities. Saffron adds an aromatic flavour and rich golden colour to this bread.

1 large potato, about 225g/8oz, peeled
5ml/1 tsp saffron threads
1 egg
450g/1lb/4 cups unbleached white bread flour
30ml/2 tbsp skimmed milk powder (non fat dry milk)
25g/1oz/2 tbsp butter
15ml/1 tbsp clear honey
7.5ml/1½ tsp salt
7.5ml/1½ tsp easy bake (rapid-rise) dried yeast

MAKES 1 LOAF

COOK'S TIP
If you have time, soak the saffron for 3–4 hours. The longer it soaks, the better the colour and flavour will be.

1 Place the potato in a pan of boiling water, reduce the heat and simmer until tender. Drain the potato, reserving 200ml/7fl oz/⅞ cup of the cooking water. Add the saffron to the hot water; leave to stand for 30 minutes. Mash the potato (without adding butter or milk) and leave to cool.

2 Add the saffron water to the bread pan. Add the mashed potato and the egg. Reverse the order in which you add the wet and dry ingredients if necessary.

3 Sprinkle over the flour, ensuring that it covers the ingredients already placed in the pan. Spoon over the milk powder. Add the butter, honey and salt in separate corners of the bread pan. Make a small indent in the centre of the flour (but not down as far as the liquid) and add the yeast.

4 Set the bread machine to the dough setting; use basic dough setting (if available). Press Start. Lightly flour a baking sheet.

5 When the dough cycle has finished, remove the dough from the machine and place on a lightly floured surface. Gently knock it back (punch it down).

6 Shape the dough into a plump ball. Place on the baking sheet, cover with oiled clear film (plastic wrap) and leave to rise for 30–45 minutes. Meanwhile preheat the oven to 200°C/400°F/Gas 6.

7 Slash the top of the loaf with three or four diagonal cuts, then rotate and repeat to make a criss-cross effect.

8 Bake the bread for 35–40 minutes, or until the bottom sounds hollow when tapped. Turn out on to a wire rack.

CARAMELIZED ONION BREAD

The unmistakable, mouthwatering flavour of golden fried onions is captured in this coburg-shaped bread. Serve with soup, cheeses or salad.

50g/2oz/¼ cup butter
2 onions, chopped
280ml/10fl oz/1¼ cups water
15ml/1 tbsp clear honey
450g/1lb/4 cups unbleached white bread flour
7.5ml/1½ tsp salt
2.5ml/½ tsp freshly ground black pepper
7.5ml/1½ tsp easy bake (rapid-rise) dried yeast

MAKES 1 LOAF

1 Melt the butter in a frying pan and sauté the onions over a low heat until golden. Remove the pan from the heat and let the onions cool slightly. Place a sieve over the bread machine pan, then tip the contents of the frying pan into it, so that the juices fall into the pan. Set the onions aside to cool completely.

2 Add the water and honey to the bread pan. Reverse the order in which you add the wet and dry ingredients if necessary. Sprinkle over the flour, covering the liquid. Place the salt and pepper in separate corners. Make a shallow indent in the centre of the flour; add the yeast.

3 Set the bread machine to the dough setting; use basic raisin dough setting (if available). Press Start. Add the onions when the machine beeps or in the last 5 minutes of kneading. Lightly flour a baking sheet.

4 When the cycle has finished, remove the dough from the bread pan and place on a lightly floured surface.

5 Knock back (punch down), then shape into a ball. Place on the baking sheet and cover with oiled clear film (plastic wrap). Leave to rise for 45 minutes. Preheat the oven to 200°C/400°F/Gas 6. Slash a 1cm/½in deep cross in the top of the loaf. Bake for 35–40 minutes. Cool on a wire rack.

Per loaf Energy 2039kcal/8639kJ; Protein 55.9g; Carbohydrate 402.3g, of which sugars 26.1g; Fat 34.2g, of which saturates 17.2g; Cholesterol 254mg; Calcium 797mg; Fibre 16.2g; Sodium 3261mg.
Per loaf Energy 2054kcal/8675kJ; Protein 46.2g; Carbohydrate 384.8g, of which sugars 35g; Fat 47.3g, of which saturates 27.9g; Cholesterol 115mg; Calcium 714mg; Fibre 18.1g; Sodium 3347mg.

ROLLS, BUNS AND PASTRIES

These hand-shaped delights include French Ham and Cheese Croissants, Swedish Saffron Braids and fruit-filled Danish Pastries. Chelsea Buns, Yorkshire Teacakes and Pikelets are British classics, while Parker House Rolls and Doughnuts are traditional American offerings. Savoury rolls using mixed grains and onions, herb and ricotta-flavoured knots or Cashew and Olive Scrolls are just a few of the characterful small breads in this section to enjoy.

CALAS

These tasty morsels are a Creole speciality, made from a rice-based yeast dough which is then deep-fried. They are delicious served warm with coffee or as a breakfast treat.

50g/2oz/generous ⅓ cup pudding rice
280ml/10fl oz/1¼ cups milk
140ml/5fl oz/⅔ cup water
2 eggs
125g/4½oz/generous 1 cup unbleached white bread flour
5ml/1 tsp grated lemon rind
2.5ml/½ tsp ground ginger
2.5ml/½ tsp freshly grated nutmeg
50g/2oz/¼ cup caster (superfine) sugar
1.5ml/¼ tsp salt
5ml/1 tsp easy bake (rapid-rise) dried yeast
oil, for deep-frying
icing (confectioners') sugar, for dusting

MAKES ABOUT 25

1 Place the rice, milk and water in a pan and slowly bring to the boil. Lower the heat, cover and simmer for 20 minutes, stirring occasionally, until the rice is soft and the liquid absorbed. Leave to cool.

2 Add the eggs to the bread machine pan. Reverse the order in which you add the wet and dry ingredients if necessary.

3 Add the rice. Sprinkle over the flour, then the lemon rind, ginger and nutmeg. Add the sugar and salt, placing them in separate corners of the bread pan. Make a small indent in the centre of the flour (but not down as far as the liquid) and add the yeast.

4 Set the bread machine to the dough setting; use basic dough setting (if available). Press Start. When the dough cycle has finished, lift out the pan containing the batter from the machine.

5 Preheat the oven to 140°C/275°F/Gas 1. Heat the oil for deep-frying to 180°C/350°F or until a cube of dried bread, added to the oil, turns golden in 45 seconds. Add tablespoons of batter a few at a time and fry for 3–4 minutes, turning occasionally, until golden.

6 Use a slotted spoon to remove the calas from the oil and drain on kitchen paper. Keep them warm in the oven while you cook the remainder. When all the calas have been cooked, dust them with icing sugar and serve warm.

COOK'S TIP
If you are using a large bread machine it is a good idea to make double the quantity of dough. If you use the quantities listed here, it is important to check that all the flour is thoroughly mixed with the liquid.

AMERICAN BREAKFAST PANCAKES

These thick, succulent breakfast pancakes are often served with a sauce made from wild cranberries, also known as lingonberries. They are equally delicious served with maple syrup and with strips of crispy bacon.

2 eggs
280ml/10fl oz/1¼ cups milk
225g/8oz/2 cups unbleached white bread flour
5ml/1 tsp salt
15ml/1 tbsp caster (superfine) sugar
15g/½oz/1 tbsp butter, melted
5ml/1 tsp easy bake (rapid-rise) dried yeast
maple syrup or wild cranberry sauce, to serve

MAKES ABOUT 15

1 Separate 1 egg and set the white aside. Place the yolk in the machine pan and add the whole egg and the milk. If the instructions for your machine specify that the yeast is to be placed in the pan first, reverse the order in which you add the liquid and dry ingredients.

2 Sprinkle over the flour, ensuring that it covers the liquid. Add the salt, sugar and butter, placing them in separate corners of the bread pan. Make a small indent in the centre of the flour (but not down as far as the liquid) and add the easy bake dried yeast.

3 Set the bread machine to the dough setting; use basic dough setting (if available). Press Start.

4 When the dough cycle has finished pour the batter into a large measuring jug. Whisk the reserved egg white; fold it into the batter. Preheat the oven to 140°C/275°F/Gas 1.

5 Lightly oil a large heavy frying pan or griddle and place over a medium heat. Add about 45ml/3 tbsp batter, letting it spread out to form a pancake about 10cm/4in wide. If room, make a second pancake alongside the first.

6 Cook each pancake until the surface begins to dry out, then turn over using a fish slice or spatula and cook the other side for about 1 minute, or until golden.

7 Stack the pancakes between sheets of baking parchment on a warm plate and keep them warm in the oven while you cook the rest of the batter. Serve the pancakes with the syrup or sauce.

Per cala Energy 80kcal/335kJ; Protein 1.6g; Carbohydrate 8.3g, of which sugars 2.7g; Fat 4.8g, of which saturates 0.7g; Cholesterol 16mg; Calcium 25mg; Fibre 0.2g; Sodium 12mg.
Per pancake Energy 81kcal/342kJ; Protein 2.9g; Carbohydrate 13.6g, of which sugars 2.2g; Fat 2.1g, of which saturates 1g; Cholesterol 29mg; Calcium 48mg; Fibre 0.5g; Sodium 159mg.

WHOLEMEAL ENGLISH MUFFINS

350ml/12fl oz/1½ cups milk
225g/8oz/2 cups unbleached white
bread flour
225g/8oz/2 cups stoneground
wholemeal (whole-wheat) bread flour
5ml/1 tsp caster (superfine) sugar
7.5ml/1½ tsp salt
15g/½oz/1 tbsp butter
7.5ml/1½ tsp easy bake (rapid-rise)
dried yeast
rice flour or fine semolina, for dusting

MAKES 9

COOK'S TIP
If you don't have a griddle, cook the muffins in a heavy frying pan. It is important that they cook slowly.

After a long walk on a wintry afternoon, come home to warm muffins, carefully torn apart and spread thickly with butter.

1 Pour the milk into the bread machine pan. If the instructions for your bread machine specify that the yeast is to be placed in the pan first, then reverse the order in which you add the liquid and dry ingredients.

2 Sprinkle over each type of flour in turn, making sure that the milk is completely covered. Add the caster sugar, salt and butter, placing each of them in separate corners of the bread pan. Then make a small indent in the centre of the flour (but do not go down as far as the liquid underneath) and add the easy bake dried yeast.

3 Set the machine to the dough setting; use basic dough setting (if available). Press Start. Sprinkle a baking sheet with rice flour or semolina.

4 When the dough cycle has finished, place the dough on a floured surface. Knock it back (punch it down) gently. Roll out the dough until it is about 1cm/½in thick.

5 Using a floured 7.5cm/3in plain cutter, cut out nine muffins. If you like, you can re-roll the trimmings, knead them together and let the dough rest for a few minutes before rolling it out again and cutting out an extra muffin or two.

6 Place the muffins on the baking sheet. Dust with rice flour or semolina. Cover with oiled clear film (plastic wrap) and leave in a warm place for 20 minutes, or until almost doubled in size.

7 Heat a griddle over a medium heat. You should not need any oil if the griddle is well seasoned; if not, add the merest trace of oil. Cook the muffins slowly, three at a time, for about 7 minutes on each side. Serve warm.

Per muffin Energy 235kcal/997kJ; Protein 7.4g; Carbohydrate 48.2g, of which sugars 3.2g; Fat 2.8g, of which saturates 0.7g; Cholesterol 2mg; Calcium 121mg; Fibre 2.5g; Sodium 351mg.

PIKELETS

Pikelets are similar to crumpets, and have the same distinctive holey tops, but crumpets are thicker and are cooked inside a ring, which supports them while they set. Serve pikelets warm with preserves and butter. They are also excellent with soft cheese and smoked salmon.

140ml/5fl oz/⅝ cup water
140ml/5fl oz/⅝ cup milk
15ml/1 tbsp sunflower oil
225g/8oz/2 cups unbleached white bread flour
5ml/1 tsp salt
5ml/1 tsp caster (superfine) sugar
7.5ml/1½ tsp easy bake (rapid-rise) dried yeast
1.5ml/¼ tsp bicarbonate of soda (baking soda)
60ml/4 tbsp water
1 egg white
MAKES ABOUT 20

5 Dissolve the bicarbonate of soda in the remaining water and stir it into the batter. Whisk the egg white in a grease-free bowl until it forms soft peaks, then fold it into the batter.

6 Cover the batter mixture with oiled clear film (plastic wrap) and leave the mixture to rise for 30 minutes. Preheat the oven to 140°C/275°F/Gas 1.

7 Lightly grease a griddle and heat it gently. When it is hot, pour generous tablespoonfuls of batter on to the hot surface, spacing them well apart to allow for spreading, and cook until the tops no longer appear wet and have acquired lots of tiny holes.

8 When the base of each pikelet is golden, turn it over, using a spatula or palette knife, and cook until pale golden.

9 Remove the cooked pikelets and layer them in a folded dishtowel. Place in the oven to keep them warm while you cook the remaining batter. Serve the pikelets immediately.

1 Pour the water into the bread machine pan, then add the milk and sunflower oil. If the instructions for your bread machine specify that the yeast is to be placed in the pan first, reverse the order in which you add the liquid and dry ingredients to the pan.

2 Sprinkle over the white bread flour, ensuring that it covers the liquid completely. Add the salt and caster sugar, placing them in separate corners of the bread pan. Make a shallow indent in the centre of the flour (but not down as far as the liquid) and add the easy bake dried yeast.

3 Set the breadmaking machine to the dough setting; use basic dough setting (if available). Press Start. Then lightly oil two baking sheets.

4 When the dough cycle has finished, carefully lift the bread pan out of the machine and pour the batter for the pikelets into a large mixing bowl.

Per pikelet Energy 48kcal/204kJ; Protein 1.4g; Carbohydrate 9.4g, of which sugars 0.8g; Fat 0.8g, of which saturates 0.2g; Cholesterol 0mg; Calcium 24mg; Fibre 0.4g; Sodium 106mg.

PETITS PAINS AU CHOCOLAT

125ml/4½fl oz/generous ½ cup water
250g/9oz/2¼ cups unbleached white
bread flour
30ml/2 tbsp skimmed milk powder
(non fat dry milk)
15ml/1 tbsp caster (superfine) sugar
2.5ml/½ tsp salt
140g/5oz/⅔ cup butter, softened
7.5ml/1½ tsp easy bake (rapid-rise)
dried yeast
225g/8oz plain (semisweet) chocolate,
broken into pieces

FOR THE GLAZE
1 egg yolk
15ml/1 tbsp milk

MAKES 9

A freshly baked petit pain au chocolat is almost impossible to resist, with its buttery, flaky yet crisp pastry concealing a delectable chocolate filling. For a special finish, drizzle melted chocolate over the tops of the freshly baked and cooked pastries.

1 Pour the water into the machine pan. If the instructions for your machine specify that the yeast is to be placed in the pan first, then reverse the order in which you add liquid and dry ingredients.

2 Sprinkle over the flour, then the skimmed milk powder, ensuring that the water is completely covered.

3 Add the caster sugar, salt and 25g/1oz/ 2 tbsp of the softened butter, placing them in separate corners of the bread pan. Make a small indent in the centre of the flour (but not down as far as the liquid) and add the yeast.

4 Set the breadmaking machine to the dough setting; use basic dough setting (if available). Press Start. Meanwhile shape the remaining softened butter into an oblong-shaped block, about 2cm/¾in thick.

5 Lightly grease two baking sheets. When the dough cycle has finished, place the dough on a floured surface. Knock back (punch down) and shape into a ball. Cut a cross halfway through the top of the dough.

6 Roll out around the cross, leaving a risen centre. Place the butter in the centre. Fold the rolled dough over the butter to enclose; seal the edges.

7 Roll to a rectangle 2cm/¾in thick, twice as long as wide. Fold the bottom third up and the top down; seal the edges with a rolling pin. Wrap in lightly oiled clear film (plastic wrap). Place in the refrigerator and chill for 20 minutes.

8 Do the same again twice more, giving a quarter turn and chilling each time. Chill again for 30 minutes.

9 Roll out the dough to a rectangle measuring 52 × 30cm/21 × 12in. Using a sharp knife, cut the dough into three strips lengthways and widthways to make nine 18 × 10cm/7 × 4in rectangles.

10 Divide the chocolate among the nine dough rectangles, placing the pieces lengthways at one short end.

11 Mix the egg yolk and milk for the glaze together. Brush the mixture over the edges of the dough.

12 Roll up each piece of dough to completely enclose the chocolate, then press the edges together to seal.

13 Place the pastries seam side down on the prepared baking sheets. Cover with oiled clear film and leave to rise in a warm place for about 30 minutes or until doubled in size.

14 Meanwhile, preheat the oven to 200°C/400°F/Gas 6. Brush the pastries with the remaining glaze and bake for about 15 minutes, or until golden. Turn out on to a wire rack to cool just slightly and serve warm.

VARIATION
Fill this flaky yeast pastry with a variety of sweet and savoury fillings. Try chopped nuts, tossed with a little brown sugar and cinnamon or, for a savoury filling, thin strips of cheese, wrapped in ham or mixed with chopped cooked bacon.

Per pain au chocolat Energy 352kcal/1473kJ; Protein 4.2g; Carbohydrate 40.1g, of which sugars 17.6g; Fat 20.6g, of which saturates 12.8g; Cholesterol 39mg; Calcium 65mg; Fibre 0.9g; Sodium 126mg.

50g/2oz/¼ cup butter
1 large onion, finely chopped
280ml/10fl oz/1¼ cups water
280g/10oz/2½ cups unbleached white
bread flour
115g/4oz/1 cup Granary
(whole-wheat) bread flour
25g/1oz/¼ cup oat bran
10ml/2 tsp salt
10ml/2 tsp clear honey
7.5ml/1½ tsp easy bake (rapid-rise)
dried yeast
corn meal, for dusting
30ml/2 tbsp millet grain
15ml/1 tbsp coarse oatmeal
15ml/1 tbsp sunflower seeds
MAKES 12

1 Melt half the butter in a frying pan. Add the chopped onions and sauté for 8–10 minutes, or until softened and lightly browned. Set aside to cool.

2 Pour the water into the machine pan. If the instructions for your machine state the yeast is to be placed in the pan first, reverse the order in which you add the wet and dry ingredients.

3 Sprinkle over the white bread flour, Granary flour and oat bran, ensuring that the water is completely covered. Add the salt, honey and remaining butter, placing them in separate corners of the bread pan. Make a small indent in the centre of the flour (but not down as far as the liquid) and add the yeast.

4 Set the bread machine to the dough setting; use basic raisin dough setting (if available). Press Start. Lightly oil two baking sheets and sprinkle them with corn meal.

MIXED GRAIN ONION ROLLS

These crunchy rolls, flavoured with golden onions, are perfect for snacks, sandwiches or to serve with soup.

5 Add the millet grain, coarse oatmeal, sunflower seeds and cooked onion when the machine beeps. If your machine does not have this facility add these ingredients 5 minutes before the end of the kneading cycle.

6 When the dough cycle has finished, remove the dough from the bread machine and place it on a surface that has been lightly floured. Knock the dough back (punch it down) gently, then divide it into 12 equal pieces.

> **VARIATION**
> If time is short you can omit the cutting in step 9 and cook as round shaped rolls.

7 Shape each piece into a ball, making sure that the tops are smooth. Flatten them slightly with the palm of your hand or a small rolling pin. Place the rolls on the prepared baking sheets and dust them with more corn meal.

8 Cover the rolls with oiled clear film (plastic wrap) and leave them in a warm place for 30–45 minutes, or until doubled in size. Meanwhile, preheat the oven to 200°C/400°F/Gas 6.

9 Using a pair of lightly floured sharp scissors snip each roll in five places, cutting inwards from the edge, almost to the centre. Bake for 18–20 minutes, or until the rolls are golden. Turn them out on to a wire rack to cool.

Per roll Energy 178kcal/750kJ; Protein 4.8g; Carbohydrate 28.7g, of which sugars 3.2g; Fat 5.7g, of which saturates 2.5g; Cholesterol 10mg; Calcium 51mg; Fibre 3g; Sodium 362mg.

PARKER HOUSE ROLLS

These stylish rolls were first made in a hotel in Boston, after which they are named. They are delicious served warm.

1 Pour the milk and egg into the bread machine pan. If the instructions for your bread machine specify that the yeast is to be placed in the pan first, reverse the order in which you add the liquid and dry ingredients.

2 Sprinkle over the flour, ensuring that it covers the liquid. Add the sugar, salt and 25g/1oz/2 tbsp of the melted butter, placing them in separate corners of the bread pan. Make a small indent in the centre of the flour (but do not go down as far as the liquid underneath) and add the easy bake dried yeast.

3 Set the machine to the dough setting; use basic dough setting (if available). Press Start. Lightly oil two baking sheets.

4 When the dough cycle has finished, remove the dough from the machine, place it on a lightly floured surface and knock it back (punch it down) gently.

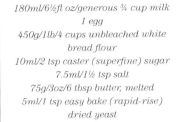

180ml/6½fl oz/generous ¾ cup milk
1 egg
450g/1lb/4 cups unbleached white bread flour
10ml/2 tsp caster (superfine) sugar
7.5ml/1½ tsp salt
75g/3oz/6 tbsp butter, melted
5ml/1 tsp easy bake (rapid-rise) dried yeast

MAKES 10 ROLLS

COOK'S TIP
If you do not have a small rolling pin – and can't borrow one from a child's cooking set – use a small clean bottle or the rounded handle of a knife to shape the rolls.

5 Roll out to a 1cm/½in thickness. Use a 7.5cm/3in cutter to make ten rounds, then use a small rolling pin to roll or flatten each across the centre in one direction, to create a valley about 5mm/¼in thick.

6 Brush with a little remaining melted butter to within 1cm/½in of the edge. Fold over, ensuring the top piece of dough overlaps the bottom. Press down lightly on the folded edge.

7 Place the rolls on the prepared baking sheets, just overlapping, brush them with more melted butter and cover with oiled clear film (plastic wrap). Leave in a warm place for 30 minutes, until doubled in size.

8 Preheat the oven to 200°C/400°F/ Gas 6. Bake the rolls for 15–18 minutes, or until they are golden. Brush the hot rolls with the last of the melted butter and transfer them to a wire rack to cool.

Per roll Energy 221kcal/932kJ; Protein 4.9g; Carbohydrate 36.9g, of which sugars 2.6g; Fat 7g, of which saturates 4.3g; Cholesterol 18mg; Calcium 86mg; Fibre 1 4g; Sodium 362mg.

BRIDGE ROLLS

Milk and egg flavour these small, soft-textured finger rolls. Use them for canapés or serve them with soup.

1 egg
100ml/3½ fl oz/7 tbsp milk
225g/8oz/2 cups unbleached white bread flour
5ml/1 tsp salt
2.5ml/½ tsp caster (superfine) sugar
50g/2oz/¼ cup butter
5ml/1 tsp easy bake (rapid-rise) dried yeast
30ml/2 tbsp milk, for glazing (optional)

MAKES 12

COOK'S TIP
Make double the quantity and freeze the surplus. You will only need the same amount of yeast.

1 Pour the egg and milk into the bread pan. If necessary for your machine, place the dry ingredients in the pan before the liquid.

2 Sprinkle over the flour, ensuring that it covers the liquid. Add the salt, sugar and butter, placing them in separate corners of the bread machine pan. Then make a small indent in the centre of the flour (but do not go down as far as the liquid) and add the easy bake dried yeast.

3 Set the bread machine to the dough setting; use basic dough setting (if available). Press Start. Lightly oil two baking sheets.

4 When the dough cycle has finished, remove the dough from the machine and place it on a lightly floured surface. Knock it back (punch it down) gently, then divide it into 12 pieces and cover with a piece of oiled clear film (plastic wrap).

5 Take one piece of dough, leaving the rest covered, and shape it on the floured surface into a tapered long roll. Repeat with the remaining dough until you have 12 evenly shaped rolls.

6 Place six rolls in a row, keeping them fairly close to each other, on each baking sheet. Cover with oiled clear film and leave in a warm place for about 30 minutes, or until the rolls have doubled in size and are touching each other. Meanwhile, preheat the oven to 220°C/425°F/Gas 7.

7 Brush the bridge rolls with milk, if you like, and bake them for 15–18 minutes, or until lightly browned. Transfer the batch to a wire rack to cool, then separate into rolls.

WHOLEMEAL BAPS

There's nothing nicer than waking up to the aroma of fresh baked bread. The wholemeal flour adds extra flavour to these soft breakfast rolls.

140ml/5fl oz/scant ⅔ cup milk
140ml/5fl oz/scant ⅔ cup water
225g/8oz/2 cups stoneground wholemeal (whole-wheat) bread flour, plus extra for dusting
225g/8oz/2 cups unbleached white bread flour
7.5ml/1½ tsp salt
10ml/2 tsp caster (superfine) sugar
5ml/1 tsp easy bake (rapid-rise) dried yeast
milk, for glazing

MAKES 10

1 Pour the milk and water into the pan. Reverse the order in which you add the wet and dry ingredients if necessary. Sprinkle over the flours, covering the liquid. Add the salt and sugar in separate corners. Make a shallow indent in the centre of the flour and add the yeast. Set the bread machine to the dough setting; use basic dough setting (if available). Press Start.

2 When the dough cycle has finished, remove the dough and place it on a lightly floured surface. Knock it back (punch it down) gently, then divide it into ten pieces and cover with lightly oiled clear film (plastic wrap).

3 Take one piece of dough, leaving the rest covered, and cup your hands around it to shape it into a ball. Place it on the lightly floured surface and roll it into a flat oval measuring 10 × 7.5cm/4 × 3in.

4 Repeat with the remaining dough so that you have ten flat oval dough pieces. Lightly oil two baking sheets.

5 Place the baps on the prepared baking sheets. Cover with oiled clear film and leave to rise in a warm place for about 30 minutes, or until the baps are almost doubled in size. Meanwhile, preheat the oven to 200°C/400°F/Gas 6.

6 Using three middle fingers, press each bap in the centre to help disperse any large air bubbles. Brush with milk and dust lightly with wholemeal flour.

7 Bake for 15–20 minutes, or until the baps are lightly browned. Turn out on to a wire rack and serve warm.

Per roll Energy 113kcal/476kJ; Protein 2.6g; Carbohydrate 17.2g, of which sugars 2.9g; Fat 4.3g, of which saturates 2.5g; Cholesterol 26mg; Calcium 40mg; Fibre 0.6g; Sodium 42mg.
Per bap Energy 157kcal/667kJ; Protein 5.4g; Carbohydrate 33.6g, of which sugars 2.6g; Fat 1g, of which saturates 0.3g; Cholesterol 1mg; Calcium 58mg; Fibre 2.7g; Sodium 304mg.

RICOTTA AND OREGANO KNOTS

The ricotta cheese adds a wonderful moistness to these beautifully shaped rolls. Serve them slightly warm to appreciate fully the flavour of the oregano as your butter melts into the crumb.

60ml/4 tbsp ricotta cheese
225ml/8fl oz/scant 1 cup water
450g/1lb/4 cups unbleached white bread flour
45ml/3 tbsp skimmed milk powder (non fat dry milk)
10ml/2 tsp dried oregano
5ml/1 tsp salt
10ml/2 tsp caster (superfine) sugar
25g/1oz/ 2 tbsp butter
5ml/1 tsp easy bake (rapid-rise) dried yeast

FOR THE TOPPING
1 egg yolk
freshly ground black pepper

MAKES 12

1 Spoon the cheese into the bread machine pan and add the water. Reverse the order in which you add the liquid and dry ingredients if necessary.

2 Sprinkle over the flour, ensuring that it covers the cheese and water. Add the skimmed milk powder and oregano. Place the salt, sugar and butter in separate corners of the bread pan. Make a small indent in the centre of the flour (but not down as far as the liquid) and add the yeast.

3 Set the bread machine to the dough setting; use basic dough setting (if available). Press Start. Lightly oil two baking sheets.

4 When the dough cycle has finished, remove the dough from the machine and place it on a lightly floured surface.

5 Knock the dough back (punch it down) gently, then divide it into 12 pieces and cover with oiled clear film (plastic wrap).

6 Take one piece of dough, leaving the rest covered, and roll it on the floured surface into a rope about 25cm/10in long. Lift one end of the dough over the other to make a loop. Push the end through the hole in the loop to make a neat knot.

7 Repeat with the remaining dough. Place the knots on the prepared baking sheets, cover them with oiled clear film and leave to rise in a warm place for about 30 minutes, or until doubled in size. Meanwhile, preheat the oven to 220°C/425°F/Gas 7.

8 Mix the egg yolk and 15ml/1tbsp water for the topping in a small bowl. Brush the mixture over the rolls. Sprinkle some with freshly ground black pepper and leave the rest plain.

9 Bake for about 15–18 minutes, or until the rolls are golden brown. Turn out on to a wire rack to cool.

Per knot Energy 160kcal/678kJ; Protein 4.3g; Carbohydrate 30.7g, of which sugars 2.1g; Fat 3.1g, of which saturates 1.8g; Cholesterol 7mg; Calcium 65mg; Fibre 1.2g; Sodium 186mg.

WHOLEMEAL AND RYE PISTOLETS

A wholemeal and rye version of this French and Belgian speciality. Unless your bread machine has a programme for wholewheat dough, it is worth the extra effort of the double rising, because this gives a lighter roll with a more developed flavour.

290ml/10¼fl oz/1¼ cups water
280g/10oz/2½ cups stoneground
wholemeal (whole-wheat) bread flour
50g/2oz/½ cup unbleached white
bread flour, plus extra for dusting
115g/4oz/1 cup rye flour
30ml/2 tbsp skimmed milk powder
(non fat dry milk)
10ml/2 tsp salt + 5ml/1tsp to glaze
10ml/2 tsp caster (superfine) sugar
25g/1oz/2 tbsp butter
7.5ml/1½ tsp easy bake (rapid-rise)
dried yeast

MAKES 12

5 Leaving the rest of the dough covered, shape one piece into a ball. Roll on the floured surface into an oval. Repeat with the remaining dough.

6 Place the rolls on the prepared baking sheets. Cover them with oiled clear film and leave them in a warm place for about 30–45 minutes, or until almost doubled in size. Meanwhile preheat the oven to 220°C/425°F/Gas 7.

7 Mix the salt with 15ml/1tbsp water for the glaze and brush over the rolls. Dust the tops of the rolls with flour.

8 Using the oiled handle of a wooden spoon held horizontally, split each roll almost in half, along its length. Replace the clear film and leave for 10 minutes.

9 Bake the rolls for 15–20 minutes, until the bases sound hollow when tapped. Turn out on to a wire rack to cool.

1 Pour the water into the bread pan. If the instructions for your machine specify that the yeast is to be placed in the pan first, reverse the order in which you add the liquid and dry ingredients.

2 Sprinkle over all three types of flour, ensuring that the water is completely covered. Add the skimmed milk powder. Then add the salt, sugar and butter, placing them in separate corners of the bread pan. Make a small indent in the centre of the flour (but do not go down as far as the water underneath) and add the easy bake dried yeast.

3 Set the bread machine to the dough setting; use wholewheat dough setting (if available). If you have only one basic dough setting you may need to repeat the programme to allow sufficient time for this heavier dough to rise. Press Start. Lightly oil two baking sheets.

4 When the dough cycle has finished, remove the dough from the bread machine pan and place it on a surface that has been lightly floured. Knock the dough back (punch it down) gently, then divide it into 12 pieces. Cover with oiled clear film (plastic wrap).

Per pistolet Energy 142kcal/601kJ; Protein 4.5g; Carbohydrate 26.8g, of which sugars 1.9g; Fat 2.6g, of which saturates 1.3g; Cholesterol 5mg; Calcium 31mg; Fibre 3.4g; Sodium 186mg.

HAM AND CHEESE CROISSANTS

*The crispy layers of yeast pastry melt in your mouth to reveal a cheese and
ham filling. Serve the croissants freshly baked and still warm.*

115ml/4fl oz/½ cup milk
30ml/2 tbsp water
1 egg
*280g/10oz/2½ cups unbleached white
bread flour*
*50g/2oz/½ cup fine French plain
(all-purpose) flour*
5ml/1 tsp salt
15ml/1 tbsp caster (superfine) sugar
*25g/1oz/2 tbsp butter, plus
175g/6oz/¾ cup butter, softened*
*7.5ml/1½ tsp easy bake (rapid-rise)
dried yeast*
1 egg yolk, to glaze
15ml/1 tbsp milk, to glaze

For the Filling
*175g/6oz Emmenthal or Gruyère
cheese, cut into thin batons*
*70g/2½oz thinly sliced dry cured
smoked ham, torn into small pieces*
5ml/1 tsp paprika

Makes 12

1 Pour the milk, water and egg into the
pan. Reverse the order in which you add
the wet and dry ingredients, if necessary.

2 Sprinkle over the flours. Place the salt,
sugar and 25g/1oz/2 tbsp butter in
separate corners. Add the yeast in an
indent in the flour. Set to the dough
setting; use basic dough setting (if
available). Press Start. Shape the
softened butter into an oblong block
2cm/¾in thick.

3 When the dough cycle has finished, place
the dough on a floured surface and knock
back (punch down) gently. Roll out to a
rectangle slightly wider than the butter
block, and just over twice as long. Place
the butter on one half of the pastry, fold it
over and seal the edges, using a rolling pin.

4 Roll out again into a rectangle 2cm/¾in
thick, twice as long as it is wide. Fold
the top third down, the bottom third up,
seal, wrap in clear film (plastic wrap) and
chill for 15 minutes. Repeat the rolling,
folding and chilling twice more, giving
the pastry a quarter turn each time. Wrap
in clear film and chill for 30 minutes.

5 Lightly oil two baking sheets. Roll out
the pastry into a rectangle measuring
52 × 30cm/21 × 12in. Cut into two 15cm/
6in strips. Using one strip, measure
15cm/6in along one long edge and
7.5cm/3in along the opposite long edge.
Using the 15cm/6in length as the base of
your first triangle, cut two diagonal lines
to the 7.5cm/3in mark opposite, using a
sharp knife. Continue along the strip,
cutting six triangles in all. You will end
up with two scraps of waste pastry, at
either end of the strip. Repeat with the
remaining strip.

6 Place a pastry triangle on the work
surface in front of you, with the pointed
end facing you. Divide the cheese and
ham into 12 portions and put one
portion on the wide end of the triangle.
Hold and gently pull each side point to
stretch the pastry a little, then roll up
the triangle from the filled end with one
hand while pulling the remaining point
gently towards you with the other hand.

7 Curve the ends of the rolled triangle
away from you to make a crescent.
Place this on one of the baking sheets,
with the point underneath. Fill and
shape the remaining croissants. Cover
with oiled clear film and leave to rise for
30 minutes, until almost doubled in size.
Preheat the oven to 200°C/400°F/Gas 6.

8 Mix the egg yolk and milk for the glaze
and brush over the croissants. Bake for
15–20 minutes, until golden. Turn out
on to a wire rack. Serve warm.

Per croissant Energy 288kcal/1202kJ; Protein 8.4g; Carbohydrate 23.4g, of which sugars 2.3g; Fat 18.4g, of which saturates 11.7g; Cholesterol 70mg; Calcium 169mg; Fibre 0.9g; Sodium 520mg.

SAFFRON BRAIDS

Delicately scented and coloured with saffron, these deep-fried braids are favourite coffee-time treats in Scandinavia.

1 Heat the milk until hot but not boiling. Pour over the saffron in a bowl. Leave for 45 minutes or until cold.

2 Pour the saffron milk into the bread machine pan, then add the eggs. If the instructions for your machine specify that the yeast is to be placed in the pan first, reverse the order in which you add the liquid and dry ingredients.

3 Sprinkle over the flour, ensuring that it covers the saffron milk completely. Add the salt, sugar and butter, placing them in separate corners of the bread machine pan. Make a small indent in the centre of the flour (but do not go down as far as the liquid) and add the easy bake dried yeast.

4 Set the bread machine to the dough setting; use basic dough setting (if available). Press Start. Lightly oil two baking sheets.

5 When the dough cycle has finished, remove the dough for the saffron braids from the bread machine and place it on a lightly floured surface. Knock it back (punch it down) gently, then divide the dough into eight pieces. Cover with a piece of oiled clear film (plastic wrap).

200ml/7fl oz/⅞ cup milk
3.5ml/¾ tsp saffron threads
2 eggs
450g/1lb/4 cups unbleached white bread flour
2.5ml/½ tsp salt
50g/2oz/¼ cup caster (superfine) sugar
50g/2oz/¼ cup butter
5ml/1 tsp easy bake (rapid-rise) dried yeast
sunflower oil, for deep-frying
caster (superfine) sugar, for sprinkling

MAKES 8

6 Take one piece of dough (leaving the rest covered). Divide into three. Roll out each small piece into a 20cm/8in rope.

7 Place the ropes next to each other, pinch the ends together and braid them from left to right. When you reach the other end, press the ends together and tuck them under.

8 Repeat with the remaining portions of dough. Place the braids on the prepared baking sheets. Cover with oiled clear film and leave in a warm place for 30–45 minutes or until almost doubled in size.

9 Preheat the oil for deep-frying to 180°C/360°F or until a cube of dried bread, added to the oil, turns golden brown in 30–60 seconds.

10 Fry the saffron braids, two at a time, for 4–5 minutes, until they have risen and are golden in colour. Drain on kitchen paper and sprinkle with caster sugar. Serve warm.

Per braid Energy 379kcal/1591kJ; Protein 7.7g; Carbohydrate 51.5g, of which sugars 8.6g; Fat 17.3g, of which saturates 5.3g; Cholesterol 63mg; Calcium 120mg; Fibre 1.7g; Sodium 203mg.

CHINESE-STYLE CHICKEN BUNS

These delectable sesame seeded buns, filled with chicken flavoured with ginger and soy sauce, are perfect for picnics.

*140ml/5fl oz/⅔ cup semi-skimmed
(low-fat) milk
225g/8oz/2 cups unbleached white
bread flour
2.5ml/½ tsp salt
2.5ml/½ tsp granulated sugar
15g/½oz/1 tbsp butter
5ml/1 tsp easy bake (rapid-rise)
dried yeast*

*FOR THE FILLING
30ml/2 tbsp sunflower oil
5cm/2in piece of fresh root ginger, grated
30ml/2 tbsp soy sauce
15ml/1 tbsp clear honey
225g/8oz chicken breast fillets, chopped
3 spring onions (scallions), chopped
15ml/1 tbsp chopped fresh
coriander (cilantro)
salt and freshly ground black pepper*

*FOR THE TOPPING
1 egg yolk
15ml/1 tbsp water
sesame seeds*

MAKES 8

1 Pour the milk into the bread machine pan. If the instructions for your bread machine specify that the yeast is to be placed in the pan first, simply reverse the order in which you add the liquid and dry ingredients.

2 Sprinkle over the flour, ensuring that the milk is completely covered. Add the salt, sugar and butter, placing them in separate corners of the bread pan. Make a small indent in the centre of the flour (but not down as far as the liquid) and add the easy bake dried yeast.

3 Set the bread machine to the dough setting; use basic dough setting (if available). Press Start. Lightly grease a baking sheet.

4 Make the filling. Mix half the oil with the grated ginger, soy sauce and honey. Add the chicken and toss to coat. Cover and set aside for 30 minutes.

5 Heat a non-stick wok or frying pan and add the remaining oil. When it is hot, add the chicken mixture and stir-fry over medium heat for 5–6 minutes. Add the spring onions and cook for 2 minutes more, or until the chicken is cooked. Stir in the coriander and seasoning. Set aside to cool.

6 When the dough cycle has finished, remove the dough from the machine and place it on a lightly floured surface. Knock it back gently, then divide it into eight pieces.

7 Roll out each piece of dough to a 13cm/5in round. Divide the chicken filling among the rounds of dough, placing in the centre of each.

8 Beat the egg yolk and water for the topping in a small bowl. Brush a little of the mixture around the edge of each dough round.

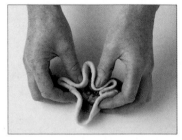

9 Bring up the sides of the dough to cover the filling and pinch the edges together firmly to seal. Place the buns seam-side down on the greased baking sheet.

10 Cover the buns with oiled clear film (plastic wrap) and leave them to rise in a warm place for about 30 minutes or until almost doubled in size. Meanwhile, preheat the oven to 200°C/400°F/Gas 6.

11 Brush the tops of the buns with the remaining egg glaze and sprinkle with the sesame seeds. Bake for about 18–20 minutes, or until the buns are golden brown.

12 Turn out on to a wire rack to cool slightly. If you like, serve immediately, while the buns are hot.

VARIATION
If you have any leftover stir-fried vegetables, use as a filling in place of the chicken filling. To make another vegetarian version of these buns, cut 225g/8oz mixed vegetables into small pieces or strips and marinade as for the chicken in step 4. Use vegetables such as carrots, broccoli, leeks, bean-sprouts and (bell) peppers.

Per bun Energy 168kcal/709kJ; Protein 9.8g; Carbohydrate 25g, of which sugars 3.2g; Fat 3.9g, of which saturates 1.6g; Cholesterol 17mg; Calcium 70mg; Fibre 1g; Sodium 383mg.

200ml/7fl oz/⅞ cup water
45ml/3 tbsp extra virgin olive oil
350g/12½oz/3 cups unbleached white
bread flour
5ml/1 tsp salt
2.5ml/½ tsp granulated sugar
5ml/1 tsp easy bake (rapid-rise)
dried yeast
30ml/2 tbsp water
15ml/1 tbsp sea salt
15ml/1 tbsp sesame seeds

MAKES ABOUT 70

COOK'S TIP
Make these tasty nibbles up to a day
in advance. Re-heat in a moderate
oven for a few minutes, to refresh.

1 Pour the water and oil into the pan.
If necessary, reverse the order in which
you add the liquid and dry ingredients.

SPANISH PICOS

*These small bread shapes, dusted with salt and sesame seeds, are often eaten
in Spain with pre-dinner drinks, but can also be served as an
accompaniment to an appetizer or soup.*

2 Sprinkle over the flour, ensuring that
it covers the liquid. Add the salt and
sugar, placing them in separate corners
of the bread pan. Make a small indent in
the centre of the flour (but not down as
far as the liquid) and add the yeast.

3 Set the machine to the dough setting;
use basic dough setting (if available).
Press Start. Then lightly oil two
baking sheets.

4 When the dough cycle has finished,
remove the dough from the machine
and place it on a lightly floured surface.
Knock it back (punch it down) gently,
then roll it out to a rectangle measuring
30 × 23cm/12 × 9in. Cut lengthways into
three strips, then cut each strip of
dough into 2.5cm/1in wide ribbons.

5 Preheat the oven to 200°C/400°F/
Gas 6. Tie each ribbon into a loose knot
and place on the baking sheets, spacing
them well apart. Cover with oiled clear
film (plastic wrap) and leave to rise in a
warm place for 10–15 minutes. Leave
the picos plain or brush with water and
sprinkle with salt or sesame seeds. Bake
for 10–15 minutes, or until golden.

CASHEW AND OLIVE SCROLLS

140ml/5fl oz/⅝ cup milk
120ml/4fl oz/½ cup water
30ml/2 tbsp extra virgin olive oil
450g/1lb/4 cups unbleached white
bread flour
5ml/1 tsp salt
2.5ml/½ tsp caster (superfine) sugar
7.5ml/1½ tsp easy bake (rapid-rise)
dried yeast
5ml/1 tsp finely chopped fresh
rosemary or thyme
50g/2oz/½ cup salted cashew nuts,
finely chopped
50g/2oz/½ cup pitted green olives,
finely chopped
45ml/3 tbsp freshly grated Parmesan
cheese, for sprinkling

MAKES 12

1 Pour the milk, water and oil into the
pan. If necessary, reverse the order in
which you add the wet and dry
ingredients.

*These attractively shaped rolls have a crunchy texture and ooze with the
flavours of olives and fresh herbs.*

2 Sprinkle over the flour, ensuring that
it covers the liquid. Add the salt and
sugar, placing them in separate corners
of the bread pan. Make a small indent in
the centre of the flour (but not down as
far as the liquid) and add the yeast.

3 Set the machine to the dough setting;
use basic raisin dough setting (if
available). Press Start. Add the herbs,
cashew nuts and olives when the
machine beeps. If your machine does
not have this facility, then add these
ingredients about 5 minutes before the
end of the kneading period. Lightly oil
two baking sheets.

4 When the dough cycle has finished,
remove the dough from the machine
and place it on a lightly floured surface.
Knock it back (punch it down) gently.

5 Divide the dough into 12 pieces of
equal size and cover with oiled clear film
(plastic wrap). Take one piece of dough,
leaving the rest covered. Roll it into a
rope about 23cm/9in long, tapering the
ends. Starting from the middle, shape
the rope into an "S" shape, curling the
ends in to form a neat spiral.

6 Transfer the spiral – or scroll – to a
prepared baking sheet. Make 11 more
scrolls in the same way. Cover with
oiled clear film and leave to rise in a
warm place for 30 minutes, or until
doubled in size.

7 Meanwhile, preheat the oven to 200°C/
400°F/Gas 6. Sprinkle the rolls with
Parmesan cheese and bake them for
18–20 minutes, or until risen and golden.
Turn out on to a wire rack to cool.

Per pico Energy 23kcal/95kJ; Protein 0.5g; Carbohydrate 4.2g, of which sugars 0.1g; Fat 0.5g, of which saturates 0.1g; Cholesterol 0mg; Calcium 8mg; Fibre 0.2g; Sodium 28mg.
Per scroll Energy 196kcal/828kJ; Protein 6.3g; Carbohydrate 30.5g, of which sugars 1.3g; Fat 6.3g, of which saturates 1.7g; Cholesterol 4mg; Calcium 116mg; Fibre 1.4g; Sodium 153mg.

210ml/7½fl oz/scant 1 cup milk
1 egg
450g/1lb/4 cups unbleached white
bread flour
7.5ml/1½ tsp mixed (apple pie) spice
2.5ml/½ tsp ground cinnamon
2.5ml/½ tsp salt
50g/2oz/¼ cup caster (superfine) sugar
50g/2oz/¼ cup butter
7.5ml/1½ tsp easy bake (rapid-rise)
dried yeast
75g/3oz/scant ½ cup currants
25g/1oz/3 tbsp sultanas (golden raisins)
25g/1oz/3 tbsp cut mixed (candied) peel

FOR THE PASTRY CROSSES
50g/2oz/½ cup plain (all-purpose) flour
25g/1oz/2 tbsp margarine

FOR THE GLAZE
30ml/2 tbsp milk
25g/1oz/2 tbsp caster sugar

MAKES 12

1 Pour the milk and egg into the bread pan. Reverse the order in which you add the liquid and dry ingredients if your machine requires this.

2 Sprinkle over the flour, ensuring that it covers the liquid. Add the mixed spice and cinnamon. Place the salt, sugar and butter in separate corners of the pan. Make a shallow indent in the centre of the flour and add the yeast.

COOK'S TIP

If preferred, to make the crosses roll out 50g/2oz shortcrust (unsweetened) pastry, and cut into narrow strips. Brush the buns with water to attach the crosses.

HOT CROSS BUNS

The traditional cross on these Easter buns originates from early civilization and probably symbolized the four seasons; it was only later used to mark Good Friday and the Crucifixion.

3 Set the bread machine to the dough setting; use basic raisin dough setting (if available). Press Start. Lightly grease two baking sheets.

4 Add the dried fruit and peel when the machine beeps or 5 minutes before the end of the kneading period.

5 When the dough cycle has finished, remove the dough from the machine and place it on a lightly floured surface. Knock it back (punch it down) gently, then divide it into 12 pieces. Cup each piece between your hands and shape it into a ball. Place on the prepared baking sheets, cover with oiled clear film (plastic wrap) and leave for 30–45 minutes or until almost doubled in size.

6 Meanwhile, preheat the oven to 200°C/400°F/Gas 6. Make the pastry for the crosses. In a bowl, rub the flour and margarine together until the mixture resembles fine breadcrumbs. Bind with enough water to make a soft pastry which can be piped.

7 Spoon the pastry into a piping bag fitted with a plain nozzle and pipe a cross on each bun. Bake the buns for 15–18 minutes, or until golden.

8 Meanwhile, heat the milk and sugar for the glaze in a small pan. Stir thoroughly until the sugar dissolves. Brush the glaze over the top of the hot buns. Turn out on to a wire rack. Serve warm or cool.

Per bun Energy 155kcal/657kJ; Protein 3.7g; Carbohydrate 29.3g, of which sugars 11.7g; Fat 3.4g, of which saturates 1.1g; Cholesterol 16mg; Calcium 55mg; Fibre 0.9g; Sodium 60mg.

HAMAN POCKETS

These delicate tricorn-shaped pastries are properly known as Hamantaschel and are traditionally eaten at the Jewish festival of Esther. They can be filled with dried fruits or poppy seeds.

1 Pour the milk and egg into the bread machine pan. However, if the instructions for your machine specify that the easy bake dried yeast is to be placed in the bread machine pan first, simply reverse the order in which you add the liquid and dry ingredients to the pan.

2 Sprinkle over the flour, ensuring that it covers the milk and egg mixture. Add the sugar, salt and butter, placing them in separate corners of the bread pan. Make a small indent in the centre of the flour (but not down as far as the liquid) and add the yeast.

3 Set the bread machine to the dough setting; use basic dough setting (if available). Press Start. Lightly grease two baking sheets.

4 Make the filling. Put the poppy seeds in a heatproof bowl, pour over boiling water to cover and leave to cool. Drain thoroughly through a fine sieve. Melt 15g/½oz/1 tbsp of the butter in a small pan, add the poppy seeds and cook, stirring, for 1–2 minutes. Remove from the heat and stir in the ground almonds, honey, mixed peel and sultanas. Cool.

5 When the dough cycle has finished, place the dough on a lightly floured surface. Knock it back (punch it down) gently and then shape it into a ball.

6 Roll out the pastry to a thickness of about 5mm/¼in. Cut out 10cm/4in circles using a plain cutter, re-rolling the trimmings as necessary. Then melt the remaining butter.

100ml/3½fl oz/7 tbsp milk
1 egg
250g/9oz/2¼ cups unbleached white bread flour
25g/1oz/2 tbsp caster (superfine) sugar
2.5ml/½ tsp salt
25g/1oz/2 tbsp butter, melted
5ml/1 tsp easy bake (rapid-rise) dried yeast
50g/2oz/4 tbsp poppy seeds
40g/1½oz/3 tbsp butter
25g/1oz/¼ cup ground almonds
15ml/1 tbsp clear honey
15ml/1 tbsp chopped mixed (candied) peel
15ml/1 tbsp sultanas (golden raisins), chopped
beaten egg, to glaze

MAKES 10–12

7 Brush each circle of dough with the melted butter and place a spoonful of filling in the centre. Bring up the edges over the filling to make tricorn shapes, leaving a little of the filling showing. Transfer the shaped pastries to the prepared baking sheets, cover them with oiled clear film (plastic wrap) and leave for 30 minutes or until the haman pockets are doubled in size.

8 Preheat the oven to 190°C/375°F/Gas 5. Brush the pastries with the beaten egg and bake for 15 minutes, or until golden. Turn out on to a wire rack.

VARIATION

For the filling, chopped ready-to-eat prunes can be used instead of poppy seeds, or use a mixture of chopped raisins and sultanas.

Per pocket Energy 156kcal/653kJ; Protein 2.8g; Carbohydrate 18.7g, of which sugars 9.1g; Fat 8.3g, of which saturates 3.6g; Cholesterol 52mg; Calcium 46mg; Fibre 0.7g; Sodium 42mg.

CHELSEA BUNS

225ml/8fl oz/scant 1 cup milk
1 egg
500g/1lb 2oz/4½ cups unbleached
white bread flour
2.5ml/½ tsp salt
75g/3oz/6 tbsp caster (superfine) sugar
50g/2oz/¼ cup butter, softened
5ml/1 tsp easy bake (rapid-rise)
dried yeast
50g/2oz/¼ cup caster (superfine)
sugar, to glaze
5ml/1 tsp orange flower water, to glaze

FOR THE FILLING
25g/1oz/2 tbsp butter, melted
115g/4oz/⅔ cup sultanas (golden raisins)
25g/1oz/3 tbsp mixed chopped
(candied) peel
25g/1oz/2 tbsp currants
25g/1oz/2 tbsp soft light brown sugar
5ml/1 tsp mixed (apple pie) spice

MAKES 12 BUNS

Chelsea buns are said to have been invented by the owner of the Chelsea Bun House in London at the end of the 17th century. They make the perfect accompaniment to a cup of coffee or tea. They are so delicious, it is difficult to resist going back for more!

4 Lightly grease a 23cm/9in square cake tin (pan). When the dough cycle has finished, remove the dough from the machine and place it on a lightly floured surface.

5 Knock the dough back (punch it down) gently, then roll it out to form a square that is approximately 30cm/12in.

6 Brush the dough with the melted butter for the filling and sprinkle it with the sultanas, candied peel, currants, brown sugar and mixed spice, leaving a 1cm/½in border along one edge.

7 Starting at a covered edge, roll the dough up, Swiss (jelly) roll fashion. Press the edges together to seal. Cut the roll into 12 slices and then place these cut side uppermost in the prepared tin.

8 Cover the dough with oiled clear film (plastic wrap). Leave to rise in a warm place for 30–45 minutes, or until the dough slices have doubled in size. Meanwhile preheat the oven to 200°C/400°F/Gas 6.

9 Bake the buns for 15–20 minutes, or until they have risen well and are evenly golden all over.

10 Leave them to cool slightly in the tin before turning them out on to a wire rack to cool further.

11 Make the glaze. Mix the caster sugar with 60ml/4 tbsp water in a small pan. Heat gently, stirring occasionally, until the sugar is completely dissolved. Then increase the heat and boil the mixture rapidly for 1–2 minutes without stirring, until syrupy.

12 Stir the orange flower water into the glaze and brush the mixture over the warm buns. Serve slightly warm.

1 Pour the milk into the bread machine pan. Add the egg. If the instructions for your machine specify that the yeast is to be placed in the pan first, reverse the order in which you add the liquid and dry ingredients.

2 Sprinkle over the flour, ensuring that it completely covers the liquid. Add the salt, sugar and butter in three separate corners of the bread machine pan. Make a small indent in the centre of the flour (but not down as far as the liquid) and add the yeast.

3 Set the bread machine to the dough setting; use basic dough setting (if available). Press Start.

COOK'S TIP
Use icing (confectioners') sugar instead of caster sugar and make a thin glaze icing to brush over the freshly baked buns.

Per bun Energy 287kcal/1208kJ; Protein 6.1g; Carbohydrate 43.5g, of which sugars 16.6g; Fat 11.1g, of which saturates 2.3g; Cholesterol 26mg; Calcium 85mg; Fibre 1.3g; Sodium 243mg.

YORKSHIRE TEACAKES

280ml/10fl oz/scant 1¼ cups milk
450g/1lb/4 cups unbleached white
bread flour
5ml/1 tsp salt
40g/1½oz/3 tbsp caster
(superfine) sugar
40g/1½oz/3 tbsp lard (shortening)
or butter
5ml/1 tsp easy bake (rapid-rise)
dried yeast
50g/2oz/¼ cup currants
50g/2oz/⅓ cup sultanas
(golden raisins)
milk, for glazing

MAKES 8–10

These fruit-filled tea-time treats are thought to be a refinement of the original medieval manchet or "handbread" – a hand-shaped loaf made without a tin. Serve them split and buttered, either warm from the oven or toasted.

1 Pour the milk into the bread machine pan. If the instructions for your machine specify that the yeast is to be placed in the pan first, then simply reverse the order in which you add the liquid and dry ingredients to the pan.

2 Sprinkle over the flour, ensuring that it covers the milk completely. Add the salt, sugar and lard or butter, placing them in separate corners of the bread machine pan. Make a small indent in the centre of the flour (but do not go down as far as the liquid underneath) and pour the easy bake dried yeast into the hollow.

3 Set the bread machine to the dough setting; use basic raisin dough setting (if available). Press Start. Add the currants and sultanas when the machine beeps. If your machine does not have this facility, simply add the dried fruits 5 minutes before the end of the kneading period.

4 Lightly grease two baking sheets. When the dough cycle has finished, remove the dough from the machine and place it on a lightly floured surface. Knock it back (punch it down) gently.

5 Divide the dough into eight or ten portions, depending on how large you like your Yorkshire teacakes, and shape into balls. Flatten out each ball into a disc about 1cm/½in thick.

6 Place the discs on the prepared baking sheets, about 2.5cm/1in apart. Cover them with oiled clear film (plastic wrap) and leave in a warm place for 30–45 minutes, or until they are almost doubled in size. Meanwhile, preheat the oven to 200°C/400°F/Gas 6.

7 Brush the top of each teacake with milk, then bake for 15–18 minutes, or until golden. Turn out on to a wire rack to cool slightly.

8 To serve, split open while still warm and spread with lashings of butter, or let the buns cool, then split and toast them before adding butter.

Per teacake Energy 239kcal/1011kJ; Protein 5.4g; Carbohydrate 47.4g, of which sugars 13.1g; Fat 4.4g, of which saturates 2.5g; Cholesterol 11mg; Calcium 107mg; Fibre 1.6g; Sodium 245mg.

DEVONSHIRE SPLITS

A summer afternoon, a scrumptious cream tea; Devonshire splits are an essential part of this British tradition.

140ml/5fl oz/⅔ cup milk
225g/8oz/2 cups unbleached white bread flour
25g/1oz/2 tbsp caster (superfine) sugar
2.5ml/½ tsp salt
5ml/1 tsp easy bake (rapid-rise) dried yeast
icing (confectioners') sugar, for dusting

FOR THE FILLING
clotted cream or whipped double (heavy) cream
raspberry or strawberry jam

MAKES 8

5 When the dough cycle has finished, remove the dough and place it on a lightly floured surface. Knock back (punch down) gently, then divide into eight portions.

6 Shape each portion of dough into a ball, using cupped hands. Place on the prepared baking sheets, and flatten the top of each ball slightly. Cover with oiled clear film (plastic wrap). Leave the dough to rise for 30–45 minutes or until doubled in size.

7 Meanwhile, preheat the oven to 220°C/425°F/Gas 7. Bake the buns for 15–18 minutes, or until they are light golden in colour. Turn out on to a wire rack to cool.

8 Split the buns open and fill them with cream and jam. Dust them with icing sugar just before serving.

1 Pour the milk into the bread pan. If your machine instructions specify it, reverse the order in which you add the liquid and dry ingredients.

2 Sprinkle over the flour, ensuring that it covers the liquid completely. Add the caster sugar and salt, placing them in separate corners of the bread machine pan.

3 Make a small indent in the centre of the flour (do not go down as far as the milk underneath) and pour the easy bake dried yeast into the hollow.

4 Set the bread machine to the dough setting; use basic dough setting (if available). Press Start. Lightly grease two baking sheets.

Per split Energy 116kcal/495kJ; Protein 3.2g; Carbohydrate 26g, of which sugars 4.6g; Fat 0.7g, of which saturates 0.2g; Cholesterol 1mg; Calcium 62mg; Fibre 0.9g; Sodium 134mg.

DOUGHNUTS

90ml/6 tbsp water
140ml/5fl oz/scant ⅔ cup milk
1 egg
450g/1lb/4 cups unbleached white
bread flour
50g/2oz/¼ cup caster (superfine) sugar
5ml/1 tsp salt
50g/2oz/¼ cup butter
7.5ml/1½ tsp easy bake (rapid-rise)
dried yeast
oil for deep-frying
caster (superfine) sugar, for sprinkling
ground cinnamon, for sprinkling

FOR THE FILLING
45ml/3 tbsp red jam
5ml/1 tsp lemon juice

MAKES ABOUT 16

The main thing to remember about doughnuts is the speed with which they disappear, so make plenty of both the cinnamon-coated rings and the round ones filled with jam.

1 Pour the water and milk into the bread machine pan. Break in the egg. If the instructions for your bread machine specify that the yeast is to be placed in the pan first, simply reverse the order in which you add the liquid and dry ingredients.

2 Sprinkle over the flour, ensuring that it covers the liquid. Add the sugar, salt and butter, placing them in separate corners of the bread pan. Make a small indent in the centre of the flour (but not down as far as the liquid) and add the easy bake dried yeast.

3 Set the bread machine to the dough setting; use basic dough setting (if available). Press Start.

4 When the dough cycle has finished, remove the dough from the machine and place it on a lightly floured surface.

5 Knock the dough back (punch it down) gently and divide it in half. Cover one half with lightly oiled clear film (plastic wrap). Divide the remaining piece into eight equal portions.

6 Take each portion in turn and use your hands to roll it into a smooth ball. Lightly oil two baking sheets.

7 Place the eight dough balls on one of the prepared baking sheets. Cover them with oiled clear film and leave in a warm place to rise for about 30 minutes, or until doubled in size.

8 Roll the remaining dough out to a thickness of 1cm/½in. Cut into circles using a 7.5cm/3in plain cutter. Then make the dough circles into rings using a 4cm/1½in plain cutter.

9 Place the rings on the remaining baking sheet, cover them with oiled clear film and leave them in a warm place for about 30 minutes, or until doubled in size.

10 Heat the oil for deep-frying to 180°C/350°F, or until a cube of dried bread, added to the oil, turns golden brown in 30–60 seconds. Add the doughnuts, three or four at a time.

11 Cook the doughnuts for about 4–5 minutes, or until they are golden. Remove from the oil using a slotted spoon and drain on kitchen paper.

VARIATION

Make oblong shaped doughnuts and split almost in half lengthways once cold. Fill with whipped cream and your favourite jam.

12 Toss the round doughnuts in caster sugar and the ring doughnuts in a mixture of caster sugar and ground cinnamon. Set aside to cool.

13 Heat the jam and lemon juice in a small pan until warm, stirring to combine. Leave to cool, then spoon the mixture into a piping (pastry) bag fitted with a small plain nozzle.

14 When the round doughnuts have cooled, use a skewer to make a small hole in each. Insert the piping nozzle and squeeze a little of the jam mixture into each doughnut.

Per doughnut Energy 192kcal/802kJ; Protein 2.5g; Carbohydrate 22.6g, of which sugars 8.3g; Fat 10.8g, of which saturates 1.4g; Cholesterol 16mg; Calcium 37mg; Fibre 0.6g; Sodium 11mg.

APPLE AND SULTANA DANISH PASTRIES

These Danish pastries are filled with fruit and are beautifully light and flaky.

FOR THE DANISH PASTRY
1 egg
75ml/5 tbsp milk
225g/8oz/2 cups unbleached white bread flour
15g/½oz/1 tbsp caster (superfine) sugar
2.5ml/½ tsp salt
140g/5oz/⅔ cup butter, softened
7.5ml/1½ tsp easy bake (rapid-rise) dried yeast

FOR THE FILLING
25g/1oz/2 tbsp butter
350g/12oz cooking apples, diced
15ml/1 tbsp cornflour (cornstarch)
25g/1oz/2 tbsp caster (superfine) sugar
30ml/2 tbsp water
5ml/1 tsp lemon juice
25g/1oz/3 tbsp sultanas (golden raisins)

TO FINISH
1 egg, separated
flaked (sliced) almonds, for sprinkling

MAKES 12

1 Place the egg and milk in the bread pan. Reverse the order in which you add the liquid and dry ingredients if necessary. Sprinkle over the flour, covering the liquid. Add the sugar, salt and 25g/1oz/ 2 tbsp of the butter in separate corners.

2 Make a shallow indent in the centre of the flour; add the yeast. Set the bread machine to the dough setting; use basic dough setting (if available). Press Start. Lightly oil two baking sheets.

3 Shape the remaining butter into a block 2cm/⅜in thick. When the dough cycle has finished, remove the prepared dough and place it on a lightly floured surface. Knock it back (punch it down) gently and then roll it out into a rectangle that is slightly wider than the butter block, and just over twice as long.

4 Place the butter on one half, fold the pastry over it, then seal the edges, using a rolling pin. Roll the butter-filled pastry into a rectangle 2cm/⅜in thick, making it twice as long as it is wide. Fold the top third down and the bottom third up, seal the edges, wrap in clear film (plastic wrap) and chill for 15 minutes. Repeat the folding and rolling process twice, giving the pastry a quarter turn each time. Wrap in clear film; chill for 20 minutes.

5 Make the filling. Melt the butter in a pan. Toss the apples, cornflour and sugar in a bowl. Add to the pan and toss.

6 Add the water and lemon juice. Cook over a medium heat for 3–4 minutes, stirring. Stir in the sultanas.

7 Leave the filling to cool. Meanwhile, roll out the pastry into a rectangle measuring 40 × 30cm/16 × 12in. Cut into 10cm/4in squares. Divide the filling among the squares, spreading it over half of each piece of pastry so that when they are folded, they will make rectangles.

8 Brush the pastry edges on each square with the lightly beaten egg white, then fold the pastry over the filling to make a rectangle measuring 10 × 5cm/4 × 2in and press the edges together firmly. Make a few cuts along the long joined edge of each pastry.

9 Place the pastries on the baking sheets, cover them with oiled clear film (plastic wrap) and leave to rise for 30 minutes.

10 Preheat the oven to 200°C/400°F/ Gas 6. Mix the egg yolk with 15ml/1 tbsp water and brush over the pastries. Sprinkle with a few flaked almonds and bake for 15 minutes, or until golden. Transfer to a wire rack to cool.

APRICOT STARS

When in season these light pastries can be decorated with fresh apricots.

1 quantity Danish pastry – see Apple and Sultana Danish Pastries

FOR THE FILLING
50g/2oz/½ cup ground almonds
50g/2oz/½ cup icing (confectioners') sugar
1 egg, lightly beaten
12 drained canned apricot halves

FOR THE GLAZE
1 egg yolk
30ml/2 tbsp water
60ml/4 tbsp apricot jam

MAKES 12

1 Roll out the pastry into a rectangle measuring 40 × 30cm/16 × 12in. Cut into 10cm/4in squares. On each square, make a 2.5cm/1in diagonal cut from each corner towards the centre. Mix the ground almonds, icing sugar and egg together. Divide the filling among the pastry squares, placing it in the centre.

2 Beat the egg yolk for the glaze with half the water. On each square, fold one corner of each cut section to the centre. Secure with the glaze. Place an apricot half, round side up on top in the centre.

3 Lightly oil two baking sheets. Place the pastries on them and cover with oiled clear film (plastic wrap). Leave to rise for 30 minutes or until doubled in size. Preheat the oven to 200°C/400°F/Gas 6.

4 Brush the pastries with the remaining egg glaze and bake them for 15 minutes, until golden. While the stars are cooking, heat the apricot jam in a small pan with the remaining water. Transfer the cooked pastries on to a wire rack, brush them with the warm apricot glaze and leave to cool.

Per pastry Energy 208kcal/869kJ; Protein 2.7g; Carbohydrate 23.6g, of which sugars 8.1g; Fat 12.1g, of which saturates 7.7g; Cholesterol 48mg; Calcium 42mg; Fibre 1.1g; Sodium 116mg.
Per star Energy 220kcal/920kJ; Protein 4.1g; Carbohydrate 22.8g, of which sugars 8.4g; Fat 13.2g, of which saturates 6.9g; Cholesterol 59mg; Calcium 58mg; Fibre 1.1g; Sodium 105mg.

CHERRY FOLDOVERS

Danish pastries are filled with a sweet cherry filling spiked with Kirsch.

FOR THE DANISH PASTRY DOUGH
1 egg
75ml/2½fl oz/⅓ cup water
*225g/8oz/2 cups unbleached white
bread flour*
2.5ml/½ tsp ground cinnamon
15ml/1 tbsp caster (superfine) sugar
2.5ml/½ tsp salt
*125g/4½oz/generous ½ cup
butter, softened*
*7.5ml/1½ tsp easy bake
(rapid-rise) dried yeast*

FOR THE FILLING AND TOPPING
*225g/8oz drained pitted morello
cherries in syrup, plus 15ml/1 tbsp
syrup from the jar or can*
25g/1oz/2 tbsp caster (superfine) sugar
15ml/1 tbsp cornflour (cornstarch)
30ml/2 tbsp Kirsch
1 egg, separated
30ml/2 tbsp water
30ml/2 tbsp apricot jam

MAKES 12

1 Pour the egg and water into the pan. Reverse the order in which you add the liquid and dry ingredients if necessary.

2 Sprinkle over the flour and cinnamon, covering the liquid. Add the sugar, salt and 25g/1oz/2 tbsp of the butter, placing them in separate corners. Make a shallow indent in the flour; add the yeast. Set the bread machine to the dough setting; use basic or pizza dough setting (if available). Press Start. When the cycle has finished, remove the dough and place on a lightly floured surface. Knock back (punch down) gently, then roll out to a rectangle about 1cm/½in thick.

3 Divide the remaining butter into three and dot one portion over the top two-thirds of the dough, leaving the edges clear. Fold the unbuttered portion of dough over half the buttered area and fold the remaining portion on top. Seal the edges with a rolling pin. Give the dough a quarter turn and repeat the buttering and folding. Wrap in clear film (plastic wrap) and chill for 30 minutes. Repeat the folding and chilling with the remaining butter, then repeat again, this time without any butter. Wrap and chill the dough for 30 minutes.

4 Make the filling. Put the cherries, cherry syrup, caster sugar, cornflour and Kirsch in a pan and toss. Cook over a medium heat for 3–4 minutes, stirring until thickened. Leave to cool.

5 Roll out the dough to a rectangle measuring 40 × 30cm/16 × 12in. Cut into 10cm/4in squares. Place a tablespoon of filling in the middle of each square. Brush one corner of each pastry square with lightly beaten egg white, then bring the opposite corner over to meet it, setting it back slightly to leave some of the cherry filling exposed. Press down to seal.

6 Place the foldovers on lightly greased baking sheets. Cover with oiled clear film and leave to rise for 30 minutes. Preheat the oven to 200°C/400°F/Gas 6.

7 Mix the egg yolk with half the water and brush over the dough. Bake for 15 minutes, or until golden. Mix the jam and remaining water in a pan; heat until warm. Brush over the pastries and turn out on to a wire rack to cool.

GINGER AND RAISIN WHIRLS

Tasty spirals of buttery pastry, studded with dried fruit and crystallized ginger.

*1 quantity Danish pastry dough –
see Cherry Foldovers*

FOR THE FILLING
40g/1½oz/3 tbsp butter, softened
40g/1½oz/3 tbsp caster (superfine) sugar
2.5ml/½ tsp grated nutmeg
*25g/1oz/2 tbsp crystallized
(candied) ginger*
25g/1oz/2 tbsp candied orange peel
75g/3oz/½ cup raisins

FOR THE GLAZE AND ICING
1 egg yolk, beaten with 15ml/1 tbsp water
*30ml/2 tbsp icing (confectioners')
sugar, sifted*
15ml/1 tbsp orange juice

MAKES 12

1 Roll the pastry into a 30 × 23cm/ 12 × 9in rectangle. Cream the butter, sugar and nutmeg together and spread over the dough. Finely chop the ginger and peel. Sprinkle over the dough with the raisins. Lightly oil two baking sheets.

2 Tightly roll up the dough from one long side, as far as the centre. Repeat with the remaining long side, so the two meet at the centre. Brush the edges where the rolls meet with egg glaze.

3 Cut into 12 slices and place, spaced well apart, on the baking sheets. Cover with oiled clear film (plastic wrap) and leave to rise for 30 minutes.

4 Preheat the oven to 200°C/400°F/ Gas 6. Brush the whirls with the egg glaze and bake for 12–15 minutes, or until golden. Turn out on to a wire rack to cool. Mix the icing sugar and orange juice together and use to ice the pastries.

Per foldover Energy 196kcal/820kJ; Protein 3g; Carbohydrate 24.4g, of which sugars 9g; Fat 9.7g, of which saturates 5.9g; Cholesterol 56mg; Calcium 38mg; Fibre 0.7g; Sodium 93mg.
Per whirl Energy 221kcal/926kJ; Protein 2.5g; Carbohydrate 27.5g, of which sugars 13.3g; Fat 12g, of which saturates 7.6g; Cholesterol 47mg; Calcium 40mg; Fibre 0.8g; Sodium 120mg.

SWEET BREADS AND YEAST CAKES

Fresh fruit-flavoured loaves and rich yeast cakes filled with nuts, dried fruits or chocolate are all part of this diverse range of breads. A bread machine is the perfect tool for mixing and proving the rich doughs of Continental specialities, which are often made for special occasions.

BLUEBERRY AND OATMEAL BREAD

The blueberries add a subtle fruitiness to this loaf, while the oatmeal contributes texture and a nutty flavour. This is best eaten on the day it is baked.

SMALL
75ml/5 tbsp water
75ml/5 tbsp milk
1 egg
325g/11½oz/scant 3 cups unbleached white bread flour, plus 30ml/2 tbsp for coating the blueberries
25g/1oz/¼ cup coarse oatmeal
5ml/1 tsp mixed (apple pie) spice
40g/1½oz/3 tbsp caster (superfine) sugar
2.5ml/½ tsp salt
25g/1oz/2 tbsp butter
5ml/1 tsp easy bake (rapid-rise) dried yeast
50g/2oz/½ cup blueberries

MEDIUM
110ml/scant 4 fl oz/scant ½ cup water
120ml/4fl oz/½ cup milk
1 egg
450g/1lb/4 cups unbleached white bread flour, plus 30ml/2 tbsp for coating the blueberries
50g/2oz/½ cup coarse oatmeal
7.5ml/1½ tsp mixed spice
50g/2oz/¼ cup caster sugar
3.5ml/¾ tsp salt
40g/1½oz/3 tbsp butter
7.5ml/1½ tsp easy bake dried yeast
75g/3oz/¾ cup blueberries

LARGE
120ml/generous 4fl oz/½ cup water
130ml/4½fl oz/½ cup + 1 tbsp milk
2 eggs
550g/1lb 4oz/5 cups unbleached white bread flour, plus 30ml/2 tbsp for coating the blueberries
50g/2oz/½ cup coarse oatmeal
10ml/2 tsp mixed spice
65g/2½oz/5 tbsp caster sugar
3.5ml/¾ tsp salt
40g/1½oz/3 tbsp butter
10ml/2 tsp easy bake dried yeast
100g/3½oz/scant 1 cup blueberries

MAKES 1 LOAF

COOK'S TIP
Use the light crust setting to avoid a rich, dark crust on this sweet loaf.

1 Pour the water, milk and egg(s) into the bread machine pan. If the instructions for your machine specify that the yeast is to be placed in the pan first, reverse the order in which you add the liquid and dry ingredients.

2 Sprinkle over the flour, ensuring it covers the liquid. Add the oatmeal and spice. Add the sugar, salt and butter in separate corners. Make a small indent in the centre of the flour (but not down as far as the liquid) and add the yeast.

3 Set the bread machine to sweet/basic, with raisin setting if available. Use light crust, 500g for small; medium crust, large/750g for medium; or medium crust 1kg/2lb for large. Press Start. Toss the berries with the extra flour and add when the machine beeps during the kneading cycle.

4 Remove the bread at the end of the baking cycle. Turn out on to a wire rack.

Per loaf Energy 1549kcal/6551kJ; Protein 43.6g; Carbohydrate 285.1g, of which sugars 13.6g; Fat 34.1g, of which saturates 16.4g; Cholesterol 252mg; Calcium 594mg; Fibre 13.1g; Sodium 1301mg.

CRANBERRY AND ORANGE BREAD

The distinctive tart flavour of cranberries is intensified when these American fruits are dried. They combine well here with orange rind and pecan nuts.

1 Pour the water, orange juice and egg(s) into the bread machine pan. If the instructions for your machine specify that the yeast is to be placed in the pan first, reverse the order in which you add the liquid and dry ingredients.

2 Sprinkle over the flour, ensuring that it covers the water. Add the milk powder. Place the sugar, salt and butter in separate corners of the bread pan. Make a small indent in the centre of the flour (but not down as far as the liquid). Add the yeast.

3 Set the machine to sweet/basic, raisin setting (if available). Use light crust, 500g for small; medium crust, large/750g for medium; or medium crust 1kg/2lb for large. Press Start. Add the rind, cranberries and nuts when the machine beeps during the kneading cycle.

4 Remove the bread from the pan at the end of the baking cycle and turn out on to a wire rack. Mix the orange juice and caster sugar in a small pan. Heat, stirring, until the sugar dissolves, then boil until syrupy. Brush over the loaf. Leave to cool.

SMALL
70ml/2½ fl oz/scant 5 tbsp water
80ml/scant 3 fl oz/⅓ cup orange juice
1 egg
375g/13oz/3¼ cups unbleached white bread flour
15ml/1 tbsp skimmed milk powder (non fat dry milk)
40g/1½oz/3 tbsp caster (superfine) sugar
2.5ml/½ tsp salt
25g/1oz/2 tbsp butter
5ml/1 tsp easy bake (rapid-rise) dried yeast
10ml/2 tsp grated orange rind
40g/1½oz/⅓ cup dried cranberries
25g/1oz/¼ cup pecan nuts, chopped

MEDIUM
120ml/4fl oz/½ cup water
120ml/4fl oz/½ cup orange juice
1 egg
500g/1lb 2oz/4½ cups unbleached white bread flour
30ml/2 tbsp skimmed milk powder
50g/2oz/¼ cup caster sugar
3.5ml/¾ tsp salt
40g/1½oz/3 tbsp butter
7.5ml/1½ tsp easy bake dried yeast
15ml/1 tbsp grated orange rind
50g/2oz/scant ½ cup dried cranberries
40g/1½oz/3 tbsp pecan nuts, chopped

LARGE
115ml/4fl oz/½ cup water
130ml/4½fl oz/½ cup + 1 tbsp orange juice
2 eggs
600g/1lb 5oz/5¼ cups unbleached white bread flour
30ml/2 tbsp skimmed milk powder
65g/2¼oz/5 tbsp caster sugar
5ml/1 tsp salt
50g/2oz/¼ cup butter
7.5ml/1½ tsp easy bake dried yeast
20ml/4 tsp grated orange rind
75g/3oz/⅔ cup dried cranberries
50g/2oz/½ cup pecan nuts, chopped

FOR GLAZING
30ml/2 tbsp each fresh orange juice and caster sugar

MAKES 1 LOAF

Per loaf Energy 2004Kcal/8475kJ; Protein 42.6g; Carbohydrate 381.3g, of which sugars 95.2g; Fat 44.8g, of which saturates 16.7g; Cholesterol 63mg; Calcium 716mg; Fibre 13.9g; Sodium 1277mg.

THREE CHOCOLATE BREAD

If you like chocolate, you'll adore this bread. The recipe suggests three specific types of chocolate, but you can combine your own favourites.

SMALL

150ml/generous 5fl oz/scant ⅔ cup water

1 egg

375g/13oz/3¼ cups unbleached white bread flour

15ml/1 tbsp caster (superfine) sugar

2.5ml/½ tsp salt

20g/¾oz/1½ tbsp butter

5ml/1 tsp easy bake (rapid-rise) dried yeast

40g/1½oz plain (semisweet) chocolate with raisins and almonds

40g/1½oz plain (semisweet) chocolate with ginger

50g/2oz Belgian milk chocolate

MEDIUM

240ml/8½fl oz/generous 1 cup water

1 egg

500g/1lb 2oz/4½ cups unbleached white bread flour

25g/1oz/2 tbsp caster sugar

5ml/1 tsp salt

25g/1oz/2 tbsp butter

7.5ml/1½ tsp easy bake dried yeast

50g/2oz plain chocolate with raisins and almonds

50g/2oz plain chocolate with ginger

75g/3oz Belgian milk chocolate

LARGE

250ml/9fl oz/generous 1 cup water

2 eggs

600g/1lb 5oz/5¼ cups unbleached white bread flour

40g/1½oz/3 tbsp caster sugar

5ml/1 tsp salt

25g/1oz/2 tbsp butter

7.5ml/1½ tsp easy bake dried yeast

65g/2½oz plain chocolate with raisins and almonds

65g/2½oz plain chocolate with ginger

100g/3½oz Belgian milk chocolate

MAKES 1 LOAF

COOK'S TIP

Gradually add the chocolate to the bread machine pan, making sure that it is mixing into the dough before adding more.

1 Pour the water into the bread pan and add the egg(s). If necessary for your machine, reverse the order in which you add the liquid and dry ingredients.

2 Sprinkle over the flour, ensuring that it covers the water. Add the sugar, salt and butter, placing them in separate corners of the bread pan. Make a small indent in the centre of the flour; add the easy bake dried yeast.

3 Set the bread machine to sweet/basic, with raisin setting if available. Use light crust, 500g for small; medium crust, large/750g for medium; or medium crust 1kg/2lb for large. Press Start. Coarsely chop all the chocolate. Add to the bread pan when the machine beeps during the kneading cycle.

4 Remove the bread at the end of the baking cycle. Turn out on to a wire rack.

Per loaf Energy 2245kcal/9473kJ; Protein 51.1g; Carbohydrate 386.4g, of which sugars 96g; Fat 65.7g, of which saturates 35.9g; Cholesterol 267mg; Calcium 778mg; Fibre 11.6g; Sodium 1327mg.

LEMON AND MACADAMIA BREAD

Originally from Australia, macadamia nuts have a buttery taste that combines well with the tangy flavour of lemon rind and yogurt in this delicious bread.

1 Pour the egg(s), yogurt and milk into the pan. If necessary, reverse the order of adding the wet and dry ingredients.

2 Sprinkle over the flour, ensuring that it covers the water. Add the sugar, salt and butter, placing them in separate corners of the bread pan. Make a small indent in the flour (but not down as far as the liquid) and add the yeast.

3 Set the machine to white/basic, raisin setting (if available), medium crust. Size: 500g for small, large/750g for medium, or 1kg/2lb for large. Press Start. Add the nuts and lemon rind when the machine beeps during the kneading cycle.

4 Remove the lemon and macadamia bread from the bread pan at the end of the baking cycle and turn out on to a wire rack to cool.

SMALL
1 egg
125ml/4½fl oz/generous ½ cup lemon yogurt
60ml/4 tbsp milk
375g/13oz/3¼ cups unbleached white bread flour
40g/1½oz/3 tbsp caster (superfine) sugar
2.5ml/½ tsp salt
25g/1oz/2 tbsp butter
5ml/1 tsp easy bake (rapid-rise) dried yeast
25g/1oz/¼ cup macadamia nuts, chopped
10ml/2 tsp grated lemon rind

MEDIUM
1 egg
175ml/6fl oz/¾ cup lemon yogurt
115ml/4fl oz/½ cup milk
500g/1lb 2oz/4½ cups unbleached white bread flour
50g/2oz/¼ cup caster sugar
3.5ml/¾ tsp salt
40g/1½oz/3 tbsp butter
7.5ml/1½ tsp easy bake dried yeast
40g/1½oz/⅓ cup macadamia nuts, chopped
15ml/1 tbsp grated lemon rind

LARGE
2 eggs
175ml/6fl oz/¾ cup lemon yogurt
100ml/3½fl oz/7 tbsp milk
600g/1lb 5oz/5¼ cups unbleached white bread flour
50g/2oz/4 tbsp caster sugar
5ml/1 tsp salt
50g/2oz/¼ cup butter
7.5ml/1½ tsp easy bake dried yeast
50g/2oz/½ cup macadamia nuts, chopped
20ml/4 tsp grated lemon rind

MAKES 1 LOAF

COOK'S TIP
Select light crust setting if your bread machine tends to produce a rich crust when you make a sweet bread.

Per loaf Energy 2021kcal/8509kJ; Protein 50.9g; Carbohydrate 359.8g, of which sugars 73.8g; Fat 52.1g, of which saturates 19.7g; Cholesterol 256mg; Calcium 860mg; Fibre 12.9g; Sodium 454mg.

RUM AND RAISIN LOAF

Juicy raisins, plumped up with dark rum, flavour this tea-time loaf.
Serve just as it is or lightly toasted, with butter.

SMALL
75g/3oz/generous ½ cup raisins
22ml/1½ tbsp dark rum
1 egg, lightly beaten
170ml/6fl oz/ 1⅔ cup + 1 tbsp milk
350g/12oz/3 cups unbleached white
bread flour
1.5ml/¼ tsp ground ginger
25g/1oz/2 tbsp caster (superfine) sugar
2.5ml/½ tsp salt
40g/1½oz/3 tbsp butter
5ml/1 tsp easy bake (rapid-rise)
dried yeast
10ml/2 tsp clear honey, warmed

MEDIUM
90g/3¼oz/⅔ cup raisins
30ml/2 tbsp dark rum
1 egg, lightly beaten
250ml/9fl oz/generous 1 cup milk
500g/1lb 2oz/4½ cups unbleached
white bread flour
2.5ml/½ tsp ground ginger
40g/1½oz/3 tbsp caster sugar
3.5ml/¾ tsp salt
50g/2oz/¼ cup butter
7.5ml/1½ tsp easy bake dried yeast
15ml/1 tbsp clear honey, warmed

LARGE
100g/3½oz/⅔ cup raisins
45ml/3 tbsp dark rum
1 egg, lightly beaten
320ml/11fl oz/1⅓ cups milk
600g/1lb 5oz/5¼ cups unbleached
white bread flour
5ml/1 tsp ground ginger
40g/1½oz/3 tbsp caster sugar
5ml/1 tsp salt
65g/2½oz/5 tbsp butter
7.5ml/1½ tsp easy bake dried yeast
15ml/1 tbsp clear honey, warmed

MAKES 1 LOAF

1 Place the raisins and rum in a small bowl and leave to soak for 2 hours. Drain any remaining liquid into the bread machine pan. Add the egg and milk. If necessary for your machine, reverse the order in which you add the liquid and dry ingredients.

2 Sprinkle over the flour, ensuring that it covers the liquid completely. Add the ground ginger. Add the caster sugar, salt and butter, placing them in separate corners of the bread machine pan. Make a small indent in the centre of the flour (but not down as far as the liquid) and pour in the dried yeast.

3 Set the bread machine to sweet/basic, with raisin setting if available, light crust. Size: 500g for small, large/750g for medium, or 1kg/2lb for large. Press Start. Add the raisins when the machine beeps during the kneading cycle.

4 Remove the bread at the end of the baking cycle and turn out on to a wire rack. Brush the top with honey and leave the loaf to cool.

Per loaf Energy 1939kcal/8198kJ; Protein 41.1g; Carbohydrate 357.7g, of which sugars 91g; Fat 43.1g, of which saturates 23.9g; Cholesterol 282mg; Calcium 573mg; Fibre 12.4g; Sodium 428mg.

MANGO AND BANANA BREAD

Tropical fruit juice, fresh banana and dried mango give this light-textured loaf its Caribbean flavour.

1 Pour the fruit juice and buttermilk into the bread machine pan. Add the mashed banana(s) to the bread pan, with the honey. If necessary for your machine, reverse the order in which you add the liquid and dry ingredients.

2 Sprinkle over the flour, ensuring that it covers the liquid. Place the salt and butter in separate corners of the bread pan. Make a shallow indent in the centre of the flour and add the yeast.

3 Set the machine to sweet/basic, with raisin setting if available, light crust. Size: 500g for small, large/750g for medium, or 1kg/2lb for large. Add the mango pieces to the automatic dispenser, if available. Press Start. If adding them manually, add when the machine beeps during the kneading cycle.

4 Remove the bread at the end of the baking cycle. Turn out on to a wire rack.

SMALL
45ml/3 tbsp orange and mango juice
150ml/generous 5fl oz/scant
⅔ cup buttermilk
150g/5oz/1 medium banana,
peeled and mashed
30ml/2 tbsp clear honey
385g/13oz/3⅓ cups unbleached
white bread flour
5ml/1 tsp salt
25g/1oz/2 tbsp butter
5ml/1 tsp easy bake (rapid-rise)
dried yeast
25g/1oz/¼ cup dried mango, chopped

MEDIUM
60ml/2fl oz/¼ cup orange and
mango juice
200ml/7fl oz/⅞ cup buttermilk
175g/6oz/1 large banana, peeled
and mashed
45ml/3 tbsp clear honey
500g/1lb 2oz/4½ cups unbleached
white bread flour
5ml/1 tsp salt
40g/1½oz/3 tbsp butter
5ml/1 tsp easy bake dried yeast
40g/1½oz/⅓ cup dried mango, chopped

LARGE
75ml/2½fl oz/⅓ cup orange and
mango juice
230ml/8fl oz/1 cup buttermilk
225g/8oz/1½ bananas, peeled
and mashed
60ml/4 tbsp clear honey
600g/1lb 5oz/5¼ cups unbleached
white bread flour
7.5ml/1½ tsp salt
50g/2oz/¼ cup butter
7.5ml/1½ tsp easy bake dried yeast
50g/2oz/½ cup dried mango, chopped

MAKES 1 LOAF

COOK'S TIP
The small loaf may be cooked before the end of the programme. Check 5–10 minutes before the end and remove if well browned. Leave to stand for 5 minutes before turning out.

Per loaf Energy 1869kcal/7880kJ; Protein 44.2g; Carbohydrate 385.3g, of which sugars 88.5g; Fat 26.4g, of which saturates 14.6g; Cholesterol 63mg; Calcium 750mg; Fibre 14.6g; Sodium 2257mg.

MAPLE AND PECAN GLUTEN-FREE BREAD

This delicious tea-time bread can be served sliced and buttered, or toasted first. Use other dried fruits and nuts instead of sultanas and pecan nuts, if you like.

SMALL
140ml/5fl oz/⅝ cup milk
150ml/5¼fl oz/⅔ cup water
1 egg
30ml/2 tbsp maple syrup
60ml/4tbsp sunflower oil
5ml/1 tsp cider vinegar
400g/14oz/3½ cups Doves Farm
gluten- and wheat-free white
bread flour blend
5ml/1 tsp salt
10ml/2 tsp sugar
7.5ml/1½ tsp easy bake (rapid-rise)
dried yeast
40g/1½oz/⅓ cup pecan nuts, chopped
40g/1½oz/⅓ cup sultanas
(golden raisins)

MEDIUM
170ml/6fl oz/¾ cup milk
180ml/6½fl oz/generous ¾ cup water
2 eggs
45ml/3 tbsp maple syrup
75ml/5 tbsp sunflower oil
5ml/1 tsp cider vinegar
500g/1lb 2oz/4½ cups Doves Farm
gluten- and wheat-free white
bread flour blend
5ml/1 tsp salt
15ml/1 tbsp sugar
10ml/2 tsp easy bake dried yeast
50g/2oz/⅔ cup pecan nuts, chopped
50g/2oz/⅔ cup sultanas

LARGE
170ml/6fl oz/¾ cup milk
200ml/7fl oz/scant ⅞ cup water
2 eggs
60ml/4 tbsp maple syrup
90ml/6 tbsp sunflower oil
7.5ml/1½ tsp cider vinegar
600g/1lb 5oz/5¼ cups Doves Farm
gluten- and wheat-free white
bread flour blend
5ml/1 tsp salt
22.5ml/1⅓ tbsp sugar
12.5ml/2½ tsp easy bake dried yeast
60g/2½oz/⅝ cup pecan nuts, chopped
60g/2½oz/⅝ cup sultanas

MAKES 1 LOAF

1 Pour the milk and water into the bread machine pan. Add the egg(s), maple syrup, sunflower oil and vinegar. If the instructions for your machine specify that the yeast is to be placed in the pan first, reverse the order in which you add the liquid and the dry ingredients. Check with your manufacturer's instructions as you may need to add the water first for the gluten-free programme.

2 Sprinkle over the flour, ensuring that it covers the water. Add the salt and sugar in separate corners of the bread pan. Make a small indent in the centre of the flour (but not down as far as the liquid) and add the yeast.

3 Add the pecan nuts and sultanas, if using the gluten-free setting. If using the basic setting, add them to the automatic dispenser, if available. If adding them manually, add them when the machine beeps during the kneading cycle.

4 Set the bread machine to the gluten-free or white/basic setting, medium crust, if available. Select size: 500g for small, large/750g for medium, or 1kg/2lb for large. The weight setting is not available on some gluten-free cycles. Check the amount of gluten-free mix your machine handles. The large size may need to be cooked on the white/basic setting. You may need to scrape down the mixture after 5 minutes. Only use a plastic spatula, as metal may damage the surface.

5 Remove the bread at the end of the baking cycle. Turn out on to a wire rack.

Per loaf Energy 2400kcal/10108kJ; Protein 53.6g; Carbohydrate 378.5g, of which sugars 73.1g; Fat 85.3g, of which saturates 11.3g; Cholesterol 199mg; Calcium 962mg; Fibre 15.1g; Sodium 2161mg.

HAZELNUT TWIST CAKE

*Easy to make yet impressive, this sweet bread consists of layers of ground
nuts, twisted through a rich dough, topped with a maple-flavoured icing.*

230ml/8fl oz/1 cup water
1 egg
*450g/1lb/4 cups unbleached white
bread flour*
*45ml/3 tbsp skimmed milk powder
(non fat dry milk)*
grated rind of 1 orange
2.5ml/½ tsp salt
50g/2oz/¼ cup caster (superfine) sugar
75g/3oz/6 tbsp butter, melted
*7.5ml/1½ tsp easy bake (rapid-rise)
dried yeast*
*flaked (sliced) almonds or slivered
hazelnuts, to decorate*

FOR THE FILLING
115g/4oz/1 cup ground hazelnuts
100g/3½oz/1 cup ground almonds
*100g/3½oz/scant ½ cup light
muscovado (brown) sugar*
2.5ml/½ tsp freshly grated nutmeg
2 egg whites
15ml/1 tbsp brandy

FOR THE TOPPING
*60ml/4 tbsp icing
(confectioners') sugar*
15ml/1 tbsp hot water
30ml/2 tbsp natural maple syrup

SERVES 6–8

1 Pour the water and egg into the bread
pan. Reverse the order in which you add
the wet and dry ingredients if necessary.
Sprinkle over the flour, covering the
liquid. Add the milk powder and orange
rind. Place the salt, sugar and butter in
separate corners. Make a shallow indent
in the centre of the flour; add the yeast.

2 Set the bread machine to the dough
setting; use basic dough setting (if
available). Press Start. Lightly oil a
23cm/9in springform ring cake tin (pan).

3 When the dough cycle has finished,
place the dough on a lightly floured
surface. Knock it back (punch it down)
gently, then roll it out to a 65 × 45cm/
26 × 18in rectangle. Cut the dough in
half lengthways.

4 Make the filling by mixing all of the
ingredients in a bowl. Divide the filling in
half. Spread one portion over each piece
of dough, leaving a 1cm/½in clear border
along one long edge of each piece.

5 Starting from the other long edge, roll
up each piece of dough, Swiss (jelly)
roll fashion. Place the two pieces next
to each other and twist them together.

6 Brush the ends of the dough rope
with a little water. Loop the rope in
the prepared springform tin and gently
press the ends together to seal.

7 Cover the tin with lightly oiled clear
film (plastic wrap) and then leave the
dough in a warm place for 30–45
minutes, or until it has risen and is puffy.
Preheat the oven to 200°C/400°F/Gas 6.

8 Bake for 30–35 minutes, or until
golden and well risen. Leave to cool
slightly, then turn out on to a wire rack.

9 Make the icing by mixing the icing
sugar, hot water and maple syrup in a
bowl. Drizzle over the warm cake.
Sprinkle with a few flaked almonds or
slivered hazelnuts and leave to cool
completely before serving.

Per serving Energy 557kcal/2337kJ; Protein 12.3g; Carbohydrate 73.8g, of which sugars 30.3g; Fat 25.3g, of which saturates 6.7g; Cholesterol 46mg; Calcium 171mg; Fibre 3.6g; Sodium 233mg.

150ml/5fl oz/⅔ cup water
1 egg
75g/3oz/¾ cup grated tart green
eating apple
450g/1lb/4 cups unbleached white
bread flour
30ml/2 tbsp skimmed milk powder
(non fat dry milk)
50g/2oz/¼ cup caster (superfine) sugar
40g/1½oz/3 tbsp butter, melted
7.5ml/1½ tsp easy bake (rapid-rise)
dried yeast
225g/8oz cherries, pitted
225g/8oz white almond paste, grated
5ml/1 tsp ground cinnamon

FOR THE TOPPING
beaten egg white
15ml/1 tbsp demerara (raw) sugar
30ml/2 tbsp flaked (sliced) almonds

MAKES 1 CAKE

1 Pour the water and egg into the bread machine pan. Sprinkle over the grated apple. If the instructions for your machine specify that the yeast is to be placed in the pan first, simply reverse the order in which you add the liquid and dry ingredients.

2 Sprinkle over the flour, ensuring that it covers the water, egg and apple completely. Add the skimmed milk powder then add the sugar and butter, placing them in separate corners of the bread pan.

3 Make a small indent in the centre of the flour (but not down as far as the liquid underneath) and pour the easy bake dried yeast into the hollow.

AUSTRIAN COFFEE CAKE

This attractive cake is layered with marzipan and fresh cherries and has just a hint of cinnamon and apple. It is a rich cake, perfect with freshly made coffee, or try it warm as a tasty dessert, served with cream, crème fraîche or yogurt.

4 Set the bread machine to the dough setting; use basic dough setting (if available). Press Start.

5 When the dough cycle has finished, remove the dough from the machine and place it on a lightly floured surface. Knock it back (punch it down) gently, then roll it out to form a 40cm/16in square.

6 Arrange the cherries on top and then sprinkle the grated almond paste and ground cinnamon over the fruit.

7 Carefully roll the dough up, as you would when making a Swiss (jelly) roll, then gently roll and stretch the sausage shape until it is 55cm/22in long. Twist the roll into a loose coil and place in a 23cm/9in non-stick springform cake tin (pan).

COOK'S TIP
Try this cake layered with thick slices of fresh apricots or plums when cherries are out of season.

8 Cover the tin with lightly oiled clear film (plastic wrap) and leave in a warm place for about 30–45 minutes, to allow the dough to rise. Meanwhile, preheat the oven to 190°C/375°F/Gas 5.

9 Brush the top of the risen dough with egg white and sprinkle with demerara sugar and flaked almonds.

10 Bake for 30–35 minutes, or until the cake is golden and well risen. Let it cool for a few minutes in the tin, then transfer the cake to a wire rack to cool. Serve warm or cold, cut into wedges.

Per cake Energy 3419kcal/14443kJ; Protein 72.9g; Carbohydrate 609.3g, of which sugars 265.6g; Fat 90g, of which saturates 28.3g; Cholesterol 286mg; Calcium 1072mg; Fibre 23.7g; Sodium 494mg.

85ml/3fl oz/⅜ cup milk
1 egg
225g/8oz/2 cups unbleached white
bread flour
2.5ml/½ tsp salt
25g/1oz/2 tbsp caster (superfine) sugar
25g/1oz/2 tbsp butter, melted
5ml/1 tsp easy bake (rapid-rise)
dried yeast
icing (confectioners') sugar, to dust

FOR THE FILLING
120ml/4fl oz/½ cup single (light) cream
2 eggs
25g/1oz/2 tbsp caster (superfine) sugar
2.5ml/½ tsp freshly grated nutmeg
3 pears, peeled, halved and cored
50g/2oz/⅓ cup redcurrants

SERVES 6–8

SWISS PEAR AND REDCURRANT TART

Juicy pears and redcurrants in a nutmeg cream custard provide an unforgettable filling for this Swiss tart.

1 Pour the milk and egg into the bread machine pan. If the instructions for your bread machine specify it, reverse the order in which you add the liquid and dry ingredients.

2 Sprinkle over the flour, ensuring that it covers the liquid completely. Add the salt, sugar and butter, placing them in separate corners of the bread pan. Make a small indent in the centre of the flour (but not down as far as the liquid) and add the yeast.

3 Set the bread machine to the dough setting; use basic dough setting (if available). Press Start. Lightly oil a 25cm/10in pizza pan, shallow pie pan or flan tin.

4 When the dough cycle has finished, remove the dough from the machine and place it on a lightly floured surface. Knock it back (punch it down) gently.

5 Roll out the dough to a 28cm/11in round. Place it in the oiled pizza pan or pie or flan tin. With your fingers, press the dough outwards and upwards so that it covers the base and sides of the tin evenly. Then preheat the oven to 190°C/375°F/Gas 5.

6 Make the filling by beating the cream with the eggs, sugar and nutmeg in a bowl. Pour it into the dough-lined tin, then arrange the pears on top, placing them cut side down. Sprinkle the redcurrants in the centre.

7 Bake the tart for 35–40 minutes, or until the filling has set and the crust is golden. Let it cool for a few minutes in the tin, then sprinkle it with sugar. Cut it into wedges and serve immediately.

Per serving Energy 212kcal/892kJ; Protein 4.4g; Carbohydrate 35.6g, of which sugars 14.1g; Fat 6.7g, of which saturates 3.8g; Cholesterol 40mg; Calcium 83mg; Fibre 2.3g; Sodium 171mg.

APRICOT AND VANILLA SLICES

Fresh apricots are perfect for these fruit slices, but there's no need to deny yourself when they are out of season. Just use well-drained canned ones.

115ml/4fl oz/½ cup water
225g/8oz/2 cups unbleached white bread flour
2.5ml/½ tsp salt
25g/1oz/2 tbsp caster (superfine) sugar
25g/1oz/2 tbsp butter, melted
5ml/1 tsp easy bake (rapid-rise) dried yeast

FOR THE FILLING
40g/1½oz/3 tbsp caster (superfine) sugar
15ml/1 tbsp cornflour (cornstarch)
140g/5oz/⅔ cup mascarpone cheese
175g/6oz/¾ cup curd (farmer's) cheese
2 eggs, lightly beaten
2.5ml/½ tsp vanilla essence (extract)
30ml/2 tbsp apricot conserve
9 apricots, halved and stoned (pitted)

MAKES ABOUT 14

1 Pour the water into the bread machine pan. If the instructions for your bread machine specify that the yeast is to be placed in the pan first, simply reverse the order in which you add the liquid and dry ingredients.

2 Sprinkle over the flour, ensuring that it covers the water. Add the salt, sugar and butter, placing them in separate corners of the bread pan.

3 Make a small indent in the centre of the flour (but not down as far as the liquid underneath) and add the yeast.

4 Set the bread machine to the dough setting; use basic dough setting (if available). Press Start. Then lightly oil a 33 × 20cm/13 × 8in Swiss (jelly) roll tin (pan).

5 When the dough cycle has finished, remove the dough from the machine and place it on a lightly floured surface.

6 Knock the dough back (punch it down) gently, then roll out to a rectangle, measuring 35 × 23cm/14 × 9in. Lift it on to the Swiss roll tin. Using your fingers, press the dough outwards and upwards so that it covers the base and sides of the tin evenly. Cover with oiled clear film (plastic wrap). Set aside.

7 Preheat the oven to 200°C/400°F/ Gas 6. Make the filling. Mix the sugar and cornflour in a cup or small bowl. Put the mascarpone and curd cheese into a large mixing bowl and beat in the sugar mixture, followed by the eggs and vanilla essence.

8 Spread the apricot conserve evenly over the base of the dough, then spread the vanilla mixture on top. Arrange the apricots over the filling, placing them cut-side down.

9 Bake for 25–30 minutes, or until the filling is set and the dough has risen and is golden.

10 Leave to cool slightly before cutting into slices. Serve warm

Per slice Energy 149kcal/626kJ; Protein 5.5g; Carbohydrate 22.4g, of which sugars 9.2g; Fat 4.9g, of which saturates 2.8g; Cholesterol 38mg; Calcium 48mg; Fibre 0.9g; Sodium 150mg.

100ml/3½fl oz/7 tbsp milk
1 egg
250g/9oz/2¼ cups unbleached white
bread flour
2.5ml/½ tsp salt
40g/1½oz/3 tbsp caster (superfine) sugar
25g/1oz/2 tbsp butter, melted
5ml/1 tsp easy bake (rapid-rise)
dried yeast
4 peaches, halved and stoned (pitted)

FOR THE TOPPING
75g/3oz/¾ cup plain (all-purpose) flour
40g/1½oz/⅓ cup ground almonds
50g/2oz/¼ cup butter, diced
and softened
40g/1½oz/4 tbsp caster sugar
5ml/1 tsp ground cinnamon

SERVES 8

PEACH STREUSELKUCHEN

This peach-filled German yeast cake is finished with a crunchy almond and cinnamon topping which is quite irresistible.

1 Pour the milk and egg into the bread pan. If the instructions for your bread machine specify that the yeast should go in first, reverse the order of wet and dry ingredients.

2 Sprinkle over the flour, ensuring that it covers the milk and egg completely. Then add the salt, sugar and butter, placing them in three separate corners of the bread pan. Make a small indent in the centre of the flour (but not down as far as the liquid) and add the easy bake dried yeast.

3 Set the bread machine to the dough setting; use basic dough setting (if available). Press Start. Lightly oil a 25cm/10in springform cake tin (pan).

4 When the dough cycle has finished, remove the dough from the pan and place it on a lightly floured surface. Knock it back (punch it down) gently, then roll it out to fit the tin. Ease it into position.

5 Slice the peaches thickly and arrange them on top of the dough. Next, make the topping. Rub the flour, ground almonds and butter together until the mixture resembles coarse breadcrumbs. Stir in the caster sugar and cinnamon. Sprinkle the topping over the peaches.

6 Cover the dough with lightly oiled clear film (plastic wrap) and leave in a warm place for about 20–25 minutes, to rise slightly. Meanwhile, preheat the oven to 190°C/375°F/Gas 5.

7 Bake the cake for 25–30 minutes, or until evenly golden. Leave it to cool in the tin for a few minutes and serve warm, or turn out on to a wire rack to allow to cool completely.

Per serving Energy 313kcal/1319kJ; Protein 6.8g; Carbohydrate 47.7g, of which sugars 16.7g; Fat 12g, of which saturates 5.7g; Cholesterol 46mg; Calcium 99mg; Fibre 2.6g; Sodium 89mg.

BAVARIAN PLUM CAKE

As this bakes, the juices from the plums trickle through to the base, making a deliciously succulent, fruity cake. Serve it with crème fraîche or ice cream.

90ml/6 tbsp milk
1 egg
225g/8oz/2 cups unbleached white bread flour
5ml/1 tsp ground cinnamon
2.5ml/½ tsp salt
40g/1½oz/3 tbsp caster (superfine) sugar
25g/1oz/2 tbsp butter, melted
5ml/1 tsp easy bake (rapid-rise) dried yeast
675g/1½lb plums
icing (confectioners') sugar, for dusting

SERVES 8

3 Make a small indent in the centre of the flour (but not down as far as the liquid) and add the yeast.

4 Set the bread machine to the dough setting; use basic dough setting (if available). Press Start. Lightly oil a 27 × 18cm/10½ × 7in rectangular baking tin (pan) that is about 4cm/1½in deep.

5 When the dough cycle has finished, remove the dough and place it on a lightly floured surface. Knock it back (punch it down) gently, then roll it out to fit the tin. Ease it into position.

1 Pour the milk into the bread machine pan and add the egg. If the instructions for your machine specify that the yeast is to be placed in the pan first, simply reverse the order in which you add the liquid and dry ingredients.

6 Cut the plums into quarters and remove the stones (pits). Arrange on the dough, so that they overlap slightly. Cover with lightly oiled clear film (plastic wrap) and leave in a warm place for 30–45 minutes, to rise. Meanwhile, preheat the oven to 190°C/375°F/Gas 5.

VARIATION
Replace the plums with apple wedges or nectarine slices. Use dessert apples as cooking apples will be too tart. Allow four to five depending on their size. Sprinkle the top with demerara (raw) sugar 5 minutes before the end of baking, and return to the oven.

2 Sprinkle over the flour, ensuring that it covers the milk and egg completely. Add the ground cinnamon. Place the salt, sugar and butter in separate corners of the bread pan.

7 Bake the cake for 30–35 minutes, or until golden and well risen. Dust with icing sugar and serve warm.

Per serving Energy 311kcal/1307kJ; Protein 6.4g; Carbohydrate 44.5g, of which sugars 15.9g; Fat 13.2g, of which saturates 7.4g; Cholesterol 89mg; Calcium 86mg; Fibre 2.4g; Sodium 102mg.

5ml/1 tsp saffron threads
200ml/7fl oz/⅞ cup milk
2 eggs
500g/1lb 2oz/4½ cups unbleached
white bread flour
5ml/1 tsp ground cardamom seeds
2.5ml/½ tsp salt
50g/2oz/¼ cup caster (superfine) sugar
55g/2oz/¼ cup butter, melted
5ml/1 tsp easy bake (rapid-rise)
dried yeast
1 egg yolk, to glaze
15ml/1 tbsp water, to glaze

FOR THE TOPPING
45ml/3 tbsp flaked (sliced) almonds
40g/1½oz/3 tbsp granulated sugar
15ml/1 tbsp rum
15ml/1 tbsp candied lime peel,
chopped (optional)

SERVES 8–10

VARIATION

Instead of candied lime peel, other ingredients can be used for the topping, if preferred. Try angelica or candied orange peel instead. Glacé fruits such as cherries or peaches are also good, or you could use dried mango or dried pear.

1 Place the saffron threads in a small mixing bowl. Heat half of the milk in a small pan, pour it over the saffron and leave to infuse (steep) until the milk is at room temperature.

FINNISH FESTIVE WREATH

This traditional sweet bread, enriched with egg and delicately scented with saffron and cardamom, is called pulla in its native Finland. For festive occasions, elaborately shaped versions of the bread, like this pretty wreath, are prepared.

2 Pour the saffron milk into the bread machine pan, then add the remaining milk and the eggs. However, if the instructions for your bread machine specify that the yeast is to be placed in the bread pan first, simply reverse the order in which you add the liquid and dry ingredients.

3 Sprinkle over the flour, ensuring that it covers the liquid completely, then add the cardamom seeds.

4 Add the salt, caster sugar and butter, placing them in separate corners of the bread pan. Make a shallow indent in the centre of the flour (but not down as far as the milk and eggs) and add the easy bake dried yeast.

5 Set the bread machine to the dough setting; use basic dough setting (if available). Press Start. Lightly oil a baking sheet.

6 When the dough cycle has finished, remove the dough from the bread machine pan and place it on a surface that has been lightly floured. Knock the dough back gently, then divide it into three equal (punch it down) pieces.

7 Roll each piece of dough into a rope, about 65cm/26in long. Place the ropes lengthways, next to each other, to begin the braid.

8 Starting from the centre, braid the pieces together, working towards yourself and from left to right. Turn the dough around and repeat the braiding process. Bring the ends of the plait together to form a circular wreath and pinch to seal.

9 Place the wreath on the baking sheet. Cover with lightly oiled clear film (plastic wrap) and leave for 45–60 minutes, or until almost doubled in size.

10 Meanwhile, preheat the oven to 190°C/375°F/Gas 5. Make the glaze by mixing the egg yolk and water in a bowl. In a separate bowl, mix the almonds, sugar, rum and peel for the topping. Brush the glaze over the loaf and sprinkle the almond mixture on top.

11 Bake for 20 minutes, then reduce the oven temperature to 180°C/350°F/Gas 4 and bake for 10–15 minutes more, or until the wreath is golden and well risen. Turn out on to a wire rack to cool.

Per serving Energy 298kcal/1257kJ; Protein 7.6g; Carbohydrate 49.6g, of which sugars 11.3g; Fat 9.1g, of which saturates 3.8g; Cholesterol 52mg; Calcium 116mg; Fibre 1.9g; Sodium 167mg.

MOCHA PANETTONE

30ml/2 tbsp instant coffee powder
140ml/5fl oz/scant ⅔ cup milk
1 egg, plus 2 egg yolks
400g/14oz/3½ cups unbleached white bread flour
15ml/1 tbsp cocoa powder (unsweetened)
5ml/1 tsp ground cinnamon
2.5ml/½ tsp salt
75g/3oz/6 tbsp caster (superfine) sugar
75g/3oz/6 tbsp butter, softened
7.5ml/1½ tsp easy bake (rapid-rise) dried yeast
115g/4oz plain Continental chocolate, coarsely chopped
45ml/3 tbsp pine nuts, lightly toasted
melted butter, for glazing

SERVES 8–10

COOK'S TIP

The dough for this bread is quite rich and may require a longer rising time than that provided for by your bread machine. Check the dough at the end of the dough cycle. If it does not appear to have risen very much in the bread pan, leave the dough in the machine, with the machine switched off and the lid closed, for a further 30 minutes to allow it to rise to the required degree.

Panettone is the traditional Italian Christmas bread from Milan. This tall domed loaf is usually filled with dried fruits; for a change try this coffee-flavoured bread studded with chocolate and pine nuts.

2 Sift the flour and cocoa powder together. Sprinkle the mixture over the liquid, ensuring that it is completely covered. Add the ground cinnamon. Place the salt, sugar and butter in separate corners of the bread pan. Make a small indent in the centre of the flour (but not down as far as the liquid) and add the yeast.

3 Set the bread machine to the dough setting; use basic dough setting (if available). Press Start. Lightly oil a 15cm/6in deep cake tin (pan) or soufflé dish. Using a double sheet of baking parchment that is 7.5cm/3in wider than the depth of the tin or dish, line the container so that the excess paper creates a collar.

1 In a small bowl, dissolve the coffee in 30ml/2 tbsp hot water. Pour the mixture into the bread machine pan and then add the milk, egg and egg yolks. If the instructions for your bread machine specify that the yeast is to be placed in the pan first, simply reverse the order in which you add the liquid and dry ingredients.

4 When the dough cycle has finished, remove the dough from the machine and place it on a lightly floured surface. Knock it back (punch it down) gently. Gently knead in the chocolate and pine nuts and shape the dough into a ball. Cover it with lightly oiled clear film (plastic wrap) and leave it to rest for 5 minutes.

5 Shape the dough into a plump round loaf which has the same diameter as the cake tin or soufflé dish, and place in the base of the container. Cover with oiled clear film and leave the dough to rise in a slightly warm place for 45–60 minutes, or until the dough has almost reached the top of the greaseproof paper collar.

6 Meanwhile, preheat the oven to 200°C/400°F/Gas 6. Brush the top of the loaf with the melted butter and cut a deep cross in the top. Bake the bread for about 10 minutes.

7 Reduce the oven temperature to 180°C/350°F/Gas 4 and continue to bake the panettone for 30–35 minutes more, or until it is evenly golden all over and a metal skewer inserted in the centre comes out clean without any crumb sticking to it.

8 Leave the panettone in the tin or dish for 5–10 minutes, then turn out on to a wire rack and leave it until it is quite cold before slicing.

Per serving Energy 336kcal/1412kJ; Protein 6.7g; Carbohydrate 47.3g, of which sugars 16.5g; Fat 14.7g, of which saturates 6.8g; Cholesterol 57mg; Calcium 90mg; Fibre 1.8g; Sodium 76mg.

STRAWBERRY CHOCOLATE SAVARIN

100ml/3½fl oz/7 tbsp milk
4 eggs
225g/8oz/2 cups unbleached white
bread flour
40g/1½oz/3 tbsp cocoa powder
(unsweetened)
2.5ml/½ tsp salt
25g/1oz/2 tbsp caster (superfine) sugar
100g/3½oz/7 tbsp butter, melted
5ml/1 tsp easy bake (rapid-rise)
dried yeast
115g/4oz/½ cup granulated sugar
75ml/2½fl oz/scant ⅓ cup white wine
45ml/3 tbsp brandy
physalis and strawberry leaves,
to decorate

FOR THE FILLING
150ml/5fl oz/⅔ cup double (heavy)
cream, whipped, or crème fraîche
225g/8oz/2 cups strawberries, halved
115g/4oz/1 cup raspberries

SERVES 6–8

Strawberries and chocolate are the ultimate indulgence. This light spongy cake is soaked in a wine and brandy syrup before being filled with succulent fresh strawberries to make an exquisite dessert.

VARIATION
The savarin can be filled with other fruits, such as grapes, raspberries, currants, peaches or blackberries. Alternatively, fill with chantilly cream, (slightly sweetened, vanilla flavoured whipped cream) and sprinkle chopped nuts over the top.

1 Pour the milk and eggs into the bread pan. If your machine specifies that the yeast is to be placed in the pan first, reverse the order in which you add the liquid and dry ingredients.

2 Sift the flour and cocoa powder together. Sprinkle the mixture over the liquid in the pan, covering it completely. Place the salt, sugar and butter in separate corners. Make a shallow indent in the centre of the flour; add the yeast.

3 Set the machine to the dough setting; use basic dough setting (if available). Press Start. Lightly oil a 1.5 litre/2½ pint/6¼ cup savarin or ring mould.

4 When the machine has finished mixing the ingredients, leave it on the dough setting for 20 minutes then stop the machine. Pour the dough mixture into the mould, cover with oiled clear film (plastic wrap) and leave in a warm place for 45–60 minutes, or until the dough almost reaches the top of the tin.

5 Meanwhile, preheat the oven to 200°C/400°F/Gas 6. Bake for 25–30 minutes, or until the savarin is golden and well risen. Turn out on to a wire rack to cool, with a plate beneath the rack.

6 Make the syrup. Place the sugar, wine and 75ml/2½fl oz/⅓ cup water in a pan. Heat gently, stirring until the sugar dissolves. Bring to the boil then lower the heat and simmer for 2 minutes. Remove from the heat and stir in the brandy.

7 Spoon the syrup over the savarin. Repeat with any syrup which has collected on the plate. Transfer to a serving plate and leave to cool. To serve, fill the centre with the cream or crème fraîche and top with the strawberries and raspberries. Decorate with physalis and strawberry leaves.

Per serving Energy 335kcal/1396kJ; Protein 4.9g; Carbohydrate 25.6g, of which sugars 21.7g; Fat 22.4g, of which saturates 13.1g; Cholesterol 146mg; Calcium 66mg; Fibre 0.8g; Sodium 116mg.

PEACH BRANDY BABAS

These light, delicate sponges are moistened with a syrup flavoured with peach brandy before being filled with whipped cream and fruit. You can vary the flavour of the syrup by using orange or coconut liqueur or dark rum.

1 Pour the milk and eggs into the bread pan. If the instructions for your machine specify that the yeast is to be placed in the pan first, reverse the order in which you add the liquid and dry ingredients to the pan.

2 Sprinkle over the flour, ensuring that it covers the liquid. Add the cinnamon, then place the salt and sugar in separate corners. Make a small indent in the centre of the flour (but not down as far as the liquid) and add the yeast.

3 Set the bread machine to the dough setting; use basic dough setting (if available). Press Start. Lightly oil eight small savarin tins, each with a diameter of 10cm/4in.

4 When the machine has finished mixing the dough, let the dough cycle continue for a further 15 minutes, then stop the machine and scrape the dough into a large measuring jug (cup). Gradually beat in the melted butter.

5 Pour the batter into the prepared tins, half filling them. Cover with lightly oiled clear film (plastic wrap). Leave in a warm place until the batter reaches the tin tops.

6 Meanwhile, preheat the oven to 190°C/375°F/Gas 5. Bake for 20 minutes, or until golden and well risen. Turn out on to a wire rack to cool. Slide a large tray under the rack.

7 To make the syrup for the babas, place the granulated sugar and water in a small pan and heat gently, stirring occasionally, until the sugar has dissolved. Bring to the boil and boil hard for 2 minutes without stirring. Remove the syrup from the heat and stir in the peach brandy. Spoon the syrup over the babas. Then scrape up any syrup which has dripped on to the tray with a spatula and repeat the process until all the syrup is absorbed.

8 When the babas are cold, whip the cream, sugar and vanilla essence in a bowl until the cream just forms soft peaks. Fill the babas with the flavoured cream and decorate them with the fresh fruits of your choice.

100ml/3½fl oz/7 tbsp milk
4 eggs
225g/8oz/2 cups unbleached white bread flour
5ml/1 tsp ground cinnamon
2.5ml/½ tsp salt
25g/1oz/2 tbsp caster (superfine) sugar
5ml/1 tsp easy bake (rapid-rise) dried yeast
100g/3½oz/7 tbsp butter, melted
115g/4oz/½ cup granulated sugar
150ml/5fl oz/⅔ cup water
90ml/6 tbsp peach brandy

FOR THE DECORATION
150ml/5fl oz/⅔ cup double (heavy) cream
15ml/1 tbsp caster (superfine) sugar
3–4 drops natural vanilla essence (extract)
fresh fruits, to decorate

MAKES 8

Per baba Energy 415kcal/1735kJ; Protein 6.7g; Carbohydrate 43.2g, of which sugars 21.8g; Fat 23.6g, of which saturates 13.3g; Cholesterol 149mg; Calcium 90mg; Fibre 0.9g; Sodium 145mg.

EASTER TEA RING

90ml/6 tbsp milk
1 egg
225g/8oz/2 cups unbleached white
bread flour
2.5ml/½ tsp salt
25g/1oz/2 tbsp caster (superfine) sugar
25g/1oz/2 tbsp butter
5ml/1 tsp easy bake (rapid-rise)
dried yeast
50g/2oz/⅓ cup ready-to-eat
dried apricots
15g/½oz/1 tbsp butter
50g/2oz/¼ cup light muscovado
(brown) sugar
7.5ml/1½ tsp ground cinnamon
2.5ml/½ tsp allspice
50g/2oz/⅓ cup sultanas (golden raisins)
milk, for brushing

FOR THE DECORATION
45ml/3 tbsp icing (confectioners')
sugar
15–30ml/1–2 tbsp orange liqueur or
orange juice
pecan nuts and candied fruits

SERVES 8–10

*This Easter tea ring is too good to serve just once a year. Bake it as
a family weekend treat whenever you feel self-indulgent.
Perfect for a mid-morning coffee break or for tea time.*

3 Set the bread machine to the dough setting; use basic dough setting (if available). Press Start. Then lightly oil a baking sheet.

4 When the dough cycle has finished, remove the dough from the bread pan. Place it on a surface that has been lightly floured. Knock the dough back (punch it down) gently, then roll it out into a 30 × 45cm/12 × 18in rectangle.

5 Chop the dried apricots into small pieces. Melt the butter for the filling and brush it over the dough. Then sprinkle the dough with the muscovado sugar, ground cinnamon, allspice, sultanas and chopped apricots.

6 Starting from one long edge, roll up the rectangle of dough, as when making a Swiss (jelly) roll. Turn the dough so that the seam is underneath.

8 Using a pair of scissors, snip through the circle at 4cm/1½in intervals, each time cutting two-thirds of the way through the dough. Twist the sections so they start to fall sideways.

9 Cover the ring with lightly oiled clear film (plastic wrap) and leave in a warm place for about 30 minutes, or until the dough is well risen and puffy.

10 Preheat the oven to 200°C/400°F/ Gas 6. Bake the ring for 20–25 minutes, or until golden. Turn out on to a wire rack to cool.

11 While the tea ring is still warm, make the decoration by mixing together the icing sugar and liqueur or orange juice. Drizzle the mixture over the ring, then arrange pecan nuts and candied fruit on top. Cool completely before serving.

1 Pour the milk and egg into the bread machine pan. If the instructions for your bread machine specify that the yeast is to be placed in the pan first, simply reverse the order in which you add the liquid and dry ingredients.

2 Sprinkle over the flour, ensuring that it covers the liquid. Add the salt, sugar and butter, placing them in separate corners of the bread pan. Make a small indent in the centre of the flour (but not down as far as the liquid) and add the easy bake dried yeast.

7 Curl the dough into a circle, brush the ends with a little milk and seal. Place on the prepared baking sheet.

> **VARIATION**
> There is a vast range of dried fruits available in the supermarkets.
> Vary the sultanas and apricots; try dried peaches, mango, melon, cherries and raisins, to name a few. Just make sure that the total quantity stays the same as in the recipe.

Per serving Energy 244kcal/1028kJ; Protein 4.4g; Carbohydrate 38.6g, of which sugars 18.2g; Fat 9.1g, of which saturates 4.5g; Cholesterol 44mg; Calcium 87mg; Fibre 1.1g; Sodium 65mg.

POLISH BABKA

Vodka is the surprise ingredient in this classic Polish cake, made at Eastertime. The dough is enriched with eggs and flavoured with citrus peel and raisins.

60ml/4 tbsp vodka
2.5ml/½ tsp saffron threads
15ml/1 tbsp grated orange rind
15ml/1 tbsp grated lemon rind
115g/4oz/½ cup butter, softened
75g/3oz/6 tbsp caster (superfine) sugar
3 eggs
30ml/2 tbsp water
400g/14oz/3½ cups unbleached white bread flour
2.5ml/½ tsp salt
10ml/2 tsp easy bake (rapid-rise) dried yeast
75g/3oz/½ cup raisins
75g/3oz/½ cup dried sour cherries
115g/4oz/1 cup icing (confectioners') sugar
15ml/1 tbsp lemon juice

FOR THE DECORATION
toasted flaked almonds
pared orange rind or candied orange peel

SERVES 8–10

1 Steep the vodka, saffron and citrus rinds together for 30 minutes. Beat the butter and sugar in a bowl until pale and creamy. Tip the saffron mixture into the bread pan, then add the eggs and water. If necessary, reverse the order in which you add the liquid and dry ingredients.

2 Add the flour, covering the liquid. Add the salt in a corner. Make an indent in the flour; add the yeast. Set to the dough setting; use basic raisin dough setting (if available). Press Start.

3 Mix for 5 minutes, then add the creamed butter and sugar mixture.

4 Tip in the raisins and dried sour cherries when the machine beeps, or 5 minutes before the end of the kneading cycle. Lightly oil a brioche tin. When the cycle has finished, remove the dough from the pan and place on a floured surface.

5 Knock back (punch down) gently, and shape into a plump round ball. Place in the prepared tin, cover with lightly oiled clear film (plastic wrap) and leave in a warm place for about 2 hours, or until it has risen almost to the top of the tin.

6 Preheat the oven to 200°C/400°F/Gas 6. Bake the babka for 20 minutes. Reduce the oven temperature to 190°C/375°F/Gas 5 and continue to bake for 15–20 minutes more, until golden.

7 Turn the babka out on to a wire rack to cool. Meanwhile, make the icing. Place the icing sugar in a small bowl and add the lemon juice and 15ml/1 tbsp hot water. Mix well, then drizzle the icing over the cake. Sprinkle over the almonds and pared orange rind or candied orange peel to decorate.

Per serving Energy 349kcal/1473kJ; Protein 4.2g; Carbohydrate 61.2g, of which sugars 30.7g; Fat 10g, of which saturates 6.3g; Cholesterol 26mg; Calcium 78mg; Fibre 1.5g; Sodium 94mg.

SPICED FRUIT KUGELHOPF

Sultanas steeped in spiced rum flavour this brioche-style bread, which is baked in a special fluted mould with a central funnel.

1 Mix the rum, ginger, cloves, cinnamon stick and nutmeg in a small pan and place over a medium heat until hot, but not bubbling. Remove from the heat, add the sultanas and set aside in the pan for 30 minutes.

2 Pour the milk into the machine pan. Add three of the eggs, then separate the remaining eggs, setting the whites aside, and add the egg yolks to the pan.

3 Remove the cloves and cinnamon from the pan and discard (although the cinnamon stick can be dried for re-use later). Place a sieve over the bread pan and drain the sultanas in it so that the juices fall through into the pan. Set the sultanas aside. If the instructions for your bread machine specify that the yeast is to be placed in the machine pan first, then simply reverse the order in which you add the liquid and dry ingredients to the pan.

4 Sprinkle over the flour, ensuring that it covers the liquid mixture completely. Add the salt and sugar in separate corners of the bread pan. Make a small indent in the centre of the flour (but not down as far as the liquid) and add the easy bake dried yeast.

5 Set the bread machine to the dough setting; use basic dough setting (if available). Press Start. Mix for 5 minutes, then gradually add the melted butter. Lightly oil a non-stick kugelhopf tin.

6 When the dough cycle has finished, put the dough in a large mixing bowl. In a separate, grease-free bowl, whisk the egg whites to soft peaks. Add the reserved sultanas and cut mixed peel to the dough and fold in, using your hands. Gradually fold in the egg whites to form a soft dough.

7 Spoon the dough into the kugelhopf tin in three or four batches, making sure it is evenly distributed. Cover with lightly oiled clear film (plastic wrap) and leave in a slightly warm place for 1–1½ hours, or until the dough has risen and is almost at the top of the tin.

8 Preheat the oven to 190°C/375°F/Gas 5. Bake the kugelhopf for 50–60 minutes or until it has browned and is firm to the touch. You can cover the surface with baking parchment if it starts to brown too quickly. Turn out on to a wire rack to cool. Dust with icing sugar.

100ml/3½fl oz/7 tbsp dark rum
5ml/1 tsp ground ginger
3 whole cloves
1 cinnamon stick
5ml/1 tsp freshly grated nutmeg
*115g/4oz/⅔ cup sultanas
(golden raisins)*
30ml/2 tbsp milk
5 eggs
*500g/1lb 2oz/4½ cups unbleached
white bread flour*
2.5ml/½ tsp salt
*75g/3oz/6 tbsp caster
(superfine) sugar*
*10ml/2 tsp easy bake (rapid-rise)
dried yeast*
75g/3oz/6 tbsp butter, melted
*75g/3oz/½ cup cut mixed
(candied) peel*
*icing (confectioners') sugar,
for dusting*

MAKES 1 LOAF

Per loaf Energy 3635kcal/15330kJ; Protein 83.3g; Carbohydrate 592.5g, of which sugars 211.5g; Fat 97.2g, of which saturates 49.5g; Cholesterol 1126mg; Calcium 1101mg; Fibre 21.4g; Sodium 1180mg.

TEABREADS AND CAKES

Traditional teabreads and cakes use baking powder rather than yeast as a raising agent, giving them a light texture and a good flavour. Classic cakes, such as Madeira Cake, Marble Cake and Gingerbread can easily be baked in a bread machine. For more exotic combinations, there are recipes for Tropical Fruit Loaf, flavoured with pineapple, papaya, mango and melon; fresh Raspberry and Almond Teabread or sugar-topped Crunchy Pear and Cherry Cake.

MADEIRA CAKE

Delicately flavoured with vanilla, this classic plain cake has a firm yet light texture. Serve the traditional way with a glass of its namesake.

SMALL

115g/4oz/½ cup butter, cut into pieces
115g/4oz/generous ½ cup caster
(superfine) sugar
a few drops vanilla essence (extract)
150g/5½oz/1⅓ cup self-raising
(self-rising) flour
15g/½oz/2 tbsp plain
(all-purpose) flour
2 eggs, lightly beaten
15–30ml/1–2 tbsp milk

MEDIUM

140g/5oz/⅔ cup butter, cut into pieces
140g/5oz/¾ cup caster sugar
1.5ml/¼ tsp vanilla essence
165g/5½oz/generous 1¼ cups
self-raising flour
40g/1½oz/6 tbsp plain flour
3 eggs, lightly beaten
15–30ml/1–2 tbsp milk

LARGE

175g/6oz/¾ cup butter, cut into pieces
175g/6oz/⅞ cup caster sugar
1.5ml/¼ tsp vanilla essence
200g/7oz/1¾ cups self-raising flour
25g/1oz/¼ cup plain flour
3 eggs, lightly beaten
15–30ml/1–2 tbsp milk

MAKES 1 CAKE

1 Remove the kneading blade from the bread pan, if it is detachable, then line the base of the bread pan with baking parchment.

2 Cream the butter and sugar together in a large bowl until the mixture is very light and fluffy, then beat in the vanilla essence.

3 Sift the flours together. Gradually beat the eggs into the creamed mixture, beating well after each addition, and adding a little flour if the mixture starts to curdle.

COOK'S TIP

Cakes cooked in a bread pan tend to have browner sides than when cooked conventionally, in an oven, as the cooking element is around the sides of the bread pan. Cakes such as this, which have a high proportion of fat and sugar, need to be watched closely, as the edges will easily overcook.

4 Fold in the remaining flour mixture, using a metal spoon, then add enough of the milk to give a dropping consistency.

5 Spoon the mixture into the prepared pan and set the bread machine to the bake/bake only setting. Set the timer, if possible, for the recommended time. If, on your bread machine, the minimum time on this setting is for longer than the time suggested here, set the timer and check the cake after the shortest recommended time. Bake the small Madeira cake for 40–45 minutes, the medium for 50–55 minutes and the large cake for 60–65 minutes. Use the light crust setting, if available.

6 The cake should be well risen and firm to the touch. Test by inserting a skewer into the centre of the cake. It should come out clean. If necessary, bake for a few minutes more.

7 Remove the pan from the machine. Leave to stand for 5 minutes, then turn the cake out on to a wire rack to cool.

Per cake Energy 2264kcal/9472kJ; Protein 30.4g; Carbohydrate 257.1g, of which sugars 149.9g; Fat 131.3g, of which saturates 77.4g; Cholesterol 776mg; Calcium 368mg; Fibre 4.4g; Sodium 1040mg.

CRUNCHY PEAR AND CHERRY CAKE

Made from quick all-in-one cake mixture, this cake is filled with juicy pears and cherries, and has a crunchy demerara topping.

1 Remove the kneading blade from the bread pan, if it is detachable, then line the base of the bread pan with baking parchment.

2 Mix the margarine and caster sugar in a large bowl. Add the eggs, milk, flour and baking powder. Beat the mixture together for 1–2 minutes. Fold in the pears, cherries and ginger, using a metal spoon.

3 Spoon the mixture into the prepared pan. Sprinkle half the demerara sugar over the top. Set the machine to the bake/bake only setting. Set the timer, if possible, for the recommended time. If, on your bread machine, the minimum time on this setting is for longer than suggested here, set the timer and check the cake after the shortest recommended time. Bake the small cake for 45–50 minutes, the medium cake for 50–55 minutes and the large cake for 60–65 minutes.

4 Sprinkle the remaining sugar over after 25 minutes for the small cake, 30 minutes for medium, and 35 minutes for large. Insert a skewer into the centre to test if it is cooked: it should come out clean.

5 Remove the pan from the machine. Leave the cake to stand for 5 minutes, then turn out on to a wire rack to cool.

SMALL
75g/3oz/6 tbsp soft margarine
75g/3oz/scant ½ cup caster (superfine) sugar
2 eggs
30ml/2 tbsp milk
170g/6oz/1½ cups plain (all-purpose) flour
7.5ml/1½ tsp baking powder
50g/2oz/½ cup ready-to-eat dried pears, chopped
40g/1½oz/2 tbsp glacé (candied) cherries, quartered
25g/1oz/2 tbsp crystallized (candied) ginger, chopped
22ml/1½ tbsp demerara (raw) sugar

MEDIUM
100g/3½oz/7 tbsp soft margarine
100g/3½oz/½ cup caster sugar
2 eggs
60ml/4 tbsp milk
225g/8oz/2 cups plain flour
10ml/2 tsp baking powder
65g/2½oz/generous ½ cup ready-to-eat dried pears, chopped
65g/2½oz/generous ¼ cup glacé cherries, quartered
40g/1½oz/3 tbsp crystallized ginger, chopped
30ml/2 tbsp demerara sugar

LARGE
140g/5oz/⅔ cup soft margarine
140g/5oz/¾ cup caster sugar
3 eggs
60ml/4 tbsp milk
280g/10oz/2½ cups plain flour
12.5ml/2½ tsp baking powder
75g/3oz/¾ cup ready-to-eat dried pears, chopped
75g/3oz/scant ½ cup glacé cherries, quartered
50g/2oz/4 tbsp crystallized ginger, chopped
30ml/2 tbsp demerara sugar

MAKES 1 CAKE

Per cake Energy 1905kcal/8019kJ; Protein 31.4g; Carbohydrate 295.6g, of which sugars 166.1g; Fat 74.8g, of which saturates 3.4g; Cholesterol 381mg; Calcium 422mg; Fibre 9g; Sodium 775mg.

SODA BREAD

This quick Irish bread is perfect for a tea-time treat. It is best served warm with lashings of butter.

SMALL
240g/8½oz/generous 2 cups plain (all-purpose) flour
2.5ml/½ tsp salt
65g/2½oz/generous ½ cup coarse oatmeal
25g/1oz/2 tbsp butter
5ml/1 tsp bicarbonate of soda (baking soda)
5ml/1 tsp cream of tartar
10ml/2 tsp sugar
225ml/8fl oz/scant 1 cup buttermilk

MEDIUM
320g/11½oz/generous 2¾ cups plain flour
2.5ml/½ tsp salt
85g/3oz/¾ cup coarse oatmeal
40g/1½oz/3 tbsp butter
7.5ml/1½ tsp bicarbonate of soda
7.5ml/1½ tsp cream of tartar
10ml/2 tsp sugar
300ml/10½fl oz/1¼ cups buttermilk

LARGE
400g/14oz/3½ cups plain flour
5ml/1 tsp salt
100g/3½oz/scant 1 cup coarse oatmeal
50g/2oz/4 tbsp butter
10ml/2 tsp bicarbonate of soda
10ml/2 tsp cream of tartar
15ml/1 tbsp sugar
375ml/13½fl oz/1½ cups + 1 tbsp buttermilk

MAKES 1 LOAF

1 Remove the kneading blade from the bread pan, if it is detachable, then line the base of the bread pan with baking parchment.

2 Sift the flour and salt together into a mixing bowl. Stir in the oatmeal. Add the butter and rub into the flour until the mixture resembles fine breadcrumbs.

3 Add the bicarbonate of soda, cream of tartar and sugar, and mix together. Add the buttermilk and quickly mix together to a soft dough.

4 Place the mixture in the prepared bread pan. Set the bread machine to the bake/bake only setting, medium crust, if available. Set the timer, if possible, for the recommended time. If not, check the bread after the shortest recommended time. Bake the small bread for 45–50 minutes, the medium bread for 50–55 minutes and the large bread for 65–70 minutes.

5 Test by inserting a skewer in the centre of the bread: it should come out clean. If necessary, bake the bread for a few minutes more.

6 Remove the pan from the bread machine and leave to stand for 2–3 minutes. Turn out on to a wire rack. Serve warm.

Per loaf Energy 1235kcal/5253kJ; Protein 40.7g; Carbohydrate 273.9g, of which sugars 16.6g; Fat 5.2g, of which saturates 1g; Cholesterol 10mg; Calcium 793mg; Fibre 10.5g; Sodium 1600mg.

GINGERBREAD

This tea-time favourite can be baked easily in your bread machine. Store it in an airtight tin for a couple of days to allow the moist sticky texture to develop.

*175g/6oz/1½ cups plain
(all-purpose) flour
3.5ml/¾ tsp ground ginger
5ml/1 tsp baking powder
1.5ml/¼ tsp bicarbonate of soda
(baking soda)
2.5ml/½ tsp mixed (apple pie) spice
75g/3oz/6 tbsp light muscovado
(brown) sugar
50g/2oz/¼ cup butter, cut into pieces
75g/3oz/scant ⅓ cup golden
(light corn) syrup
40g/1½oz black treacle (molasses)
105ml/7 tbsp milk
1 egg, lightly beaten
40g/1½oz/¼ cup drained preserved
stem ginger, thinly sliced*

MEDIUM

*225g/8oz/2 cups plain flour
5ml/1 tsp ground ginger
7.5ml/1½ tsp baking powder
2.5ml/½ tsp bicarbonate of soda
2.5ml/½ tsp mixed spice
115g/4oz/½ cup light muscovado sugar
75g/3oz/6 tbsp butter, cut into pieces
100g/3½oz/generous ⅓ cup
golden syrup
50g/2oz black treacle
150ml/5fl oz/⅔ cup milk
1 egg, lightly beaten
50g/2oz/⅓ cup drained preserved
stem ginger, thinly sliced*

LARGE

*250g/9oz/2¼ cups plain flour
7.5ml/1½ tsp ground ginger
7.5ml/1½ tsp baking powder
3.5ml/¾ tsp bicarbonate of soda
3.5ml/¾ tsp mixed spice
115g/4oz/½ cup light muscovado sugar
100g/3½oz/scant ½ cup butter,
cut into pieces
115g/4oz/scant ½ cup golden syrup
50g/2oz black treacle
175ml/6fl oz/¾ cup milk
1 egg, lightly beaten
50g/2oz/⅓ cup drained preserved
stem ginger, thinly sliced*

1 Remove the kneading blade from the bread pan, if it is detachable, then line the base of the pan with baking parchment. Sift the flour, ginger, baking powder, bicarbonate of soda and mixed spice together into a large bowl.

2 Melt the sugar, butter, syrup and treacle in a pan over a low heat.

3 Make a well in the centre of the dry ingredients and pour in the melted mixture. Add the milk, egg and stem ginger and mix thoroughly.

4 Pour the mixture into the bread pan and set the machine to the bake/bake only setting. Set the timer, if possible, for the recommended time. If, on your machine, the minimum time on this setting is for longer than suggested here, set the timer and check the loaf after the shortest recommended time. Bake the small loaf for 40–45 minutes, medium for 50–55 minutes and large for 60–65 minutes, or until well risen.

5 Remove the bread pan. Leave to stand for 5 minutes, then turn on to a wire rack.

MAKES 1 LOAF

Per loaf Energy 1721kcal/7215kJ; Protein 14g; Carbohydrate 222g, of which sugars 221.4g; Fat 92.7g, of which saturates 57g; Cholesterol 401mg; Calcium 1154mg; Fibre 0g; Sodium 1048mg.

COCONUT CAKE

Desiccated coconut gives this simple, speedy cake a wonderful moist texture and delectable aroma.

SMALL
75g/3oz/6 tbsp butter or
margarine, softened
115g/4oz/generous ½ cup caster
(superfine) sugar
2 eggs, lightly beaten
115g/4oz/1⅓ cups desiccated (dry
unsweetened shredded) coconut
85g/3oz/¾ cup self-raising
(self-rising) flour
55ml/2fl oz/¼ cup sour cream
5ml/1 tsp grated lemon rind

MEDIUM
100g/3½oz/7 tbsp butter or
margarine, softened
140g/5oz/¾ cup caster sugar
2 large eggs, lightly beaten
140g/5oz/1⅔ cups desiccated coconut
100g/3½oz/scant 1 cup self-raising flour
70ml/2½fl oz/scant ⅓ cup sour cream
7.5ml/1½ tsp grated lemon rind

LARGE
115g/4oz/½ cup butter or
margarine, softened
150g/5½oz/⅔ cup caster sugar
3 eggs, lightly beaten
150g/5½oz/1⅞ cups desiccated coconut
115g/4oz/1 cup self-raising flour
85ml/3fl oz/⅜ cup sour cream
10ml/2 tsp grated lemon rind

MAKES 1 CAKE

1 Remove the kneading blade from the bread pan, if detachable. Line the base of the pan with baking parchment.

2 Cream the butter or margarine and sugar together until pale and fluffy, then add the eggs a little at a time, beating well after each addition.

3 Add the desiccated coconut, flour, sour cream and lemon rind. Gradually mix together, using a non-metallic spoon.

4 Spoon into the pan and set the machine to the bake/bake only setting. Set the timer, if possible, for the recommended time. If, on your bread machine, the minimum time on this setting is longer than suggested here, set the timer and check after the shortest recommended time. Bake the small or medium cake for 40–50 minutes; large for 55–60 minutes.

5 Test if the cake is cooked after the recommended time by inserting a skewer into the centre of it. It should come out clean. If necessary, bake the cake for a few minutes more.

6 Remove the bread pan from the machine. Leave the cake to stand for 5 minutes, then turn the cake out on to a wire rack to cool.

COOK'S TIP
This cake is delicious with a lemon syrup drizzled over the top once it is cooked. Heat 30ml/2 tbsp lemon juice with 100g/3½oz/scant ½ cup granulated sugar and 85ml/3fl oz/ 6 tbsp water in a small pan, stirring constantly until the sugar has dissolved. Bring to the boil, then simmer for 2–3 minutes before drizzling the syrup over the warm coconut cake.

Per cake Energy 2205kcal/9244kJ; Protein 30.4g; Carbohydrate 277.5g, of which sugars 220.5g; Fat 116.3g, of which saturates 82.4g; Cholesterol 611mg; Calcium 313mg; Fibre 16.2g; Sodium 506mg.

RASPBERRY AND ALMOND TEABREAD

Fresh raspberries and almonds combine perfectly to flavour this mouthwatering cake. Toasted flaked almonds make a crunchy topping.

1 Remove the kneading blade from the bread machine pan, if it is detachable, then line the base of the pan with baking parchment.

2 Sift the self-raising flour into a large bowl. Add the butter and rub in with your fingertips until the mixture resembles fine breadcrumbs.

3 Stir in the caster sugar and ground almonds. Gradually beat in the egg(s). If making the small or large teabread, beat in the milk.

4 Fold in the raspberries, then spoon the mixture into the prepared pan. Sprinkle over the flaked almonds.

SMALL
140g/5oz/1¼ cups self-raising (self-rising) flour
70g/2½oz/5 tbsp butter, cut into pieces
70g/2½oz/generous ⅓ cup caster (superfine) sugar
25g/1oz/¼ cup ground almonds
1 large egg, lightly beaten
30ml/2 tbsp milk
115g/4oz/1 cup raspberries
22ml/1½ tbsp flaked (sliced) almonds

MEDIUM
175g/6oz/1½ cups self-raising flour
90g/3½oz/7 tbsp butter, cut into pieces
90g/3½oz/½ cup caster sugar
40g/1½oz/⅓ cup ground almonds
2 large eggs, lightly beaten
140g/5oz/1¼ cups raspberries
30ml/2 tbsp flaked almonds

LARGE
225g/8oz/2 cups self-raising flour
115g/4oz/½ cup butter, cut into pieces
115g/4oz/generous ½ cup caster sugar
50g/2oz/½ cup ground almonds
2 large eggs, lightly beaten
45ml/3 tbsp milk
175g/6oz/1½ cups raspberries
30ml/2 tbsp flaked almonds

MAKES 1 TEABREAD

5 Set the bread machine to the bake/ bake only setting. Set the timer, if possible, for the recommended time. If not, set the timer and check after the shortest recommended time. Bake the small loaf for 40–45 minutes, the medium for 55–60 minutes and the large for 65–70 minutes or until well risen. Use the light crust setting, if available.

6 Test by inserting a skewer into the centre of the teabread. It should come out clean.

7 Remove the pan from the machine. Leave to stand for 5 minutes, then turn out on to a wire rack to cool. This cake is best eaten on the day it is made, when the fresh raspberries will be at their best.

Per cake Energy 1722Kcal/7212kJ; Protein 34.3g; Carbohydrate 192.5g, of which sugars 84.4g; Fat 96.1g, of which saturates 42.6g; Cholesterol 353mg; Calcium 469mg; Fibre 11.3g; Sodium 631mg.

PASSION CAKE

Don't be misled into assuming this cake contains passion fruit. It is actually a carrot and walnut cake and a very good one, too. Topped with a tangy lemon cheese icing, it makes the perfect tea-time treat.

SMALL

115g/4oz/½ cup butter
115g/4oz/½ cup soft light brown sugar
2 eggs, separated
5ml/1 tsp lemon juice, plus 5ml/1 tsp
for the topping
115g/4oz/1 cup self-raising flour
2.5ml/½ tsp baking powder
25g/1oz/¼ cup ground almonds
65g/2½oz/generous ½ cup walnut
pieces, chopped
175g/6oz/scant 1¼ cups grated carrot
115g/4oz/½ cup mascarpone cheese
25g/1oz/2 tbsp icing
(confectioners') sugar
22ml/1½ tbsp walnut pieces,
to decorate

MEDIUM

140g/5oz/scant ⅔ cup butter
140g/5oz/scant ⅔ cup soft light
brown sugar
2 eggs, separated
10ml/2 tsp lemon juice, plus 5ml/1 tsp
for the topping
15ml/1 tbsp milk
140g/5oz/1¼ cups self-raising flour
3.5ml/¾ tsp baking powder
40g/1½oz/⅓ cup ground almonds
75g/3oz/¾ cup walnut
pieces, chopped
200g/7oz/scant 1½ cups grated carrot
140g/5oz/⅔ cup mascarpone cheese
40g/1½oz/3 tbsp icing sugar
30ml/2 tbsp walnut pieces, to decorate

LARGE

150g/5½oz/⅔ cup butter
150g/5½oz/⅔ cup soft light brown sugar
3 eggs, separated
15ml/1 tbsp lemon juice, plus
5ml/1 tsp for the topping
150g/5½oz/1⅓ cups self-raising flour
5ml/1 tsp baking powder
50g/2oz/½ cup ground almonds
100g/3½oz/⅞ cup walnut
pieces, chopped
200g/7oz/scant 1½ cups grated carrot
140g/5oz/⅔ cup mascarpone cheese
40g/1½oz/3 tbsp icing sugar
30ml/2 tbsp walnut pieces, to decorate

MAKES 1 CAKE

1 Remove the kneading blade from the bread machine pan, if it is detachable. Line the base of the bread pan with baking parchment.

2 Place the butter and sugar together in a large mixing bowl and cream until light and fluffy. Beat in the egg yolks, one at a time, then beat in the lemon juice. If making the medium cake, beat in the milk.

3 Sieve the flour and baking powder together and fold in. Add the ground almonds and chopped walnut pieces.

4 Meanwhile, whisk the egg whites in a grease-free bowl until stiff.

5 Fold the egg whites into the creamed cake mixture, together with the grated carrot and mix.

6 Spoon the mixture into the prepared pan and set the machine to the bake/ bake only setting. Set the timer, if possible, for the recommended time. If, on your bread machine, the minimum time on this setting is for longer than the time suggested here, set the timer and check after the shortest recommended time. Bake the small and the medium cake for 40–50 minutes and the large cake for 65–70 minutes.

7 The passion cake should be well risen and firm to the touch. Test by inserting a skewer into the centre of the cake. It should come out clean. If necessary, bake for a few minutes more.

8 Remove the pan from the machine. Leave the cake to stand for 5 minutes, then turn out on to a wire rack to cool.

9 To finish the passion cake, beat the mascarpone cheese with the icing sugar and lemon juice. Spread the topping mixture over the top of the cake and sprinkle with the walnut pieces.

COOK'S TIP
If you can't locate mascarpone cheese, use cream cheese instead. It doesn't matter whether it is full-fat or a light cheese.

Per cake Energy 2643kcal/11041kJ; Protein 31.2g; Carbohydrate 279.3g, of which sugars 184.2g; Fat 163.7g, of which saturates 88.2g; Cholesterol 545mg; Calcium 488mg; Fibre 9g; Sodium 1088mg.

LEMON AND GINGER CAKE

This cake is quick to make, as your machine will mix as well as bake it for you. Just add the liquid ingredients followed by the dry ones, press start and the machine will do the rest.

SMALL
125g/4½oz/generous ½ cup butter,
melted and cooled
2 eggs
10ml/2 tsp lemon juice
25g/1oz/2 tbsp candied lemon
peel, chopped
40g/1½oz/3 tbsp crystallized
ginger, chopped
175g/6oz/generous 1½ cups plain
(all-purpose) flour
7.5ml/1½ tsp baking powder
125g/4½oz/½ cup + 1 tbsp caster
(superfine) sugar

MEDIUM
150g/5½oz/⅔ cup butter, melted
and cooled
3 eggs
10ml/2 tsp lemon juice
35g/1¼oz/3 tbsp candied lemon
peel, chopped
50g/2oz/4 tbsp crystallized
ginger, chopped
215g/7½oz/1⅞ cup plain flour
10ml/2 tsp baking powder
150g/5½oz/⅔ cup caster sugar

LARGE
175g/6oz/¾ cup butter, melted
and cooled
3 eggs
15ml/1 tbsp lemon juice
40g/1½oz/3 tbsp candied lemon
peel, chopped
65g/2½oz/5 tbsp crystallized
ginger, chopped
265g/9½oz/2⅓ cups plain flour
15ml/1 tbsp baking powder
175g/6oz/¾ cup caster sugar

FOR THE LEMON ICING
10ml/2 tsp lemon juice
40-50g/1½-2oz icing
(confectioners') sugar

MAKES 1 CAKE

1 Mix the butter, eggs and lemon juice together and pour into the bread machine pan. Add the candied peel and crystallized ginger.

2 Sift the flour and baking powder together. Stir in the caster sugar and add to the bread machine pan.

3 Set the bread machine to the cake setting, light crust, 500g, if available.

4 Remove the bread pan at the end of the cycle. Leave to stand for 5 minutes, then turn out the cake on to a wire rack to cool. Mix the lemon juice and icing sugar together and drizzle over the cake. Leave to set.

Per cake Energy 2367kcal/9931kJ; Protein 30.5g; Carbohydrate 320.7g, of which sugars 187.3g; Fat 116.1g, of which saturates 70.9g; Cholesterol 668mg; Calcium 479mg; Fibre 8.5g; Sodium 1273mg.

VANILLA-CHOCOLATE MARBLE CAKE

White and dark chocolate, marbled together, make a cake that tastes as good as it looks. Serve it for tea, or cut it into chunks, mix it with fresh peach slices and add a sprinkling of orange or peach liqueur for an impressive dessert.

SMALL

115g/4oz/½ cup margarine or butter
115g/4oz/generous ½ cup caster
(superfine) sugar
2 eggs, lightly beaten
40g/1½oz white chocolate, in pieces
40g/1½oz plain (semisweet)
chocolate, in pieces
1.5ml/¼ tsp vanilla essence (extract)
175g/6oz/1½ cups self-raising
(self-rising) flour
icing (confectioners') sugar and
cocoa powder (unsweetened),
for dusting

MEDIUM

125g/4½oz/generous ½ cup
margarine or butter
125g/4½oz/scant ¾ cup caster sugar
2 eggs, lightly beaten
50g/2oz white chocolate, in pieces
50g/2oz plain chocolate, in pieces
2.5ml/½ tsp vanilla essence
200g/7oz/1¾ cups self-raising flour
icing sugar and cocoa powder,
for dusting

LARGE

175g/6oz/¾ cup margarine
or butter
175g/6oz/⅞ cup caster sugar
3 eggs, lightly beaten
65g/2½oz white chocolate, in pieces
65g/2½oz plain chocolate, in pieces
2.5ml/½ tsp vanilla essence
250g/9oz/2¼ cups self-raising flour
icing sugar and cocoa powder,
for dusting

MAKES 1 CAKE

1 Remove the kneading blade from the bread pan, if detachable. Line the base of the pan with baking parchment. Cream the margarine or butter and sugar together until light and fluffy. Slowly add the eggs, beating thoroughly. Place half the mixture in another bowl.

2 Place the white chocolate in a heatproof bowl over a pan of simmering water. Stir until the chocolate is melted.

3 Melt the plain chocolate in a separate bowl, in the same way. Stir the white chocolate and the vanilla essence into one bowl of creamed mixture and the plain chocolate into the other. Divide the flour equally between the two bowls and lightly fold it in with a metal spoon.

4 Put alternate spoonfuls of the two mixtures into the prepared bread pan. Use a round-bladed knife to swirl the mixtures together to marble them.

5 Set the bread machine to the bake/bake only setting. Set the timer, if possible, for the recommended time. If not check after the shortest recommended time. Bake the small cake for 45–50 minutes, medium for 50–55 minutes and large for 65–70 minutes. Use the light crust setting if available.

6 The cake should be just firm to the touch. Test by inserting a skewer into the centre of the cake. It should come out clean. If necessary, bake for a few minutes more.

7 Remove the pan from the machine. Leave to stand for 5 minutes, then turn the cake out on to a wire rack. Dust with icing sugar and cocoa powder and serve in slices or chunks.

Per cake Energy 2379kcal/10077kJ; Protein 15.7g; Carbohydrate 493.8g, of which sugars 439.6g; Fat 51.7g, of which saturates 30.6g; Cholesterol 231mg; Calcium 393mg; Fibre 2.6g; Sodium 366mg.

BANANA AND PECAN TEABREAD

This moist, light teabread is flavoured with banana, lightly spiced with nutmeg and studded with sultanas and pecan nuts. Weigh the bananas after peeling them – it is important to use the precise quantities given.

SMALL

75g/3oz/6 tbsp butter, softened
150g/5½oz/generous ¾ cup caster (superfine) sugar
2 eggs, lightly beaten
175g/6oz/1½ cups self-raising (self-rising) flour, sifted
150g/5½oz peeled ripe bananas
70ml/2½fl oz/5 tbsp buttermilk
1.5ml/¼ tsp baking powder
2.5ml/½ tsp freshly grated nutmeg
100g/3½oz/generous ½ cup sultanas (golden raisins)
65g/2½oz/generous ½ cup pecan nuts, chopped
15ml/1 tbsp banana or apricot jam, melted
15ml/1 tbsp banana chips

MEDIUM

100g/3½oz/7 tbsp butter, softened
175g/6oz/⅞ cup caster sugar
2 large eggs, lightly beaten
200g/7oz/1¾ cups self-raising flour, sifted
200g/7oz peeled ripe bananas
85ml/3fl oz/6 tbsp buttermilk
2.5ml/½ tsp baking powder
5ml/1 tsp freshly grated nutmeg
125g/4½oz/⅔ cup sultanas
75g/3oz/¾ cup pecan nuts, chopped
30ml/2 tbsp banana or apricot jam, melted
30ml/2 tbsp banana chips

LARGE

115g/4oz/½ cup butter, softened
200g/7oz/1 cup caster sugar
3 eggs, lightly beaten
225g/8oz/2 cups self-raising flour, sifted
200g/7oz peeled ripe bananas
100ml/3½fl oz/7 tbsp buttermilk
2.5ml/½ tsp baking powder
5ml/1 tsp freshly grated nutmeg
140g/5oz/scant 1 cup sultanas
75g/3oz/¾ cup pecan nuts, chopped
30ml/2 tbsp banana or apricot jam, melted
30ml/2 tbsp banana chips

MAKES 1 TEABREAD

1 Remove the kneading blade from the bread pan, if detachable. Line the base of the pan with baking parchment.

2 Cream the butter and caster sugar in a mixing bowl until pale and fluffy. Gradually beat in the eggs, beating well after each addition, and adding a little of the flour if the mixture starts to curdle.

3 Mash the bananas until completely smooth. Beat into the creamed mixture with the buttermilk.

4 Sift the remaining flour and the baking powder into the bowl. Add the nutmeg, sultanas and pecans; beat until smooth.

5 Spoon the mixture into the prepared pan and set the bread machine to the bake/bake only setting. Set the timer, if possible, for the recommended time. If not check the cake after the shortest recommended time. Bake the small or medium cake for 50–60 minutes, and the large cake for 65–70 minutes. Use the light crust setting if available.

6 Remove the pan from the bread machine. Leave it to stand for about 5 minutes, then turn the cake out on to a wire rack.

7 While the cake is still warm, brush the top with the melted jam and sprinkle over the banana chips. Leave to cool completely before serving.

Per cake Energy 3277kcal/13745kJ; Protein 52.8g; Carbohydrate 413.7g, of which sugars 239.9g; Fat 168.2g, of which saturates 69.2g; Cholesterol 1263mg; Calcium 1056mg; Fibre 13.1g; Sodium 1701mg.

GOJI BERRY AND YOGURT TEABREAD

*Packed full of fruit and nuts, this healthy teabread is equally delicious
served as a mid-morning snack or a tea-time treat. Goji berries are
vitamin-rich and are becoming more popular and widely available.*

1 Mix the yogurt and egg(s) together
and pour into the bread machine pan.

2 Sift the flour and baking powder
together. Stir in the nutmeg. Add the
butter and rub in with your fingers until
the mixture resembles fine
breadcrumbs. Stir in the sugars.

3 Mix in the goji berries, walnuts and
apricots. Add to the bread machine pan.

4 Set the machine to the cake setting,
light crust, 500g, if available. Remove
the bread pan at the end of the cycle.
Leave to stand for 5 minutes, then turn
out the cake on to a wire rack to cool.

COOK'S TIP

If your machine does not have a cake
setting, or if you prefer, you can mix
the cake by hand, then bake it in the
machine. Mix the yogurt and egg into
the dry mixture. Stir in the nuts and
fruits. Remove the kneading blade from
the bread pan, line the pan with baking
parchment and place the mixture in
the pan. Cook on the bake setting for
45 minutes for small, 50 minutes for
medium and 60–65 minutes for large, or
until risen and firm to the touch. Test it
is cooked by inserting a skewer into the
centre: it should come out clean.

SMALL
120ml/generous 4fl oz/½ cup natural
(plain) live yogurt
1 egg
200g/7oz/1¾ cups plain
(all-purpose) flour
10ml/2 tsp baking powder
2.5ml/½ tsp ground nutmeg
65g/2½oz/5 tbsp butter
35g/1¼oz/3 tbsp light muscovado
(brown) sugar
25g/1oz/2 tbsp caster (superfine) sugar
40g/1½oz/⅓ cup goji berries
40g/1½oz/¼ cup walnuts, chopped
50g/2oz/⅜ cup ready-to-eat dried
apricots, chopped

MEDIUM
200ml/7fl oz/⅞ cup natural
live yogurt
1 egg
280g/10oz/2½ cups plain flour
12.5ml/2½ tsp baking powder
4ml/⅘ tsp ground nutmeg
75g/3oz/6 tbsp butter, softened
45g/1¾oz/3 tbsp light muscovado sugar
30g/generous 1oz/2¼ tbsp caster sugar
50g/2oz/⅜ cup goji berries
50g/2oz/½ cup walnuts, chopped
75g/3oz/generous ½ cup ready-to-eat
dried apricots, chopped

LARGE
210ml/7½fl oz/scant 1 cup natural
live yogurt
2 eggs
350g/12½oz/3 cups plain flour
15ml/3 tsp baking powder
5ml/1 tsp ground nutmeg
85g/3oz/6 tbsp butter, softened
45g/1¾oz/3 tbsp light muscovado sugar
45g/1¾oz/3 tbsp caster sugar
65g/2½oz/¾ cup goji berries
65g/2½oz/generous ½ cup
walnuts, chopped
75g/3oz/generous ½ cup ready-to-eat
dried apricots, chopped

MAKES 1 TEABREAD

Per cake Energy 1928kcal/8007kJ; Protein 04.0g; Carbohydrate 274.4g, of which sugars 121.7g; Fat 84.8g, of which saturates 38.3g; Cholesterol 151mg; Calcium 642mg; Fibre 11.6g; Sodium 631mg.

TROPICAL FRUIT LOAF

*There's a tempting tropical taste in every slice of this wonderfully moist loaf.
Speckled with delicious little chunks of papaya, mango, melon and
pineapple, it is topped with a tangy lime soft cheese icing and finished
with fresh toasted coconut.*

SMALL
*125g/4½oz/1 cup plain (all-purpose) flour
5ml/1 tsp baking powder
40g/1½oz/½ cup desiccated (dry
unsweetened shredded) coconut
65g/2½oz/5 tbsp butter, diced
65g/2½oz/5 tbsp caster (superfine) sugar
100g/3½oz/generous ½ cup ready-to-eat
dried tropical fruits, chopped
100ml/3½fl oz/7 tbsp milk
1 egg, lightly beaten
grated rind and juice of ½ lime*

FOR THE ICING (SMALL)
*75g/3oz/scant ½ cup full-fat soft white
(farmer's) cheese
45ml/3 tbsp icing (confectioners') sugar
juice of ½ lime*

MEDIUM
*175g/6oz/1½ cup plain flour
5ml/1 tsp baking powder
50g/2oz/⅝ cup desiccated coconut
100g/3½oz/7 tbsp butter, diced
100g/3½oz/7 tbsp caster sugar
140g/5oz/scant 1 cup ready-to-eat dried
tropical fruits, chopped
130ml/4½fl oz/½ cup + 1 tbsp milk
1 egg, lightly beaten
grated rind and juice of ½ lime*

LARGE
*225g/8oz/2 cups plain flour
7.5ml/1½ tsp baking powder
65g/2½oz/⅞ cup desiccated coconut
115g/4oz/½ cup butter, diced
125g/4½oz/⅝ cup caster sugar
160g/5¾oz/scant 1 cup ready-to-eat
dried tropical fruits, chopped
200ml/7fl oz/⅞ cup milk
1 egg, lightly beaten
grated rind and juice of ½ lime*

FOR THE ICING (MEDIUM AND LARGE)
*125g/4½oz/½ cup full-fat soft white cheese
60ml/4 tbsp icing sugar
juice of ½ lime*

FOR THE DECORATION
pared lime rind and fresh coconut shreds

MAKES 1 LOAF

1 Remove the kneading blade from the bread pan, if detachable. Line the base of the pan with baking parchment.

2 Sift the flour and baking powder into a large bowl. Then mix in the desiccated coconut. Add the butter and rub in with your fingers until the mixture resembles fine breadcrumbs.

3 Stir in the sugar and dried tropical fruits. Gradually add the milk, egg, grated lime rind and juice, beating well after each addition.

4 Spoon the mixture into the prepared pan and set the bread machine to the bake/bake only setting. Set the timer, if possible for the recommended time. If, on your bread machine, the minimum time on this setting is for longer than the time here, set the timer and check the cake after the shortest recommended time. Bake the small or medium cake for 40–50 minutes, and the large cake for 65–70 minutes. Use the light crust setting if available.

5 The fruit loaf should be well risen and firm to the touch. Test by inserting a skewer into the centre of the loaf. It should come out perfectly clean.

6 Remove the bread pan from the bread machine. Leave the loaf to stand for about 5 minutes, then turn it out on to a wire rack to cool.

7 Meanwhile, make the icing. Cream the soft cheese, icing sugar and lime juice together in a bowl. Spread the mixture over the top of the loaf.

8 Lightly toast the coconut shavings or shreds. Leave to cool for 2–3 minutes, then use them to decorate the top of the loaf, with the pared lime rind.

COOK'S TIP
When testing the cake with a skewer, try to avoid piercing a piece of dried fruit, or the skewer will come out sticky and might therefore give you a misleading result.

Per loaf Energy 2024kcal/8461kJ; Protein 26.8g; Carbohydrate 218.1g, of which sugars 122.9g; Fat 122.4g, of which saturates 81.5g; Cholesterol 417mg; Calcium 496mg; Fibre 10.3g; Sodium 882mg.

AMERICAN COFFEE BREAD

This quick and easy sweet bread keeps well and so makes a useful standby.

Small
175g/6oz/1½ cups plain
(all-purpose) flour
7.5ml/1½ tsp baking powder
pinch of salt
75g/3oz/6 tbsp light muscovado
(brown) sugar
50g/2oz/½ cup pecan nuts, chopped
7.5ml/1½ tsp instant coffee
20g/¾oz/1½ tbsp butter, melted
75ml/5 tbsp milk
1 egg, lightly beaten

Medium
200g/7oz/1¾ cups plain flour
10ml/2 tsp baking powder
pinch of salt
100g/3½oz/scant ½ cup light
muscovado sugar
75g/3oz/¾ cup pecan nuts, chopped
10ml/2 tsp instant coffee
25g/1oz/2 tbsp butter, melted
100ml/3½fl oz/7 tbsp milk
2 eggs, lightly beaten

Large
280g/10oz/2½ cups plain flour
15ml/1 tbsp baking powder
pinch of salt
150g/5½oz/⅔ cup light muscovado sugar
100g/3½oz/⅞ cup pecan nuts, chopped
15ml/1 tbsp instant coffee
40g/1½oz/3 tbsp butter, melted
115ml/4fl oz/½ cup milk
3 eggs, lightly beaten

Makes 1 Loaf

COOK'S TIP
For a special tea-time treat, drizzle
the loaf with coffee glacé icing and
decorate with pecan nut halves.

---

1 Remove the kneading blade from the
bread machine pan, if it is detachable.
Line the base of the bread pan with
baking parchment.

2 Sift the flour, baking powder and salt into
a large bowl. Stir in the sugar and pecan
nuts. Dissolve the coffee granules or powder
with 15ml/1 tbsp hot water in a cup.

3 Add the coffee, the melted butter,
milk and egg(s) to the dry ingredients.
Beat thoroughly to mix. Spoon the
mixture into the prepared pan and
set the bread machine to the bake/
bake only setting.

4 Set the timer, if possible, for the
recommended time. If not, set
the timer and check after the shortest
recommended time. Bake the small cake
for 40–45 minutes, the medium for
50–60 minutes and the large cake
for 65–70 minutes. Use the light crust
setting if available.

5 Test by inserting a skewer into the centre
of the loaf. It should come out clean. If
necessary, bake for a few minutes more.

6 Remove the bread pan from the
machine. Leave to stand for 5 minutes,
then turn out on to a wire rack to cool.

Per loaf Energy 1419kcal/5972kJ; Protein 24g; Carbohydrate 221g, of which sugars 86.9g; Fat 54.9g, of which saturates 14.8g; Cholesterol 50mg; Calcium 408mg; Fibre 7.8g; Sodium 202mg.

Peanut Butter Teabread

Peanut butter gives this teabread a distinctive flavour and interesting texture.

SMALL

75g/3oz/¼ cup crunchy peanut butter
65g/2½oz/⅓ cup caster
(superfine) sugar
1 egg, lightly beaten
105ml/7 tbsp milk
200g/7oz/1¾ cups self-raising
(self-rising) flour

MEDIUM

115g/4oz/½ cup crunchy
peanut butter
75g/3oz/scant ½ cup caster sugar
1 egg, lightly beaten
175ml/6fl oz/¾ cup milk
300g/10½oz/generous 2½ cups
self-raising flour

LARGE

135g/4¾oz/scant ½ cup crunchy
peanut butter
125g/4½oz/scant ¾ cup caster sugar
2 eggs, lightly beaten
200ml/7fl oz/⅞ cup milk
400g/14oz/3½ cups self-raising flour

MAKES 1 TEABREAD

1 Remove the kneading blade from the bread machine pan, if it is detachable, then line the base of the pan with baking parchment.

2 Cream the peanut butter and sugar in a bowl together until light and fluffy, then gradually beat in the egg(s).

3 Add the milk and flour and mix with a wooden spoon.

COOK'S TIP
Leave a rough finish on the top of the cake before baking to add character.

4 Spoon the mixture into the prepared bread pan and set the machine to the bake/bake only setting.

5 Set the timer, if possible for the recommended time. If, on your bread machine, the minimum time on this setting is for longer than the time here, set the timer and check the cake after the shortest recommended time. Bake the small cake for 40–45 minutes, medium for 55–60 minutes and large for 60–65 minutes. Use the light bake setting if available.

6 The teabread should be well risen and just firm to the touch. Test by inserting a skewer in the centre of the teabread. It should come out clean. If necessary, bake for a few minutes more.

7 Remove the bread pan from the bread machine. Leave to stand for 5 minutes, then turn on to a wire rack to cool.

Per cake Energy 1527kcal/6439kJ; Protein 45.8g; Carbohydrate 238.4g, of which sugars 81.2g; Fat 48.8g, of which saturates 11.8g; Cholesterol 196mg; Calcium 497mg; Fibre 10.3g; Sodium 400mg.

SMALL
115g/4oz/⅔ cup pitted dates
grated rind and juice of ½ lemon
115g/4oz/1 cup self-raising
(self-rising) flour
2.5ml/½ tsp each ground cinnamon,
ginger and grated nutmeg
50g/2oz/¼ cup butter
50g/2oz/¼ cup light muscovado
(brown) sugar
15ml/1 tbsp treacle (molasses)
30ml/2 tbsp golden (light corn) syrup
40ml/2½ tbsp milk
1 egg
40g/1½oz/⅓ cup chopped walnuts

MEDIUM
140g/5oz/scant 1 cup pitted dates
grated rind and juice of 1 lemon
170g/6oz/1½ cups self-raising flour
3.5ml/¾ tsp each ground cinnamon,
ginger and grated nutmeg
75g/3oz/6 tbsp butter
75g/3oz/6 tbsp light muscovado sugar
22ml/1½ tbsp treacle
45ml/3 tbsp golden syrup
60ml/4 tbsp milk
1 large egg
50g/2oz/½ cup chopped walnuts

LARGE
155g/5½oz/scant 1 cup pitted dates
grated rind and juice of 1 lemon
200g/7oz/1¾ cups self-raising flour
5ml/1 tsp each ground cinnamon,
ginger and grated nutmeg
100g/3½oz/scant ½ cup butter
100g/3½oz/scant ½ cup light
muscovado sugar
22ml/1½ tbsp treacle
45ml/3 tbsp golden syrup
75ml/5 tbsp milk
1 large egg
65g/2½oz/generous ½ cup chopped walnuts

TOPPING FOR ALL SIZES OF LOAF
25g/1oz/2 tbsp butter
50g/2oz/¼ cup light muscovado sugar
22ml/1½ tbsp plain (all-purpose) flour
3.5ml/¾ tsp ground cinnamon
40g/1½oz/⅓ cup chopped walnuts
MAKES 1 CAKE

TREACLE, DATE AND WALNUT CAKE

Layered with date purée and finished with a crunchy sugar and walnut topping, this cake is absolutely irresistible.

1 Remove the kneading blade from the bread pan, if it is detachable. Line the base of the pan with baking parchment. Place the dates, lemon rind and juice in a saucepan, add 60ml/4 tbsp water and bring to the boil. Simmer until soft. Purée in a blender or food processor until smooth.

2 Sift the flour and spices together. Cream the butter and sugar until pale and fluffy. Warm the treacle, golden syrup and milk in a pan, until just melted then beat into the creamed butter mixture. Add the egg and beat in the flour mixture, then stir in the chopped walnuts.

> **COOK'S TIP**
> You could try decreasing the topping ingredients by 25 per cent if you are making a small cake.

3 Place half the mixture in the bread pan. Spread over the date purée, leaving a narrow border of cake mix all round. Top with the remaining cake mixture, spreading it evenly over the date purée.

4 Set the bread machine to the bake/bake only setting. Set the timer, if possible for the recommended time. If not, set the timer and check after the shortest recommended time. Bake the small cake for 30 minutes, medium for 40 minutes and large for 50 minutes. Use the light bake setting if available.

5 Mix the topping ingredients together, sprinkle over the nearly baked cake and cook for 15–20 minutes more, until the topping bubbles and the cake is cooked.

6 Remove the bread pan from the machine. Leave to stand for 15 minutes, then turn out on to a wire rack to cool.

Per cake Energy 1771kcal/7445kJ; Protein 29.7g; Carbohydrate 256.9g, of which sugars 169g; Fat 76.6g, of which saturates 31.4g; Cholesterol 457mg; Calcium 447mg; Fibre 9.6g; Sodium 573mg.

Strawberry Teabread

Perfect for a summertime treat, this hazelnut-flavoured teabread is laced with luscious fresh strawberries.

SMALL
115g/4oz/1 cup strawberries
115g/4oz/½ cup butter, softened
115g/4oz/generous ½ cup caster
(superfine) sugar
2 eggs, beaten
140g/5oz/1¼ cups self-raising
(self-rising) flour, sifted
25g/1oz/¼ cup ground hazelnuts

MEDIUM
170g/6oz/1½ cups strawberries
140g/5oz/⅔ cup butter, softened
140g/5oz/⅔ cup caster sugar
2 eggs, beaten
15ml/1 tbsp milk
155g/5½oz/1⅓ cups self-raising
flour, sifted
40g/1½oz/⅓ cup ground hazelnuts

LARGE
175g/6oz/1½ cups strawberries
150g/5½oz/⅔ cup butter, softened
150g/5½oz/⅔ cup caster sugar
3 eggs, beaten
175g/6oz/1½ cups self-raising
flour, sifted
40g/1½oz/⅓ cup ground hazelnuts

MAKES 1 TEABREAD

1 Remove the kneading blade from the bread machine pan, if it is detachable, then line the base of the pan with baking parchment.

3 Gradually beat in the eggs and milk (if you are making the medium cake), beating well after each addition to combine quickly without curdling.

5 Fold in the strawberries and spoon the mixture into the pan. Set the bread machine to the bake/bake only setting. Set the timer, if possible, for the recommended time. If, on your machine, the minimum time on this setting is for longer than the time suggested here, set the timer and check the cake after the shortest recommended time. Bake the small cake for 40–45 minutes, medium for 50–55 minutes and large for 55–60 minutes. Use the light bake setting if available.

6 Test by inserting a skewer in the centre of the teabread. It should come out clean. If necessary, bake for a few minutes more.

2 Hull the strawberries and chop them roughly. Set them aside. Cream the butter and sugar in a mixing bowl until pale and fluffy.

4 Mix the self-raising flour and the ground hazelnuts together and gradually fold into the creamed mixture, using a metal spoon.

7 Remove the bread pan. Leave the teabread to stand for 5 minutes, then turn out on to a wire rack to cool.

Per cake Energy 9119kcal/0002kJ; Protein 31.3g; Carbohydrate 237.4g, of which sugars 130.2g; Fat 122.9g, of which saturates 66.7g; Cholesterol 645mg; Calcium 385mg; Fibre 7.2g; Sodium 1022mg.

SUPPLIERS

UK

BREAD MACHINE MANUFACTURERS

KENWOOD
1 Kenwood Business Park
New Lane
Havant
PO9 2NH
Tel: 023 9247 6000

MORPHY RICHARDS
Talbot Road
Mexborough
S64 8AJ
Helpline: 0344 871 0944
www.morphyrichards.co.uk

PANASONIC
Panasonic House
Willoughby Road
Bracknell
RG12 8FP
Tel: 0844 844 3899

PULSE HOME PRODUCTS LTD
Vine Mill
Middleton Road
Royton
OL2 5LN
Tel: 0161 652 1211
Helpline: 0800 525 089
Brand: Breville

SALTON EUROPE
Salton House
Failsworth
Manchester
M35 0HS
Tel: 0161 947 3000
Brand: Russell Hobbs

FLOURS

DOVES FARM FOODS LTD
Salisbury Road
Hungerford
RG17 0RF
Tel: 01488 684 880
www.dovesfarm.co.uk

JUVELA
19 Havilland Drive
Liverpool
L24 8RN
Tel: 0800 783 1992
www.juvela.co.uk

RETAILERS

Bread machines are available from many electrical shops, department stores, kitchenware shops and some of the larger supermarkets. Please ring for details of your local store and the brands of bread machines available.

ARGOS
Helpline: 0345 640 2020

CURRYS
Helpline: 0344 561 1234

DEBENHAMS
Tel: 0844 800 8877

HARRODS (LONDON)
Tel: 020 7730 1234

HOUSE OF FRASER
Tel: 0345 602 1073

JOHN LEWIS PARTNERSHIP
Helpline: 08456 049 049

SELFRIDGES (LONDON)
Tel: 0800 123 400

UNITED STATES

MANUFACTURERS

OSTER
Tel: (800) 438-0935
www.oster.com

PANASONIC
Tel: (800) 211-7262
www.panasonic.com

REGAL WARE
Tel: (262) 626-2121
www.regalware.com

SPECTRUM BRANDS
Tel: (800) 566-7899
www.spectrumbrands.com

WEST BEND HOUSEWARES
Tel: (866) 290-1851
www.westbend.com

ZOJIRUSHI
Tel: (800) 733-6270
www.zojirushi.com

RETAILERS

DEAN & DELUCA
Tel: (800) 221-7714
www.deandeluca.com

JCPENNEY
Tel: (800) 322-1189
www.jcpenney.com

MACY'S
www.macys.com

WILLIAMS-SONOMA
Tel: (877) 812-6235
www.williams-sonoma.com

ARROWHEAD MILLS
Tel: (866) 595-8917
www.arrowheadmills.com

BOB'S RED MILL
Tel: (800) 349-2173
www.bobsredmill.com

KENYON'S GRIST MILL
P.O. Box 221
West Kingston, RI 02892
Tel: (401) 783-4054
www.kenyonsgristmill.com

KING ARTHUR FLOUR
Tel: (800) 827-6836
www.kingarthurflour.com

BREAD BAKER'S GUILD OF AMERICA
670 West Napa St, Suite B
Sonoma, CA 95476
Tel: (707) 935-1468
www.bbga.org

AUSTRALIA

RETAILERS

BETTA ELECTRICAL
Tel: (07) 3414 8700
www.betta.com.au

DAVID JONES
Tel: 1800 354 663
www.davidjones.com.au

HARVEY NORMAN
Tel: 1300 4642 7839
www.harveynorman.com.au

MYER
Tel: 1800 811 611
www.myer.com.au

RETRAVISION
Tel: 1300 173 872
www.retravision.com.au

USEFUL HOTLINES AND WEBSITES

WESTON MILLING
Tel: 1800 649 494
www.westonmilling.com.au

BREVILLE
Tel: 1300 139 798
www.breville.com.au

PANASONIC
Tel: 13 26 00
www.panasonic.com/au

SUNBEAM
Tel: 1300 881 861
www.sunbeam.com.au

ACKNOWLEDGEMENTS

The author and publishers would like to thank the following companies who lent equipment and supplied flours:

Kenwood
Morphy Richards
Pulse Home Products Ltd
Salton Europe Ltd
Dove Farm Foods Ltd.
West Mill Foods Ltd
Magimix

INDEX